Almost 30

Almost 30

A DEFINITIVE GUIDE TO A LIFE YOU LOVE FOR THE NEXT DECADE AND BEYOND

LINDSEY SIMCIK AND KRISTA WILLIAMS

ST. MARTIN'S
ESSENTIALS
NEW YORK

First published in the United States by St. Martin's Essentials, an imprint of St. Martin's Publishing Group

ALMOST 30. Copyright © 2025 by Almost 30, LLC. All rights reserved. Printed in the United States of America. For information, address St. Martin's Publishing Group, 120 Broadway, New York, NY 10271.

www.stmartins.com

Library of Congress Cataloging-in-Publication Data

Names: Simcik, Lindsey, author. | Williams, Krista, (Podcaster) author.
Title: Almost 30 : a definitive guide to a life you love for the next decade and beyond / Lindsey Simcik and Krista Williams.
Other titles: Almost thirty
Description: First edition. | New York : St. Martin's Essentials, 2025. | Includes bibliographical references.
Identifiers: LCCN 2024058113 | ISBN 9781250327208 (hardcover) | ISBN 9781250411471 (signed) | ISBN 9781250327215 (ebook)
Subjects: LCSH: Women—Life skills guides. | Self-actualization (Psychology) | Adulthood.
Classification: LCC HQ1221 .S56 2025 | DDC 646.70084/4—dc23/eng/20250214
LC record available at https://lccn.loc.gov/2024058113

Our books may be purchased in bulk for promotional, educational, or business use. Please contact your local bookseller or the Macmillan Corporate and Premium Sales Department at 1-800-221-7945, extension 5442, or by email at MacmillanSpecialMarkets@macmillan.com.

First Edition: 2025

10 9 8 7 6 5 4 3 2 1

To the *Almost 30* community, podcast guests,
our friends and family, and anyone and everyone
who has believed in and been impacted by
the conversations that started with
just two girls who wanted to feel less alone

CONTENTS

INTRODUCTION

We should have been enjoying our lives. It was our twenties! Life was supposed to be serving us a fun, glitzy montage of bachelorette parties, hot dates, fun adventures, cool corporate outfits with chic stilettos, and rooftop happy hours galore with coworkers we loved. We were young, living in Los Angeles, seemingly healthy, with fresh blond highlights and endless career opportunities in front of us. Life should have been good. Things should have made sense. We were supposed to be *thriving*—but we were far from it. In actuality, we were just two late-twentysomethings with bad skin flare-ups, relationship issues, credit card debt, hormonal imbalances, heartbreak, and no career or purpose in sight. We were lost, and no one was coming to save us.

The lives we had envisioned for ourselves by this point in our twenties weren't really shaking out. Our journeys were different, but they reeked of a similar sort of disappointment. The dream of becoming a Broadway-star-turned-series-regular-on-an-Emmy-Award-winning-TV-show was fading with every rejection Lindsey got, while that corner office dream, cool corporate ladder climb didn't feel how Krista had hoped it would. Our stories merged in Los Angeles at the point when each of us had moved on from our original visions with less of a plan than ever. On the outside, it may have looked like things were fine. Yes, Lindsey had put acting on hold, but she was thriving as a SoulCycle instructor, teaching the most popular fitness class in LA, whipping her hair back and forth while pedaling away in front of a sold-out crowd day after day. Krista was in a serious relationship, traveling all over the world when she wasn't working her corporate gig, and documenting the journey along the way in Hefe-filtered pics for both the 'Gram and her blog. Based on our social media accounts, you'd think we were both killing it. But behind our handles was a reality that was much less Instagrammable.

Our misery wasn't casual. It wasn't just a talking point over mimosas at Sunday brunch. No, we were desperate, emotional, and vocal (at least to each other) about this feeling that we were somehow wasting our time on the wrong things, moving in the wrong direction, or stalled out altogether. The majority of our conversations centered around this feeling that life was happening without us, and that we were doing all the things, but the wrong ones. Let's be real: our early to midtwenties gives way to a period of time that no one prepares us for. These existential questions we were asking were warranted, just like they are for you. *Will I ever feel good in my body? Who am I meant to be with? What's my purpose? What am I doing with my life anyway?* It's a time when we are launched from a period of invincibility, lack of responsibility, and the blissful ignorance of our younger years into the abyss of adulthood. In our early twenties, it's all about what's happening outside of ourselves, from the parties to the pressure to get the job of our (parents') dreams to dating in the "real world." It's about how we can *be more like that* and *I hope they like me,* rather than about trusting our own intuition and desires.

Like all good love stories, we first met ~~on Hinge~~ over FaceTime when a mutual friend connected us because she thought that Lindsey, who was a current SoulCycle instructor, might be of some help to Krista, who had an audition scheduled to try to become one. We felt a spark immediately, and started hanging out IRL. There was something different about our relationship; it felt like kismet, the kind of instant, deep, and comfortable bond that happens so rarely. We went on walks together, worked out together, and couch surfed together. Our connection got stronger the more we realized just how similarly we were feeling about our lives. Being in the thick of it together felt reassuring and safe.

It was early on a Monday morning, and the West Side fog had yet to burn off. Lindsey was driving Krista home after a SoulCycle class because she had yet to get a car following her recent move from New York. (Figuring out how to navigate a driving city like Los Angeles without a car was a true feat!) Sweaty leggings and empty water bottles littered Lindsey's Nissan Sentra, and the smell of yogurt might as well have been the air freshener scent. Linds had no choice but to eat her meals in her car before and after teaching upward of four classes per day all over LA. Krista, a vegan at that time, gagged at the sight and smell of the goat's milk yogurt, but sucked it up for the sake of a free ride and in-depth talks. We pulled into Krista's vacant parking spot in the wooden carport behind her small Venice apartment and decided to hang for a little while longer. Misery does love company, and sometimes you just can't be alone. Plus, we didn't have much else to do that morning; Lindsey was done teaching until that evening and Krista miraculously had a day off from the multi-job schedule she was juggling in the wake of quitting her corporate gig to find her real calling.

Inside the small one-bedroom apartment by the beach, with no AC or dishwasher and some cheap boho decor, it felt like *Groundhog Day* as we sat down to discuss the current state of our lives. Lindsey plopped down in the corner on the "new" L-shaped couch Krista had found on Craigslist for $300. Krista sat across from her in the squeaky desk chair that liked to roll itself across the uneven floor. As we did weekly, we began to unpack what was going on in our lives in this safe space we had created to share how we were feeling truthfully and from our hearts. In a time when life generally felt difficult, this felt so easy. Krista explained her hormone health struggles, which she had just learned about through testing. It was also the first time she learned what hormones were. The verdict? Not good. She felt uncomfortable in her body and out of sorts, and not only was she not feeling like herself she wasn't looking like it, either. Then it was Lindsey's turn: dating was torturous, and she felt unable to be her goofy, vibrant self with the latest gym trainer she was dating. More and more, it felt like settling was her only option. From there, our conversation turned to our credit card debt (oops!), which felt shameful and embarrassing, and also never-ending.

Something had to give. There had to be a reason for this confusion, chaos, and series of unfortunate events we were experiencing. There also had to be an answer, or at least some sort of support group we could join? We tried to jigsaw answers together for ourselves, but it seemed like the whole world lacked the vocabulary to understand how painful and intense the mid-to-late twenties really are. No one taught us how to be

adults, or the skills that would actually serve us in life. We were struggling, lost, and stuck in a haze.

But at least we had each other. As it turned out, that was enough to
put us on the right path.

The Birth of *Almost 30*

One day as we were sitting at Bulletproof Café sipping a butter-laden
vanilla latte (an LA trend we hopped on early) after a workout, Krista asked
Lindsey if we should start a podcast about all the things we spent our
time talking about anyway. The real vision for the show wasn't clear just
yet, but the desire for connection was. Krista was a podcast devotee and
listened to them religiously as a way of pursuing her interests and finding
inspiration while navigating LA traffic. Lindsey is always down to create
something, even if the end goal isn't clear, so she was in.

The podcast had almost the same gestation period as a human baby,
which is fitting because it grew to be our shared child—in this and so
many ways, our relationship has become like a marriage over the years.
We spent the next eight months figuring out what the heck we were doing. Back then, in 2016, podcasting wasn't what it is today. Most people
thought it was "radio," and those exploring the medium were making
their own rules without any expectation for their podcast to become a
"thing." It was a really exciting time, almost like the entire industry was
one big start-up, with lots of promise and very few rules. There were very
few female podcasters on the scene (and even fewer duos), so we didn't
necessarily have a template or anyone to look up to. Instead, we had to
be that for ourselves. We started brainstorming different segment ideas
by listing things we wanted to talk about (because shows need to have
segments, right?). Some of these make us cringe now: Shit That Stuck
(things we learned that week and wanted to share); 100, Not 100 (which
was an homage to Krista's first mildly successful blog, *Hundred Blog*);
and a segment where we took a question from "the audience" (that we
didn't have yet). These questions came from friends, who were technically

our only audience at the time, but we fudged that they had "written in." Lindsey bought a $15 recorder, and we started practicing whenever and wherever we could—in our closets, at an abandoned WeWork (the door was unlocked, soooo . . .), and sometimes even out in the wild (we interviewed a fertility doctor at a café once; the sound was horrible).

The elements of a show started to come together. A friend of Lindsey's made our podcast cover art for free using photos we had taken to try to legitimize ourselves a few weeks earlier. It was during the days when an "artistic" photoshoot required nothing more than a graffiti wall in the background. We tried to capture the confused-twentysomething vibe by dressing in cutoff jean shorts, bikinis, and trucker hats, a look that we felt represented this in-between time well. Another *criiiiinge*-worthy decision, but today we kind of respect the clarity and confidence of the vision. We hired a voiceover artist on Fiverr to be our hype man in the podcast intro (would love to meet him one day!) and had a friend edit our episodes for $50, the first of which we recorded on Lindsey's trusty state-of-the-art recorder, sitting on the floor of the closet of Krista's studio apartment next to her boyfriend's smelly gym shoes. We closed the door while we were recording because we were professionals and wanted the best sound quality possible. This meant we had to take frequent breaks to swing open the door and gasp since we were totally oxygen deprived (which may have affected the quality of our conversation and the show, lol).

We held our breath when we launched *Almost 30* in September 2016. Were we ready? Absolutely not! But we weren't willing to wait any longer. We had done the practice and the prep, and now it was time to let our little podcast baby go out and live a little bit. *Almost 30* gave us a place to relax, be ourselves, and hang up the idea (at least temporarily) that we had to be further along in our lives than we were; we hoped that the show would find its legs and make other people feel similarly. We had no long-term plan and chose to trust that what felt good for us to create would serve others in some way too.

In those early days, *Almost 30* was, uh, less than polished. A sampling of some of our earliest episodes include wacky titles like: "(Boy) friends with Benefits"; "Destuffing Bras + Stuffing Faces"; and "Card

Chip Readers Suck, Self-Awareness Rules." We were raunchy, doling out tips about the proper poses for taking nudes for the person you're seeing and oversharing about dating, family drama, and sexcapades. Go back and listen to a few if you dare; we can't listen without hiding underneath the table and earmuffing ourselves. But, hey! It was an honest snapshot of that moment in time. And we *had* to start there. Thankfully, the podcast evolved along with us. As we navigated our almost-thirties and then moved into our actual thirties, the podcast mirrored our evolution. The podcast had been the teacher we needed and the purpose that we had been praying for. Over the years, it became more centered on health and wellness, then career and entrepreneurship, and then we were called to explore all things spirituality. We started to include conversations with guests and bring on experts in the field we were most interested in at any given moment. Today it's a mix of all those things—and, mainly, it's about transformation or, as we put it, being almost *something*. We have always committed to honesty and saying the things that others are afraid to say, to leading with our own truth, and to connecting with others in a way that we would have never thought possible once upon a time. As a result, we have amassed millions of downloads and a community of like-hearted people all over the world who are so ready and so willing to learn, grow, and commit to living lives that they love.

Perhaps our messes made us seek the awakening, or maybe the messes *were* our awakening. Either way, we were open and hungry for knowledge and support, and for feeling less alone and (mostly) less crazy. Through our conversations, we found the teachings, experiences, modalities, and tools that could support us—and now *you*!—during this intense season. We look back and realize that although we didn't see it at the time, we really did understand our assignment from the Universe. We've moved through this intense period of almost-thirty and learned an incredible amount about ourselves. Dare we say, we've come out better on the other side. More whole, happy, and set up for a life that we love. We now know how someone like you can feel more equipped, confident, and empowered to navigate this too.

Despite the fact that we didn't plan for this to be anything beyond a fun project created in our closets, today *Almost 30* is our full-time dream, complete with an amazing team—and, yes, we have surpassed thirty. It's been hard work, yes, and we really figured it out as we went along, and although we're over that hill, the name has stuck. Thankfully, we did move our recording sessions out of the dark, cramped closet we started in and built ourselves a spacious, elevated *Almost 30*–style studio that has been featured in press outlets like *Architectural Digest* and Apartment Therapy. Over the years, the pod has been written up all over the place, in publications like *Oprah Daily, The Hollywood Reporter, Entrepreneur, Women's Health,* and more, and has been nominated for iHeartPodcast Awards a few times in both the health and spirituality spaces. We've sold out global tours and spoken on stages around the world, hosted immersive wellness retreats, expanded our biz to influential courses and online learning, and have had the incredible opportunity to interview and learn from some of the most impactful experts and thought leaders of our time, including people like Mel Robbins, Lilly Singh, Jessie Inchauspé, Jenna Kutcher, Gabby Bernstein, Glennon Doyle, Lalah Delia, and Jay Shetty, to name just a few—many of whom you'll hear from in this book.

Those twenty-seven-year-olds driving around in Lindsey's Nissan Sentra would've been so in awe and proud of the fact that we've gone on to build an entire career (and empire) out of our belly laughs, genuine curiosity, and explorative musings. But back then we were just trying to figure out what it meant to be almost thirty.

Welcome to the Club

As you approach thirty, you might be feeling disoriented and scared, as if you've just woken up to your life after having been on autopilot, fueled by familial and societal influences. You may be looking around and realizing that what you do, who you're in relationship with, where you live, or how your life looks is no longer aligned with who you are (if you even know who that is at this point). Friends begin to split off in their own directions, whether that means moving to a new location or to a different phase of life. The relationships that were once so important to you suddenly aren't feeling aligned anymore, and the things you once loved doing don't bring you that same satisfaction and fulfillment they used to. You don't feel the financial security you'd hoped for by this point; in fact, you might suddenly be confronted by daunting adult financial responsibilities and pressure to strategize for your future. To top it all off, things change from a health and body perspective, and the old ways of relating to yourself are no longer working for you. While you might feel like you want to crawl into a hole and just keep doing what you've been doing for fear of the unknown, there is a very big and powerful part of you that won't allow that to happen. And *we* won't allow that to happen either.

Without certain milestones in place by twenty-nine, for us the promise (impending doom?) of thirty felt more agonizing than exciting. If you're reading this book, you probably relate in some way. Maybe you're feeling anxious and alone like we were. Or maybe you've already hit the thirty milestone and are looking back and connecting the dots of your Saturn Return (Saturn, what?! Uh-huh, we'll explain in the next chapter), looking back on what all that transition, change, and growth meant then and means today. Whether you've already experienced your Saturn Return, are anticipating it, or are somewhere in the middle of it, we hope this book will validate your experience while offering ways to remain centered through change. Because, let's be honest, change definitely isn't limited to your late twenties. Knowing yourself is a lifelong process and commitment, and this is just the beginning. Your relationship with change sets the stage for your relationship with life.

Whatever the case, because this book is in your hands, we can safely assume that you're asking yourself some of the same questions we were asking ourselves during our Saturn Return, as we were simultaneously seeking and rejecting change: *What the heck am I doing with my life? Aren't I supposed to have things figured out by now? Is it normal to feel disconnected from people I was once close to? Where should I settle down? Where is "my person"? Am I running out of time to get it together? Will I ever get out of debt? Should I change careers? What's my purpose, and how can I pursue it?*

Media, social media, society in general, and maybe even family and friends lead you to believe that by the time you reach your thirties, you'll have it all figured out. You'll be a *real* adult, with a *real* job (maybe even your own six- or seven-fig biz that allows you to work from AnYwHeRe!), financial stability, a partner you love, and a clear purpose and path ahead. You'll be in complete control of your life, know exactly who you are and where you're heading.

Um, sorry, but *whaaaaat?!*

You might have a few of these items on the life to-do list checked off by then, sure. But it is completely unrealistic and counter to the nature of who we are as humans to have it ALL together by any age, really. Who you are is always changing, especially during this period in your late twenties. So if you lock in any of these areas of your life early on, expect them to be reevaluated as you decondition yourself, as you let go of patterns and beliefs that are not yours. To have it all "figured out" by thirty would make the rest of life, well, boring in our opinion.

If we have learned anything over the years interviewing some of the best and brightest in the world, it's that *no one* has it figured out. Your late twenties are a time of massive shifts, when at least one and, quite possibly, many or all significant areas of your life are called into question and in a state of transition: your sense of self, where and how you live, your beliefs, your lifestyle, your relationships, and your career. It might feel totally chaotic, like the anchors that once held you in a comfortable place in life have suddenly been cut loose, and you're floating in the open ocean, sunburnt and thirsty, in desperate need of shelter and a razor. Is the visual as dramatic as your life feels right now?! Mm-hmm, it's A LOT.

Even if you've been out in the world on your own for a while, chances are that there were structure and familiarity up to this point: you were at college, perhaps, then living with roommates, hanging out with the same friends all the time. Everyone around you was more or less on the same page. Most of us have fond memories of this time, because who doesn't love whipped vodka shots after hours at your favorite bar on a Monday night, only to sneak in late to the Tuesday morning meeting because you wound up in someone else's bed far, far downtown (hands-over-face emoji)? And then, as your twenties start to wrap up and the door to your thirties creaks open, things begin to *change*.

So what gives with all the change, confusion, and chaos happening right now? The truth is that change is constant, yet we find it so hard to embrace and live it. That's because the physiology of our brains is primal, and change signals a threat. Our brains convince us to resist, tell us that change is all for the worst, and that we should just run and hide. Whether it's the changes that our body goes through, the shifts in our closest relationships, or the transitions we experience many times over within our careers, it's rarely easy. Yet, when change comes knocking on our door, we have been conditioned to feel and think in a way that's totally counter to the intention that change itself has. It's what we *think* about change that colors our experience of it. To avoid change is to avoid being human.

What we know now is that if you are experiencing the same sort of feelings we did, you have been gifted with something extraordinary. This late-twenties portal and all the change that comes with it is a request from the universe for you to come close, listen intently, and be open to unexpected pleasures, fulfillment, and transformation. When you awaken to more of who you really are (we'll talk about what this means in the chapters ahead), you'll realize that so much *must* change in order for you to align with your becoming. We're here to hold your hand and cheer you on as you work through these defining life changes—changes within, changes in your body, changes in your career, and changes in your relationships.

Whether it feels like it or not, there is a part of you that's ready to initiate change, or you wouldn't be reading this book, but you're probably also afraid to or don't know how. Maybe you're feeling like we were: ready to find the career and purpose that lights you up, to meet a partner, to move somewhere new, or to connect more deeply with who you are, but doing things differently feels overwhelming. You might feel that strong desire for something different but still find it hard to trust yourself and change enough to take action. You might feel seriously stuck and currently lack the confidence or clarity to make a move.

Wherever you find yourself, the truth of the matter is that this time of life can bring you to your knees. Know that you're not alone and, in fact, *you're exactly where you're supposed to be* right now. This strong current of change is happening *for you*. And it'll bring on all the feels with it: frustration, elation, anxiety, directionlessness, isolation, excitement, sadness, confusion, and more. Your feelings will light the path to deeper alignment. In other words, your willingness and commitment to feel and be present will open up a whole new experience that you will learn to love and appreciate and be proud to call your own. We know that feeling the big emotions that come up can sometimes be scary, and we are here to help guide you through it so that you can find yourself more free on the other side of this intense time frame.

Here's another truth: for all the directionlessness, confusion, and frustration you feel right now, there's also a lot of magic in this late-twenties portal. For all the things you don't know and answers you don't have, chances are that if you use this time as an opportunity to get to know yourself—your *real* self—more intimately, ride the waves of life, listen to your heart and soul, and follow those things both big and small that call to you, when you look back you may very well realize that this period marked the beginning of a future that's even better than anything you can begin to dream of from where you stand right now.

Before we go any further, let's just take a moment and give it up for *you*. Take a deep breath of gratitude for what you've set in motion. IT'S A BIG DEAL. A book like this doesn't land in your hands by accident. There was a part of you that sent out a bat signal to the Universe because you desire and are open to guidance, support, and connection during this period of your life. Consider the two of us your Saturn Return big sisters. We're here to validate, motivate, inspire, and remind you of what's true. We'll be weeping and slow clapping in the bleachers (cue the *Mean Girls* "You're doing great, sweetie" scene) as you come back home to yourself one page at a time, because we know the impact of this exploration and the work that you are committing to. We experienced it ourselves and have come out the other side meeting our life on a soul level, and it feels so, so good.

If someone would have told us that our twenties could be a decade of liberated exploration, that we didn't have to figure out the rest of our lives, that we didn't have to find the person we would be with forever, that we weren't meant to define our career but rather experiment and let our passions lead us, the pressure wouldn't have felt so suffocating. We could have seen it all as fun and exploratory: a time for experimentation, a season to create a portfolio of our various life experiences and witness the contrast of it all. Our twenties are not meant to be a fixed point upon which everything hinges, but rather fluid and flexible. *Whew,* that would have saved us a lot of stress, tears, doubt, and self-judgment. But, alas, we had to move through it in order to land here with you, as a small but hopefully helpful part of your journey.

We hope that our personal stories, the wisdom and insight from *Almost 30* guests, and the tools and practices that support us to this day will play a part in creating a new experience of change for you. We hope that you will realize the incredible power you have in participating in your life consciously and with purpose, by working to decondition the patterns, beliefs, and behaviors that have gotten you this far, but won't get you to where you want to go. Most of all, we hope that you'll feel a little less alone as you make this important, profound, and beautiful shift from your late twenties into your thirties.

Let us be the first to welcome you to this powerful season (and life-changing opportunity) with open arms! We got you.

Chapter 1

WELCOME TO YOUR SATURN RETURN

Krista & Lindsey

Allow us to get a little Bill-Nye-the-Science-Guy on you for a moment. At around the age of twenty-five, your prefrontal cortex development plateaus. In other words, it reaches a point of maturity and is fully online. This area of the brain controls emotional maturity, thought, self-image, judgment, and action. So, while most places around the world christen you into adulthood through some arbitrary law at age eighteen, your cognitive development says otherwise.

Shortly after your prefrontal cortex comes online, you will enter an astrological transit called Saturn Return, which ushers you into adulthood on a cosmic level. If astrology feels like a big eye roll to you, know that you don't have to be super New Age-y to accept that the transition to your thirties is inevitable and that you will benefit from having tools to embrace it in a healthy, productive, and exciting way. At the end of the day, that's what this book is all about. Personally, we've found comfort in understanding this period of transition into the thirties through the lens of Saturn Return (you might prefer to see it through neuroscience!), and we hope this cosmic lens is helpful for you too. For us, it feels good to know that we are all attending the same cosmic Earth school, learning lessons together. Whether you attribute the traditional rites of passage to Saturn Return or not, there's no denying that the issues we're talking about here are *definitely* markers of the late-twenties through early-thirties experience.

Ironically, we didn't start to learn about our Saturn Return until we were almost out of it. When an astrologer explained it to us during an interview on the pod, we felt instantly validated. We weren't #Astrology-Girlies at that time but had just moved to Los Angeles and were open to learning about anything that could help us. As it turned out, there was a reason and a purpose for all the things we'd been feeling and experiencing over the previous couple of years (and, BTW, definitely not a coincidence that the two of us met when we were twenty-seven, right at the beginning of our respective Saturn Returns)! Since then, we've learned a lot about Saturn Return: from experts, from our own experiences, and from the various guests and community members we've discussed this deeply transformational period with. There's a lot to be said about it, but the most important thing to know to begin is that everything changes.

The Initiation

One of the biggest periods of change in our entire lives occurs during Saturn Return, which you can think of as a cosmic rite of passage. It happens every twenty-seven to thirty years of your life, when the planet Saturn finds its way back to the same place it was when you were born. Every single planet in our solar system has a particular duration of orbit around the sun, and each one of those planets was in a very specific place in its orbit at the point when you were born. This is what you see if you run what's known as a birth or natal chart (if you're curious, you can see if you're in your own Saturn Return at almost30.com/saturnreturn). The point in time when a planet circles back to where it was at your birth is called a *return*. Each planet returns, some frequently and some not so frequently. In fact, some planets, such as Pluto (which still counts as a full-fledged planet in the world of astrology, even if it's technically considered a dwarf planet these days), which takes 248 years to orbit, won't return to where it was when you were born in your lifetime. Mercury, on the other hand, returns to the point where it was when you were born every eighty-eight days. Saturn takes approximately twenty-nine and a half years to orbit the sun and remains in that station (in other words, it "stands still") for somewhere between two and a half to three years. This is why your late twenties and early thirties are marked by some life-changing events that will force you to get real about who you are, your values, your relationships, your career, and your health, and to take full ownership of and responsibility for your life. While Saturn will make this return two or three times in most of our lifetimes, this first Saturn Return in your late twenties is the point when you will become your own person. It's sort of like your astrological bat mitzvah because it is when you finally become an adult. It's during this period when you will learn to truly take care of yourself.

Much like an ex, each planet has its own distinct personality and impacts specific areas of your life and experience. Saturn is the planetary dad, the kind who sets a strict curfew, puts your new potential partner through a series of twenty questions, and isn't afraid of giving tough love. Saturn Return affects each of us differently, but for every one of us, it's a life-shaker, truth-teller, and wise guide all rolled into one. During your Saturn Return, you will experience a great deal of pressure to lean into what's hard, let go of anything that is out of alignment, and fully embody and own the potential within and around you. Depending on how authentically you've been living your life leading up to the point of your Saturn Return, this planet of karma can be a sweet, encouraging source of support or a super-serious, no-bullshit, alignment-obsessed life leader, tasked with whipping you into shape. That's why this time is often marked by change and a call to get very honest in every aspect of your life. Your late twenties are an inflection point—the great reorganization, a time when your life experiences so far begin to influence the adult life you will lead. Are you unsatisfied with your career path? Questioning whether or not the guy you've been with since college is actually who you're meant to be with? Maybe the city you've been living in your whole life is no longer challenging you. Are you living in alignment? If not, Saturn will force change with the intention of supporting your growth and alignment. Think of Saturn Return as sort of checks and balances for whether or not you're doing the work necessary to be fully and uniquely you.

However, if you are already living a life of alignment and clarity and feel locked and loaded for your future, then congratulations—Saturn Return can be incredibly fruitful and usher in milestones of maturity in your life, like buying your first home or accepting a career-making role! But if you're resisting growing up or stepping into yourself (which, let's be honest, is most of us), Saturn will bring you face-to-face with both your talents and deficits.

Pass the Mic

Saturn in astrology is a feared planet, but I don't think we should fear it. It's *the* great teacher. It's the one that absolutely has our best interests in mind. It says, "I'm so sorry about what has been done to you, but I need you to do better." So it's compassion with accountability. It's that moment where you understand, "If I want to be healthy, I've got to be healthy. If I want to be successful, I've got to go do some work." I think Saturn is about reparenting.

Saturn Return is a dark night of the soul for many of us. For other people it's a breakdown; for other people it's a breakthrough. Everyone navigates Saturn in a different way.

One of my favorite things to consider with astrology is determinism versus self-will. I'm a huge believer that it's a dance of both. So it's up to you. How much do you want to integrate this sign? How much do you want to meet your maker? How much are you willing to listen to Saturn?

Saturn says, "I think you could do better. I'm not going to knock at your door again, though. I'm not going to bug you for another twenty-nine years. If you would like to do this dance with me, I will make your life so much more integrated. If you don't, I'll see you in another twenty-nine years."

—Nadine Jane, author of *Magic Days*
ALMOST 30, EPISODE 590

Since Saturn Return serves as an initiatory transition into adulthood, you might be feeling called to make a more conscious choice to individuate during this season. This probably isn't an entirely new concept. You might have made previous attempts to differentiate yourself in college or even earlier than that as a rebellious preteen or teenager. In all these instances, you're saying goodbye to your old identity and starting to create the next. But the difference with your Saturn Return is the *conscious* part of this process of individuation. Rather than just going along with what everyone else is doing, getting the safe job your parents wanted for you, and drinking until the wee hours on weekends, you're looking at the world around you and your place in it, deciding what *you* like. What do *you* want outside of anyone else's desires, opinions, and perspectives? Do you feel that? That pull to shift and figure out who you are and what you want? This feeling means you are no longer living in reaction to others or what's come before, but from a truth within that's bubbling up to the surface. It's about trusting yourself to discern what parts of your upbringing you'd like to carry forward and which parts you want to tend to, heal, let go of, or commit to as a way of being.

During this Saturn Return period of your life, nearly everything feels in flux, from your relationships to your career, lifestyle, belief systems, and more. The list is endless, really. In order to navigate this intense period of transition, it's imperative to first explore within: What were you raised to believe about the world? About yourself? How have these beliefs guided you to this point? Do these beliefs still feel true to you? It's only with this understanding that true transformation can begin. These are exactly the growth points we're going to work through in this book. The truth of the matter is that these years are going to feel intense and confusing at points, but know that everything that seems to be breaking down and falling apart right now is presenting you with an incredible, exciting opportunity to cultivate a life that reflects who you really are and what you really want. Along the way, it's normal—and even important—to question everything (we sure did!), even though it might feel uncomfortable and downright scary sometimes.

This season is less about copy-paste routines and more about creating your own rituals. Saturn is jokingly known as the "taskmaster" planet, so it's offering you this big moment as a juncture during which you can choose to either settle into a life you don't desire or become brave enough to create one you love—to challenge the norms, to do it differently, to stop doing all the things that are out of alignment, and to choose yourself over the status quo. This can mean so many things. For us it meant leaving the corporate world to eventually go full time with *Almost 30*, losing and gaining friends, finding peace and healing within our family units, consciously connecting with our bodies, transitioning in and out of relationships, redefining who we were in the world, getting out of a debt cycle, and shedding outdated ways of thinking, believing, and behaving.

It's all worth it, though, because at the end of this, the goal is to become your own person. A person who is no longer a construct of your parents, teachers, or what society wants you to be. The goal coming out of this season is to be *you*, the divine soul blueprint version of you, a one-and-only edition.

The Only Constant

While everyone's Saturn Return and almost-thirty experience is different, there are a few things you can expect as you navigate this monumental period of your life. We've found these to be consistent both in our own experience and in that of our *Almost 30* community. There's some comfort in normalizing these feelings and experiences that can feel so unique (sometimes in a what's-wrong-with-me and is-this-going-to-be-okay type of way) when you're going through it.

Lots of change. There is no shortage of transition and transformation during this time, and you won't be able to moonwalk out the other side of this one. But by being aware of all the shifts either already underway or coming your way soon, you'll be better prepared to ride the waves through the various storms you shall weather. Rather than worry too much about the future, you can acknowledge that this is both the beginning of something new and an ending. Look at where you've been before you try to sort through where you're going. Slow down. Rest. This is a time to take stock, to sort through your past, just as it is a time to look ahead with courage and excitement. The lessons of your past must be honored, but you are free to release the past as an identity.

Tests and triggers. The tests you'll encounter during this period are exactly what they sound like: pop quizzes from the Universe to see (and allow *you to see*) what you're made of. It's like being in school all over again, except now you're in life school. These tests will reveal your growth edges and highlight where an epic leveling up will soon take place.

No one *enjoys* being triggered, but it's actually a helpful and necessary part of growth. As annoying as they may be, triggers are a treasure trove of information for you to review and reckon with and a way of understanding yourself more deeply. Like birthmarks, triggers are unique to you, placed specifically to enhance your signature way of moving about the world. There will be lots of triggering moments as you brush up against your previous identities and unconscious ways of living throughout your Saturn Return. Know that they're offering you a moment to consciously slow down, check in, and ask if these triggers are pointing to something that still feels like you or if they're simply activating an old version of you that just needs some time, love, and attention. Consider your data collection mode activated so that you can see all the ways of being that currently exist and that you're growing out of.

Pass the Mic

Triggers are opportunities. Triggers are a reason to celebrate, like you're ready to go to the next level.

—Bethany Webster, author of
Discovering the Inner Mother
ALMOST 30, EPISODE 407

Challenges and confronting moments. No matter how tempting it might feel, you don't want to take a shortcut to avoid the challenges and confronting moments you will have during your Saturn Return. There will be times when you find yourself wanting to give up, move to a cabin in the woods, and forget about your life as it is today in favor of a new existence feeding chickens and baking spelt loaf in rural New York. While this quaint, remote life could be the best thing for you (and your nervous system), we also want to recognize that life in your twenties is disorienting, and you *will* have moments of wanting to burn it all down, throw in the proverbial towel, and start a whole new life because yours feels like such a disaster. Before you take drastic measures, remember that while leaving your life behind might temporarily feel like relief, as if you can completely start anew and everything will be better (starting tomorrow, of course), "wherever you go, there you are." No matter where you try to run—whether it's away from a job, a relationship, or a city—if you don't heal, transform, and shift on the inside, you will continue to run up against the same lessons.

Where there were once structure and goals in school, there are now loose expectations and financial obligations. Where there was emphasis on "impractical" knowledge (mitochondria is the powerhouse of the cell, anyone?), there is now a need for very practical skill sets required to keep you *alive*. Where there were once friends and community in abundance, there are now thousands of miles between you and your besties. Where there were once demands that you follow the prescribed goals for life, there is now an expectation that you define your own (with no guidance or support, we might add). But you can face your challenges head-on. As you get more accustomed to keeping your cool, maintaining your center, and clarifying your values, you can meet each moment with kindness and grace so that confrontation starts to feel comfortable (or *more* comfortable, at least).

Existential moments. With so much happening, life can start to feel jarring, unsettling, or out of control, which might bring up some of life's larger questions. This often happens when we move from one chapter to another, like from childhood to adulthood, or from parenthood to empty nesting. You want to move, but sometimes it feels like you can't: it's like you're stuck by cultural norms, constant comparison to others, meaningless jobs you are told you're supposed to love, or an utter lack of opportunity to do what you want. You become trapped by economics and social expectations that feel reminiscent of the times you were once trapped at home as a teenager. During this time, big questions come up around your purpose and priorities, and you can't help but perform a life review. *How far have I come in life up to this point? Is this really what I envision for myself? Why isn't what worked before working anymore? Where do I want to go from here?* When you awaken in this way during this time, it's so normal to question your purpose and the meaning of life. By understanding more about the journey and the ways in which you are experiencing your Saturn Return, you can approach the experience with more joy, levity, and play, and less fear.

Growth and abundant opportunities. It's not all bad, friends! A big reason for writing this book was to recognize the gifts and bright spots of our own journey through Saturn Return. In retrospect it will become clear to you that all this growth isn't just for growth's sake, but for a profound purpose. There is nothing more important than the discovery of who you are in life, so to be in a space where growth and opportunity are abundant is a beautiful thing. Opportunities will present themselves not because the Universe is bending to your will, but because you are shifting, changing, and approaching life differently. Saturn leaves rewards in its wake, but you have to earn them. Where you once may not have been able to clearly see the opportunities in your life and all they potentially offered for your future, now you see the magic of all the potential in front of and within you. Where previously you may have had purpose and goals predefined in your life, it's now time to define them for yourself.

The chance to become the person you are meant to be. Take a deep breath, folks. What if the Universe created this beautiful moment for you to step into who you are, and what if it was all working toward your greatest good? What if everything that feels turbulent right now is paving the way for smooth sailing later on? This time is a doorway to the life and existence of your dreams. As is often the case with suffering here on earth, this is a gift for you to alchemize in the long run.

Over the years, Saturn Return has gotten a bad rap—like the grumpy old neighbor here to shut down the party. That's not really the case at all. Saturn Return is not just a sticky period you have to get through; instead, it's a time when you get to remove yourself from the expectations of the world to regroup, recharge, and *grow through*. To become—again and again. When you are waking up and following the guidance of your higher self, you're simply shedding the energies and relationships that no longer match your frequency. It is important that you choose your own growth over any relationships that drain your energy. Choose courageous and clear boundaries over the other "easier" comforts you might have chosen up to this point. See the space between what was and what is now becoming as the chance to recalibrate to your unique and specific blueprint.

Answering Saturn's Call

You're not sending Saturn's call to voicemail. You are ready, and the fact that this book is in your hands validates it. The trust with which you lean in now is directly proportional to the leveling up you will experience in all areas of your life moving forward. This process can just last for these formidable years marked by Saturn Return if you do the work being asked of you, *or* the cycle can and will repeat itself. This can be a painful process, but it is also a tremendous growth opportunity that can help you to live a more meaningful, happy life. Now that you understand what's happening, why it's happening, *aaaand* that you have us by your side, you are ready to begin this adventure.

Deep breath . . . LET'S DO THIS.

Within

The exploration of your inner world is a brave commitment. What you unearth might surprise you. The dots you connect might overwhelm you. But the reward for your dedication to understanding yourself on a much deeper level is a life you will love. You will love it not just for the "things" and the "successes" that manifest because of your inner work (and they will), but mostly for the profound peace, confidence, and inner connectedness you will cultivate, exude, and spread to others.

Within each of us lies a sacred key that will point to relationships, experiences, and opportunities that our soul *loves*. It will unlock synchronicities and revelations that make life so exciting and sweet. Your profound attunement to your inner world translates to an alignment in the world around you. So when your outer world does not reflect what you desire, take that as an invitation to dive within rather than first changing the circumstances around you. Now is your chance to use the energy of the cosmos to get straight to the issues in your life, beginning with your inner self, then extending outward to your body, your career, your relationships, and more. While it's normal to feel the inclination to change your outside circumstances first, it's important to know that you literally cannot experience change in your life without first making changes within yourself.

We will begin by questioning what we have been taught and modeled as *the way* and explore our origins. Not as a way to disparage how we got here, but to understand our path and ourselves more deeply. Together we will make our way to the most sacred and deep part of you—your soul, your most electric collaborator in this life and beyond. She will be a guiding force as you explore the medicine sent to you in the form of your Saturn Return.

Chapter 2

QUESTION EV-ERY-THING

Lindsey

'm hunched over my toilet bowl in my tiny Manhattan apartment as the sun rises over the city. It's 2012, I'm twenty-five, about a year and a half out from the official start of my Saturn Return, and life is far from what I had envisioned for myself at this age. Through the shakes and purging, I suddenly heard a voice. That voice asked me a series of rapid-fire questions. (Like, *really*? Right now? I'm puking.)

Who are you without a couple shots to kick off your work night?
Does your relationship reflect what you really desire in a partnership?
Why are you afraid to feel?
What makes you think this is the only way to be successful?

I found myself in this position in part thanks to severe food poisoning from a grilled cheese sandwich I'd picked up on my way home from bartending in the wee hours of the morning. But there was more than just the cheese to blame for this vomitous inquisition. Really, I found myself here thanks to a whole pile of misalignments that were dominating my life at the time.

My earliest career goal was to be a dancing tennis player who rescued manatees in her spare time. She's dynamic and philanthropic! Around the time I was a preteen, when I realized that probably wasn't going to happen, I switched my focus to performing—I wanted to be a famous actress. As a kid, you could catch me creating theater-worthy drama everywhere, from the small brick hearth of our living room fireplace to the grocery store, and I seemed to get a lot of praise for performing. I honed my talent throughout high school and then followed the track my parents, teachers, and mentors guided me toward to make my dreams possible. Eventually, I landed at a prestigious liberal arts college where I double majored in theater and English.

My love for theater didn't change once I entered college—there's nothing else I would have rather studied, and I still adored performing. What *did* change was my environment and the scope of what was readily available to me. There were so many things vying for my attention: my college sweetheart, my new friends, football games, wine flowing from plastic bags. Like so many college students, I was trying to figure out how to juggle it all. All these cool people, events, and situations were so new to me. *I can go out to a bar on Tuesday? I wouldn't have to sneak out?* The novelty sucked me in and was a constant temptation, pulling me away from both my center and my academic goals. I graduated, and I was proud. But no one prepared me for the leap from the college bubble life to actually living life as a responsible adult. Did I miss that class?

Alas, soon after college, I moved to New York City, where I spent the first few weeks after I arrived searching for a bartending job . . . because that's what you do when you want to become an actress, right? The seed had been planted in me long ago that multiple side jobs were necessary to support myself while I pursued my acting career. I subconsciously adopted the identity of a "starving artist," and the fear that came with that made me prioritize making enough money to survive over nurturing my craft and acting career.

A list of the things I "should" do quickly overtook my own instincts and sense of what was right for me. My focus landed on staying within the box that had been created and perpetuated well before my time. You know: the starving artist *should* have a side gig to support their living expenses while leaving room for auditions, classes, and any job they were lucky enough to book. If the artist wants to be seen and remembered, she *should* schmooze with the casting director. The artist *should* say yes to any and all gigs, regardless of pay or whether they're actually jazzed about the job because #resume and #experience. None of these shoulds are inherently bad or wrong, but can you feel the frequency of *should*? It's heavy. It's not *you*.

By week three of living in Manhattan, I had secured two bartending jobs—one at a popular sports bar downtown and the other at an Irish pub that was known for karaoke and their potpies. I was psyched. While I had taken a bartending class back home in Philadelphia a few months prior and could make a killer Sex on the Beach, nothing prepared me for being on the job like—well, like being on the job. I promptly learned that no one orders a Sex on the Beach. My mistakes were aplenty, the eye rolls from senior bartenders were nonstop, and I struggled to get used to my new hours, which consisted of working until somewhere between two a.m. and four a.m. four to five days a week, hosting karaoke, and slinging drinks until I finally found myself cross-eyed and belting out Adele tunes to the few stragglers left at last call. Probably not surprisingly, my ability to balance my pursuit of acting, my newly long-distance relationship, and the desire to get to know my new city was nonexistent. My romantic relationship began to break down under the weight of these changes.

Cut to the Thursday night that ultimately found me on my knees, head in the toilet, with my butt so close to the hot-water pipe that I burned myself more than once. Still blissfully unaware of how the night would end, I went in to work my regular shift at the karaoke bar. I stashed a folded piece of paper with lines for my audition the following day next to the register at work so that I could sneak peeks at it and (hopefully!) memorize my lines in between customer requests and pouring cocktails. As the night wore on, though, the only thing I actually accomplished was talking myself out of nailing this audition.

Next to that piece of paper, my phone was blowing up with text after text from my boyfriend. We had hit a critical point in our relationship thanks to my overwhelm with all the moving pieces of my life: trying to "make it," working hard to pay my bills, and also feeling like I was changing and growing out of our relationship. I didn't have the tools to communicate any of this to him, so instead my confusion and unhappiness manifested in being unfaithful—a graceful way of saying that I cheated on him with my manager at the bar. Classic. It seemed my boyfriend could sense this (and, also, looking back, I have the feeling I was acting weirder than I perceived myself to be at the time). But still, I thought that I *should* stay with him. I *should* marry him. I *should* be happy in this relationship. I failed to ask myself what I *actually* wanted and how I really felt.

Following my heart would have meant leaving a relationship that so many people—including me, for a long time—thought would last forever. I wish I had known back then that when you follow your heart, you will make waves. Some people close to you might be confused or bothered by your decisions, and you might disrupt some patterns, which can feel dysregulating to you and others. And all that is okay—in fact, it's more than okay: it's part of the process of growing and changing, finding your way in the world. But at the time, making waves felt wildly unsafe to me—to the degree that cheating and burning myself out seemed to be the better option.

Since my boyfriend could sense that the end of our relationship was near and he was scrambling to make sense of it, to hold it together, to blame me, and to blame others, he texted me every minute on the minute that night. It was a mess that I played a big part in creating. Finally, I texted him, *I'm working, I'll call you tomorrow.* The phone went silent, and my stomach sank, not only for his silence but for my own. As if on cue, my karaoke cohost for the evening yelled out my name as the last song of the night, "Wide Open Spaces," started to play. She tossed me the mic, and I hoisted myself up on the counter behind the bar, relieved to rest my feet for the first time that night. I sang my heart out:

> *She needs wide open spaces*
> *Room to make her big mistakes*

As I leaned back and belted "wiiiiide open spaaaces" along with the Dixie Chicks, I could almost feel in my body what it might be like to have infinite possibilities. For just a moment, I let go of the fear of what might or might not happen and, instead, felt flooded with faith in all that could possibly be. It felt amazing. Freeing. And then, as I returned to the bar and busied myself with closing duties, my anxiety reemerged and quickly extinguished the flickering feeling of freedom and potential.

After my shift, I hopped down to my favorite twenty-four-hour diner to pick up that fateful grilled cheese and fries, and started housing the fries on the taxi ride home. I was starving both physically and emotionally and was convinced the food would take care of it all. I was tired and unprepared for my audition and wondered why I would even go just to embarrass myself.

Less than an hour later that inner voice that offers insight and direction, the voice that I had been ignoring for so long, brought me to my knees, forcing me to confront all the questions I had about my life and the choices I was making. The questions I'd been trying to ignore because it somehow seemed easier to keep walking along the path I was already traveling, despite its many misalignments. Since it couldn't grab my attention any other way, that voice of mine had gone from whispering to screaming. (We'll talk more about that inner voice and how it likes to communicate with us soon.)

This night of undeniable clarity (and even more undeniable food poisoning) was the precursor to the main events that kick-started my Saturn Return. And it all began with questioning everything I had previously accepted as truth in my life.

The Questions That Will Change Everything

All this is to say: *Welcome to your Saturn Return.* It isn't for the faint of heart. But, even in those moments when it doesn't feel like it, this important and transformative time in your life is a gift. The questions your inner voice turns your attention to in these years marks the beginning of your journey back to yourself and the path that you were always meant to walk—and that path may be very different from the one you find yourself walking at this moment.

By the time you reach your Saturn Return, chances are that many aspects of your daily life are already well established and ingrained. You've probably committed to things like where you live, what you do for work, your relationships, your patterns, and your habits. But I'm talking about your *identity*—what you do, what you believe, and who you are to others. NBD, right?

If you're like most of us, one of the biggest questions that you'll have to confront during your Saturn Return is: *What would it mean to change some of the significant pieces of my life and my identity? Who would I be then?* Taking a jackhammer to and loosening the foundation of your SELF might feel like the last thing you have the energy for—I get it. And the choice, ultimately, to do so or not is most certainly yours. However, the fact that this book is in your hands right now tells me that, even if it's deep down, you have the will and energy to meet this moment.

But how will you know which areas of your life are being audited by Saturn and need your attention? *Follow the feeling that accompanies the questions Saturn is compelling you to ask yourself.*

The feeling I'm talking about here is misalignment. More specifically, misalignment might create feelings of depression, anxiety, frustration, sadness, hopelessness, jealousy, or being stuck. It can be difficult not to blame yourself or others for these feelings. Trust me, I *know*. At the point when I encountered my own questions, I was in a phase of life where I blamed rather than took responsibility; I avoided rather than faced my fears; I numbed with food, alcohol, and cheating instead of feeling what was meant to be felt; and I pretended everything was okay rather than getting real with myself. Basically, I did everything I possibly could to avoid feeling.

So, this moment of actually really *looking* at, acknowledging, and *feeling* the pain of misalignment rocked my world. I suddenly became conscious of parts of my subconscious that I had been carefully avoiding (thank you, spoiled cheese). For as difficult as the process that followed was, I'm so grateful that I learned to take stock of and accountability for my life path and choices, for sitting with the questions that had to be asked. Because blaming keeps you stuck. Taking responsibility for what you create and what you can change sets you free.

Saturn is here to demand that you do exactly this.

Pass the Mic

The twenties are a very chaotic time, and I think they're supposed to be. Even people who have accomplished a ton in their twenties are still coming out of this plasma goo of their teenage years and trying to find a form. Saturn Return comes along to show you what you've made of yourself so far. It shows your boundaries, who you're becoming, and that it's time to start to separate out from the stuff you grew up with and from needing family in the ways that you might have before. It's time to cut the cord in those psychological ways, maybe even the financial ways. Or in some way, come into your own as an adult.

—Chani Nicholas, author of *You Were Born for This*
ALMOST 30, EPISODE 299

You Were Born to Ask Questions

If you've ever observed a toddler, you might notice they navigate their little Universe so curiously, asking questions (sometimes to the point of a parent's exhaustion) about *everything*. Most likely, you too were a curious critter at one point or another in your childhood, asking, *What's that?* followed by a series of *But why*s.

"That's a cat, Lindsey."

"But why?"

My mom took hundreds of hours of home videos of me and my siblings. I'd ham it up for the camera and ask all my burning questions. I watch these often because the truth is, I miss that little girl—as my therapist refers to her, Little Lindsey—who saw so many possibilities beyond the linear thinking of the adults around her. Thanks to that aforementioned therapist, I've learned to allow Little Lindsey the space to ask questions, to express herself, and to help me understand the origins of my behaviors and beliefs.

At some point, this curious fervor that all our "littles" possess is drowned out by rules and expectations, by figures of authority who establish themselves as "the most right." They have the answers (or so they want you to believe), so you should stop asking the questions (there's that *should* again). When this happens, the pressure to figure it all out on your own becomes an internalized battle rather than an inquisitive exploration. It's like the difference between having a fight with someone in your head (in this case, yourself) versus freeing your curiosity to explore different points of view. Notice how the energy between these two things is so different. As I've gotten older, I've learned that nothing good comes from mulling thoughts over like an endless laundry cycle in my mind. I've liberated myself from that by instead unleashing Little Lindsey's curiosity. The energy of curiosity is so much more open and light, don't you think? It's also so important to nurture, because curiosity is at the very heart of living the most deeply meaningful version of your life.

Pass the Mic

Curiosity is the womb of your passion. When curiosity gives birth, then it turns into an interest, which is like a child, and then it grows up into a passion, which is like a teenager who is still trying to figure it all out. And then the purpose is our adulthood.

—Jay Shetty, author of
Think Like a Monk and *8 Rules of Love*
ALMOST 30, EPISODE 357

Saturn Return is going to raise some important questions and, for perhaps the first time in your life, you are truly free to listen to your own answers and inner voice. This makes it a perfect opportunity to get back in touch with that Little You, to ask questions to your heart's content (of yourself and of those in your life), and to allow the answers to come through a process of curiosity and exploration rather than the shoulds placed on you. To give voice to this curiosity, I've found that it's helpful to ask myself questions through journaling, in a therapy session, or (when appropriate) to bring my questions directly to the person who's likely to have answers. I've learned that it's possible to get to the truth much more quickly if you have the courage to ask the questions.

But I had to *train* myself to do this again. I had completely forgotten that the *What's that?* and *But whys?* that once helped me understand the world around me as a youngster are still accessible to me—to you too—and, honestly, more necessary than ever. By adulthood, thousands of beliefs and limitations have been impressed upon us. It is incredibly difficult to scrub this record and return to the beginner's mind we all started with. Yet it is only in this state of purity and possibility that we can imagine beyond the parameters of what our now-conditioned mind proposes.

Inquisition and exploration is a process that we adults must meet again and practice just as often as we reply to emails and texts. It's through this practice of inhabiting the beginner's mind that what your psyche might currently deem impossible becomes possible. So, let's practice!

Practice: Suspend Your Preconceived Beliefs

Try for just a moment—*literally* sixty seconds—to suspend your preconceived beliefs about a situation you're currently in that is causing you frustration, anger, confusion, or disappointment. Instead of focusing on your feelings about or reaction to the situation, see if you can experience it simply for what it is in the present moment.

For example, imagine that you are meeting up with a friend who you haven't seen in a long time, despite the fact that you live in the same city. Life has gotten busy for both of you in different ways, and making time for your friendship has not been a top priority. Leading up to the reunion, your internal narrative about this situation might skew toward your own guilt and shame for neglecting a friend. You might assume how your friend will show up, what she might say, and how it will negatively affect you. If you were to suspend these beliefs for just a moment, what would be true about this situation? How would it feel to believe it's as simple as two friends who have made time to get together to catch up? Two friends who've had life events that have required their attention during this season. Simple and true, right? Or imagine that you sent your boss a *long* email pitching a new idea, to which she replied, "Hmm, interesting. Let's discuss next week." Instead of reading into what the *hmm* means or assuming she thinks the pitch is flat, remember what is true. Your boss might have a full agenda this week and prefer to discuss your idea in person so she can ask important questions and feel your energy behind this idea; she knows that replying at length via email would be a waste of her time. Layering on our own interpretation of what is not yet revealed requires so much more energy and causes unnecessary stress on the body and spirit.

What curiosities bubble up now from this new perspective? Can you practice living these questions moment to moment? What possibilities might be available now that didn't seem to be before? Hang on to those answers. They're giving you direction and clues about where you can now focus your energy.

~~~~~~

While some questions will present themselves clearly and you will be forced to ask yourself others as you reach certain crossroads and points where you have to choose your own path, there is another brand of questions that will pop up during Saturn Return. Those are the questions that come from your inner voice. They tend to present much more quietly, and in your heart. But you have to pay attention to hear them, because as adults we are much more prone to listen to our heads than our hearts.

Despite what you might be expecting, that inner voice doesn't sound like Morgan Freeman, though it *would* be very cool if it did, and perhaps we would have an easier time paying attention to it. I've come to understand my inner voice as the voice of my soul—the part of me that knows, the part of me that is eternal and connected to all that is. Fancy, right?

The soul leads us into some pretty deep waters, so we will talk more about it in the next chapter.

For now, suffice to say that your inner voice is your internal BFF. The kind of best friend who always has your greatest and highest good in mind. The kind of BFF who is honest and clear, supportive and loving, loyal and collaborative. The inner voice is part of your innate curiosity, the part that wonders *Why?* and *For what purpose?* The inner voice won't just tell you what you want to hear to make you feel better. Far more important, the inner voice will remind you of what's true for you. The inner voice will remind you to be intentional in everything you do. That inner voice is rooted in love not fear, in faith not forcing an outcome.

At first, it might feel confusing and difficult to distinguish your inner voice from the influence or opinions and expectations of others or society in general. This is because of something called the ego. At the highest level, the ego usually refers to your sense of self or *perception* of who you are. It encompasses your thoughts, beliefs, attitudes, and values. It can be seen as a mediator between you and the external world, and seeks to find an expression for you that is most in alignment with social norms and what is seen as acceptable, good, or appropriate. I hope you can see where the ego can be problematic, if we are just allowing the part of us that is "socially acceptable" to run the show all the time. SO boring! A life UN-LIVED! we yell as we rip off our bras, throw our *Women Who Run with the Wolves* book in the air, flip the bird, and sprint off into the woods.

Pass the Mic

To get to know yourself as deeply as possible, and to get to know the divine source and allow God—or however you'd like to refer to the higher being—into your life, you have to cut out the noise, you have to get really connected to your inner voice—*How do you truly feel about this?*—and then explore it.

—Devi Brown, founder of Karma Bliss
ALMOST 30, EPISODE 399

Your body is a wonderful antenna that is constantly at your disposal to translate the internal and external world. Stop and think about that for a minute—it's pretty incredible! Here's how that works in action: An anxious thought might cause your body to contract and tighten. On the other hand, a gentle, insightful message from your inner voice might give you chills or relax you into yawning. Stay in conversation with your body, because it has the utmost intelligence to share with you on a minute-by-minute basis. You can begin to acquaint yourself with this voice by feeling whether each option or thought that it's presenting is playing to your higher self (your greatest expression, the best you) or to the ego. Does your body respond to the thought? If so, how? Also, notice how and when your inner voice prefers to reach you. Does it come in clearly when you create space and stillness, or does it fight for your attention?

As these questions from your inner voice come forward, they can feel confusing, annoying, or even scary, almost as if your autopilot setting is glitching, causing you to suddenly see beyond what is expected of you. Instead of that soothing autopilot, now you can see the cracks caused by the compromises you've made along the way, or hardly even recognize yourself when you look in the mirror. *BAM!* The ominous what-am-I-doing-with-my-life? freak-out takes hold. Generally, this freak-out begins with questions that may start out quietly, but will grow very loud if you try to ignore them (you know, kind of like a toddler).

This experience is intense, and it's real, and it happens when change wants to transform you for your highest good. It's a process that begins to take root and rock your world, most notably in your late twenties and early thirties. At this point in life, it seems that nearly everything comes into question. This can be a confusing and even painful experience to go through, but it's also deeply good and necessary. Those things that you were taught are true beyond question suddenly want to be reexamined. You are called to carefully audit your current state of affairs through a series of questions—some of which you may not initially like the answers to. Questioning can feel daunting. It might even feel like you're doing something wrong or betraying the person who you've been up to this point, not to mention all the people who have had a hand in influencing who you are—especially your parental figures.

Like me, you might find that these questions come up at what seems like the worst possible moment, when you're already feeling low or off-kilter. That's because they often arise most clearly when the ego has taken a break, the body and mind's defenses are down, and it seems like you're all alone with no relief in sight. But actually, those cracks let a bit more light in. They allow you to more easily hear your inner voice. My inner voice was just affirming and highlighting what I had known for a long time but could not bring myself to accept. I was cradling the expired version of me in order to uphold the relationships she was in and the patterning she loved to perpetuate. I was so precious with her, afraid that if she cracked, egg would splatter all over the floor, and I would be left with a whole mess to clean up. But what she actually required was less cradling and more permission to be in a healthy pot of boiling water—of pressure and challenge—to change her state. She was ready to shed the shell and reveal a glorious, resilient hard-boiled egg, primed and ready to become her ultimate destiny: an egg salad or a deviled egg or any of the 9,000-plus hard-boiled egg recipes you can find on Google. Okay, I know—a bit much, but doesn't everyone love an egg analogy?

Pass the Mic

Expansion is a process that requires containment as a sacred space. Let's think about it in terms of a caterpillar becoming a butterfly: They're in the cocoon. They have no consciousness of what the f*ck is happening. This is not really any different from any time you are invited into your own expansion. The caterpillar is sitting there, basically melting, and they actually don't know that they're becoming a butterfly. They have no clue. But evolution does, and the Universe does. And they emerge and they are still beautiful, just different.

—Mark Groves, founder of Create the Love
ALMOST 30, EPISODE 496

The point is, whether you are the egg in the boiling water, the caterpillar in the cocoon, the granule of sand in the oyster, or any other metaphor that feels right to you, you are destined to be transformed into something remarkable by way of challenge. And your willingness to question what has always been and lean into the unknown is often the catalyst for these momentous transformations.

Resistance: Your Invitation to Expansion

Ultimately, the purpose of all these questions is to lead you toward expansion—but before expansion there will always be a little (or a lot) of resistance. It can be so tempting to resist or ignore the questions that come up during this time, because they're not easy questions. They're not questions that you can answer and then go back to the way things were. But resistance does not behoove you, even though it might seem like the safer way forward in the moment, because ultimately the questions are recalibrating your GPS. Resistance just turns up the volume of the questions from a soft, gentle whisper to a relentless scream.

In part, this resistance is also coming from a very real, very primitive part of you. Change is scary, and questions can prompt change. We innately resist both of these things because we are designed for what's called *loss avoidance*. In fact, the brain is two to two and a half times as primed to avoid loss as it is to seek a reward. Like so many other quirks of human behavior, this predisposition goes back to our primitive days. If a cavewoman was hungry and wanted to gather some berries, for example, but knew there was a predator lurking nearby, her innate tendency toward loss avoidance—in this case, the threat of the loss of life—kept her in the cave and safe from harm, despite her other not immediately threatening impulse (hunger).

We are literally built to measure up our desire for reward with the risk it poses to our life and safety. Yes, the stakes are different today, but we're still deeply programmed for this loss-avoidant behavior. Although social safety was important to our ancestors as a means of survival too, even that was intimately connected to physical safety. Today, the balance has shifted.

Pass the Mic

Today the threats have changed from physical to psychological or social. The social threat of being rejected, being lonely, being abandoned is still very, very strong in our wiring. And then other things—losing your job, losing your lifestyle—have become potential threats to your safety as well. Financial and relational issues have become the biggest threats to our safety. Because that wiring has been there for so long—for generations and millennia—it's a very strong default.

—Tara Swart, MD, PhD, neuroscientist
and author of *The Source*
ALMOST 30, EPISODE 440

When you find yourself experiencing resistance, remember that it's a natural inclination and that you're safe. Give yourself a gentle reminder of the important role these tough questions have by connecting resistance to expansion rather than loss every time it comes up, every time you feel that prickly sensation, the contraction and clenching of your body and heart, and your mind shutting down so that you can hide from the questions and pretend they're not necessary. Let's instead speak to that resistance (or, more accurately, that *call to expansion*), because understanding your resistance is a vital part of understanding yourself.

Practice: Feel Into Your Resistance

Can you feel into your resistance without judgment, just for a moment? It has some weight to it, right? It has more to say, doesn't it? Resistance isn't a clear *no*. In my experience, resistance is more of a tangled web. This web might consist of some or all of the following:

- Past experiences that mask themselves as the present truth
- The judgments and projections of others
- A story passed on to you from a friend or parent that convinces you that growth and expansion are too hard and not yours to experience
- Forgetting about the divine support system we all have at all times (more on that soon)
- A part of yourself that wants to be acknowledged and tended to
- A limited perspective of what is possible
- Needing (or thinking you need) a certain outcome
- An attachment to a comfort zone

. . . to name just a few.

Let me ask you the same things I began to ask myself when I became aware of my resistance: *Does it serve you to hold it? Does it serve you to resist what you so naturally desire or are so curious to explore?* For me, the answer is almost always *no,* followed by a big sigh.

Sometimes we hold on to what we think we need to do or be in order to live the life we have so carefully envisioned for ourselves. Sometimes we choose control over change. But what if your resistance is inviting you to release and surrender your control into something better, something more expansive, something more *you*?

What if resistance is really just your expired beliefs holding on for dear life? And what *are* those beliefs? Are you even consciously aware of them? I've been there, so allow me to share some beliefs that I once held tightly to—maybe some of them will resonate with you too.

- I believed that if I questioned certain aspects of my life—including my career, relationships, sense of worth, habits, and patterns—I would then have to start from square one, and that felt too hard.
- I believed that anything that wasn't going right in my

life was due to circumstances happening *to* me and was therefore out of my control.

- I believed that if I questioned the path that I was guided to and had already chosen, I would let down people in my life.

These are all things I once believed, beliefs that ultimately came into question despite myself and that I resisted acknowledging for as long as I possibly could. Which is almost funny to look back on because, although it wasn't easy, shedding all these beliefs and the changes in direction that my life took as a result is the best thing I've ever done for myself. It also felt very, very overwhelming and scary.

Once you've identified a handful of beliefs that are fueling your resistance, you'll try on new beliefs, just to see how they feel. Don't worry, you don't have to *buy* these beliefs; you're just trying them on for size. Try on this belief, for example: *In questioning aspects of my own behavior and patterning, I am opening up to the possibility that so much more flow, joy, and fulfillment are possible by changing how I show up in the world.*

Say this out loud and, if you want, put it in your own words. How does that feel in your body? How does it feel in your mind? What does it feel like to hear yourself say and believe that questioning aspects of your behavior and patterning opens you up to possibility rather than destruction or loss?

If this idea feels good to you, next ask yourself: *What is possible now?* Notice how the question (and maybe your answer too) feels, and see where it takes you.

So often, resistance is an invitation to try on a different belief in order to allow for positive change; we just have to remain aware and open enough to accept the invite. If you are able to get to know your resistance for what it *really* is rather than letting it hold you back from knowing yourself deeply during this period of intense change, you will be rewarded. Saturn will make sure of it.

Pass the Mic

You are always being guided, and if you don't recognize that guidance, it's because of your own resistance.

—Gabby Bernstein, author of
Spirit Junkie and *Super Attractor*
ALMOST 30, EPISODE 257

When the Shoulds Run the Show

One of the most potent lessons that came up for me during my Saturn Return was around self-worth. It's funny because if someone would have asked me if I had a healthy sense of self-worth at the time, I would have said yes. I really thought I knew what I deserved and that I believed myself worthy of a great life. Oddly enough, though, as I allowed these new questions to open up my consciousness, I began to notice that my actions and subconscious beliefs were telling a different story. As a result, my Saturn Return plopped me into therapy pretty early on—thank goodness! It was there that I started to explore the roots of this worthiness wound.

Like so many other women, I was raised to be "polite," a quality that I'm thankful my parents instilled in me because it has given me the graciousness, modesty, and self-awareness that have all afforded me lots of opportunities and cultivated so many valuable relationships. But I also think that, over the years, I began to interpret "being polite" in a way that didn't serve me. And that, in fact, often worked to my detriment. I thought that to be considered polite, I had to keep my opinions and questions to myself, never rock the boat, never stand up and advocate for myself, always respect and listen to authority, and quiet that inner voice that tried to tell me there was another way to think about the issue at hand. For me, being polite became about making other people feel comfortable at the expense of my own comfort and truth.

But the truth is that I really liked being liked. It made me feel safe and confident, accepted and "good." Of course it did! Yet again, this desire—

which can sometimes even feel like a *need*—to be liked is biologically built into us as a survival mechanism. Those cavewomen ancestors of ours (and, also, their descendants for many generations forward) had a greater chance of survival—of being fed and protected—if they were liked. Loss avoidance, remember? And although being liked isn't so critical for basic survival today, social connections are proven to have a huge impact on our mental, emotional, and physical health. A landmark study published in *Science* showed that lack of social connection is a greater detriment to health than obesity, smoking, and high blood pressure.[1] So, while this need for connection (which of course involves being liked) is very real, for women, it can be all too easy to conflate being socially accepted with being good or polite, sometimes to their own detriment. For me, politeness eventually became a big part of my identity—to the point that the uninhibited, imaginative, and curious parts of myself were muted as a result. I even categorized those questioning, open parts of myself as "bad" or "weird." For the sake of being seen as polite I took the set of conditions and parameters presented to me—at school, at work, and in my relationships—as truth and followed them faithfully.

Have you ever noticed that throughout our childhood and adolescence we're subjected to conditioning with the intention of keeping us on track, of incentivizing us to aim for a desirable life? *If* you follow the rules.

Be polite and you will be liked by everyone.
Be serious and focused and you will be successful.
Be a straight-A student and you'll be able to be and get whatever you want.

I wanted to be and receive all those things, and I also truly believed there was only one way to get there—and that was by satisfying the conditions that were instilled in me. None of these conditions made space for asking questions or rocking the boat. If I fell short of the expectations I had internalized, self-judgment and disappointment rolled in like the Macy's Thanksgiving Day Parade—exaggerated and over the top, taking over every lane of my brain. Having compassion for myself wasn't even on my radar. A "polite girl" beats herself up and then tries to do better next time, with "better" being based on a set of standards and conditions that I didn't even sign on for in the first place.

By the time I hit my midtwenties, all this conditioning had mushroomed into some serious misalignment in my life that I didn't even consciously recognize, which made everything even worse. It led me to take three shots of vodka so that I felt relaxed before going out at night, which did not align with how I wanted to feel the next day. My choice to put up with less-than-stellar behavior in my relationship did not align with the open and honest communication I truly value and deserve. I was getting tired of feeling one thing and doing another, though I'm not sure I could have articulated that at the time. It was only years later in therapy that I realized how much of my distress was rooted in my preoccupation with what I thought I "should" do, according to sources like my family, friends, society, and social media. I was more keen on making those around me feel comfortable than on living in true alignment. It was easier to play the part in relationships that I had always played, and the idea of rocking the boat by being more of who I am was intimidating. Only when I started to examine my *shoulds* and got to know the part of me that held so tightly to them for safety, comfort, love, security, and validation did I start to release my grip. I could feel my conscious "adult" self coming online, helping to shepherd the more conditioned, younger parts of me into the more integrated whole of who I was becoming. Up until that point, it was difficult for me to discern whether a choice was right for me because I was so busy thinking of the many people and possibilities outside of myself, and how following my heart would affect them, that there was no way to be sure.

Did I know there was a better way all along? Deep down, yes, I did. But my relationship with my inner voice, that inner knowing, was hanging on by a thread because it had been gradually frayed by self-doubt. That self-doubt had compounded, bred by experiences like being bullied in middle school, taking on the emotional weight of others to the degree that I wasn't able to distinguish how *I* felt, and constantly being rejected in my pursuit of an acting career. The inner voice can stand to have its volume lowered for quite some time without erupting, but ignore it for long enough and it will yell, *loudly,* over the loudspeaker of your life.

Once those questions started coming, the things in my life that were not actually for me became painfully obvious, and my feelings of anxiety, depression, sadness, and disconnection reached an all-time high. It felt like my world was crumbling, and maybe it feels like yours is too (or like it *might* if you start listening to your inner voice instead of the conditioning programmed in you). But the truth is that you are being given the opportunity to look around and evaluate what's happening in your life and who you are in relationships, at work, and to yourself. This can either shock you into a more conscious state or scare you back into the comforting arms of that destructive autopilot. If you are experiencing this, let me assure you that there's nothing inherently wrong with you. Not in the slightest. In fact, your inner voice is up and running (just as it always has been, but perhaps louder now) and bringing your attention and awareness to what needs to be adjusted in order to feel the harmony that you desire. It's great news that your inner voice is getting your attention in this way, even if it feels a bit uncomfortable.

Pass the Mic

One of the reasons we stopped trusting ourselves is because we abandon ourselves during pain. If a friend comes to us and says, "I'm in pain, I'm so sad, I'm so heartbroken," we would never say, "I'm out of here. I can't take this. I'm sorry, I'm done. You should google it." We would never abandon our friend in her moment of pain, but we do it to ourselves all the time. Which is how we break trust with ourselves.

Stay with your pain. Don't run. Feel it. That changes you. The pain is like an alchemy. It literally changes who you are, but it also makes you become a woman who trusts herself because you become a woman who doesn't abandon herself in pain.

—Glennon Doyle, author of *Untamed*
ALMOST 30, EPISODE 325

As you embark on this journey, my hope is that you learn that following your heart is the safest bet. When you follow your heart, you never have to worry—you are coming back to who you really are, confronting who you are not, and answering the call of your soul. You are protected by intention and clarity. It doesn't mean that it will be easy every step of the way, but it *does* mean that you won't abandon yourself along the way.

I also hope that you do the work necessary to make sure that your sense of self-worth is as strong as it should be. Know that recalibrating and reinforcing your sense of self-worth takes work on both the conscious and subconscious levels. It's on this subconscious level that our mind stores the fears, beliefs, and memories that we aren't even aware of. An important part of doing this work on the subconscious level is taking good care of yourself in the process because, whether you realize it or not, this kind of work takes a lot of energy. It also has very real and clear effects. We'll talk more about how to do this in the Body section of the book, coming up next.

But for now, make a point of taking care of yourself in the moments when you can feel these questions rising to the surface.

Journal: Rewrite Your Beliefs

Before we go any further in this book, it's time to call some of your subconscious beliefs and stories to the surface to be seen for what they really are. Have a pen and paper nearby, but start by first closing your eyes and finding stillness.

Breathe in and out through your nose, deeply into your lower belly, and imagine that with every breath you are clearing any stagnancy and igniting truth within you, inviting your inner voice to speak. It might be helpful to observe your inhale as a green wind sweeping through your body, and your exhale as a golden liquid fire that sparks truth as it moves up and out. Repeat ten to twenty cycles of breath as you continue to visualize green wind coming in and golden liquid fire billowing out. When you feel complete, settle into a natural breath.

Gently open your eyes and write down any beliefs you currently have about your life that begin with "I can't . . ." If this feels difficult initially, reflect on areas of life that feel a bit sticky right now, that make you feel insecure or even hopeless. Here are some examples of limiting beliefs that I've experienced in the past, many of which were beliefs I had unconsciously inherited from others:

I can't make this move . . .
I can't leave my job . . .
I can't tell this person how I really feel . . .

Next, I'd like you to finish the belief with a "because." For example: *I can't find a partner* because *all the good ones are taken.*

Now explore the core feeling that justifies that belief: *This belief really speaks to the fact that I'm scared I won't find happiness in a relationship like I see other people have.* Or maybe distilled further, *. . . because I don't trust myself to choose a partner who is aligned with me on a soul level.*

Now I want you to extract the subconscious *I am* statements from your beliefs. For example, the *I am* statement to extract from "I can't find a partner because I don't trust myself to choose a partner" is: *I am untrustworthy* or *I am unworthy of being chosen.* One by one, extract these limiting beliefs and then say the *I am* statement out loud. After speaking each *I am,* pause, close your eyes, place your hands on your heart, and tune in to see if what you're saying about yourself feels like who you really are or if it feels like an expired or borrowed version of you. Remember: a single experience can imprint a belief about ourselves that lasts for years and years, so we have to check the expiration date and validity of these beliefs on the regular.

For the expired *I ams,* as well as any that feel like they never belonged to you in the first place, I want you to write down a counterbelief that's more reflective of who you are in this moment (or who you want to become). So, for example:

I can't find a new partner because I do not trust myself to pick someone who is good for me.

Becomes . . .

I haven't yet found my partner, but I trust myself to discern who I connect with on a heart level, and I trust the timing of my life.

See how it feels to say your counterbelief out loud. Close your eyes, place your hands on your heart, and tune in to the sensations in your body as you speak your new belief. Does it give you a surge of hope? Does your body relax? Does your heart feel more open?

You might write these new beliefs down where you can see them regularly, you might repeat them to yourself every morning, or you might just embody these beliefs for the next week to see how it feels to navigate the world with this belief underscoring your life. I bet you'll find that you start to naturally shed the expired beliefs about yourself and a new way of being will be revealed to you, often a way that is lighter, more present, and in flow with who you are in this moment.

Before We Proceed . . .

While I know that sometimes you just want that voice in your head and all the questions it's asking to *go away, please,* the fact that you're here makes me want to throw you a party! It truly is such a big deal. So, before you dive any further into these pages, please, *please* take a moment to honor where you are and the awareness that you already have. Sure, you might not have all the answers, you might not even have clarity about most things in your life right now—but you do have awareness. And *that* is something to celebrate.

Now that you've finished this chapter and before you move on to the next, take a victory lap around the block, draw yourself a salt bath, write yourself a love note, or turn on your favorite playlist and have a dance party. Celebrating where you are now is important fuel for the next part of your process, so don't miss it!

Chapter 3

YOU ARE A SOUL

Krista

t all seemed so magical in the movies: being chosen by a chiseled, rich hottie and whisked away to a mansion to sing to birds all day . . . so enticing, so exciting! The only problem was that this happily-ever-after relied on one thing: someone else. I figured the reason we were all here, the purpose of life, was to find The One. Why else would we suffer through the riffraff or date losers, getting ghosted by men we met on apps and going through all the pain of that first-true-love heartbreak? I was so invested in finding that one partner, a person to *complete* me. "I am looking for the other half of my soul," I used to say to my work wife, Cassidy, as I sat in her cubicle. I wanted that feeling of completion, to feel like I was living with purpose. I wanted to have all the magic and miracles in my life that I had been led to believe came when . . . well, when I had someone else alongside me in it. I lived my life thinking that all magic, purpose, and love were found not within myself but through a connection with another human being.

I was hot on my quest to find The One while I was living in Chicago on my nine-to-five grind. One steamy summer day, I swept my hair up in a pony to keep it from grazing my wet neck as I settled into a corner seat next to a tech bro. I glanced at him out of the corner of my eye: cute and maybe successful (he did have a nice watch and a collared shirt on), but *not my soulmate*, I thought, so I popped in my headphones as the number 8 bus headed up Halsted Avenue to my office. Lizzo had just made her way onto the scene, and she had a new hit song called "Soulmate." Whether it was her or the beat, I perked up.

> *I'm my own soulmate*
> *I know how to love me*

Apparently Lizzo was tired of looking for The One too, but it appeared she was further along in her journey than I was. She had already come to the point where she realized *it was her,* all along. Could I be my own one? Could *I* be the soulmate I had been looking for?

This idea that someone else completes us sets us up for a life of emptiness and desperation. The *Bachelor* and *Bachelorette* franchises are built on this idea: the contestants choose to live in a huge mansion where the cobblestone driveway always seems to be wet, guzzle cheap white wine, make out in front of the world, and spend more time in a hot tub than can possibly be considered healthy, all for the chance to find their soulmate.

We've been conditioned to think we'll complete our quest for answers, happiness, and wholeness by connecting with the soul of another. But we actually find all this wisdom and juiciness through soul collaboration with *ourselves.* It's likely the greatest collaboration you'll ever experience, and a far deeper love than you could ever experience with any other human.

Pass the Mic

No other spiritual practice matters if you're not willing to inquire about you, to be really curious about how you arrived at your current self without judgment.

—Devi Brown, author and spiritual teacher
ALMOST 30, EPISODE 399

What I didn't realize in my soulmate search was that my soul was always waiting for me—no searching necessary. If I could have a sleepover with my soul, she would probably roll her eyes at me, like, *Girl, please,* because our souls are not "pick me" girls who try to get our attention obsessively! The truth is that they are an expansive, eternal energy that lives way beyond our comprehension.

If you take or tweet (#RIP) anything from this chapter, please know that you have a soul, you are a soul, and that this most incredibly special part of yourself is the part that we humans often overlook. Your soul is your special sauce, your X factor, your magnetism, and your essence. It's also the key to living the most beautiful, epic life possible. The soul is your immaterial aspect or essence. I like to think that it's the most loving part of yourself. It's a devoted guide for your human experience and a gentle voice always ready to offer her best advice if only you get quiet enough to listen. When you look closely at our cultural idea of soulfulness, you see that it is tied to the most memorable parts of life: nourishing food, meaningful conversation, authentic relationships, and experiences that touch the heart. This feels accurate, because the soul wants to lead us to those things that will nourish us, light us up, allow us to express the fullest version of ourselves, and experience love. The soul is revealed to us in connection to others, as well as through our inner communication and personal intimacy. If you have a good therapist, sometimes they feel like the voice of your soul: gentle, patient, non-judgmental, and always there to support you. (Oh, if you don't have a therapist and feel curious about therapy, I highly recommend getting one to support you through this journey!) Your soul speaks no other language than the one you need to hear, and, as we've discussed and most important for the purpose of this chapter, it holds the blueprint of your potential. It works with both your mind and body in an incredible trinity, which we commonly call the mind-body-soul connection.

One more very important thing about the soul and your journey toward it during this period of life: no matter how disconnected from it you might feel in this moment, you don't need to search for your soul because she is never lost. It's more a matter of you being too distracted to hear her voice. I now know that all the things that I wanted to seek outside of myself to create meaning, magic, pleasure, purpose, joy, peace, and creativity were found in my relationship with my soul. All along, she was ready and waiting to give me what I thought I needed from a soulmate.

Saturn Return and Your Soul

Of all the things you stand to learn and gain through your Saturn Return, connecting with your soul is the biggest and most important, because the impact will trickle down to literally every other aspect of your life. In fact, this is some of the most important work you'll ever do, because your soul understands your own unique path, and walking that path is what you came here to do.

If you're someone who has been in touch with the whisper of your soul's voice (which we realize over time is our most loving inner voice) from a young age and haven't shut it down over time, then your Saturn Return could be a time for deepening that relationship and moving further into a more aligned and expansive life. But for those who are disconnected from their soul (which is most of us), Saturn Return is your soul's built-in wake-up call. If you haven't heard your soul's voice yet, it's time you start to listen, because without it you'll feel more lost and confused than ever during your Saturn Return. Saturn's parental guidance is intricately related to your soul because it reveals which life choices are out of sync with your soul's true desire. Basically, if your life feels like a sad Taylor Swift song, you can bet that Saturn is working its magic to acquaint you with your soul and guide you onto her path (whether or not you like how Saturn goes about it).

The good news is if you work with the energy of Saturn rather than fighting against it, this time can be rewarding and life-changing. If you listen to your soul call and allow it to point you toward your path, then Saturn will give you the discipline, focus, and grit to face your fears and fulfill your soul's mission.

Here are just a few ways that your life becomes enriched once you and your soul are in constant communion.

Deeper sense of purpose. When you feel like you have a spiritual ride-or-die with you, a constant loving companion, life can feel so much more enriching. When I started to connect with my soul in a purposeful way, I actually found my purpose (well, part of it) through *Almost 30*. As I have evolved, the depth of intimacy I share with my soul has evolved and so has the work and creativity I have brought through to the world. Your version of this experience is available to you, and your soul knows how to get you there.

Pass the Mic

I really think the single marker of human success moving forward is going to be your ability to adapt. And when you're stressed, you just don't . . . if you can get out of that state, remind yourself that you're God pretending to be human, remind yourself that you are the ocean pretending to be the wave, then all the decisions, all the demands, don't seem so overwhelming.

It's like a slow shedding, right? And bit by bit, day by day, meditation by meditation, you're sloughing off all these old layers of stress that are keeping you from the bliss and fulfillment and enlightenment that is already inside of you. The idea is that you're already perfect, you were born perfect. Everything else is stress.

—Emily Fletcher, founder of Ziva meditation
ALMOST 30, EPISODE 423

More satisfaction. A connection to something greater than yourself and the feeling you'll get from making that connection is powerful. According to the American Psychological Association, people of varying religious and spiritual beliefs (including a quarter of whom identified as atheist) who have a sense of "oneness"—a feeling that everything, including themselves, is connected to a higher purpose—appear to have a greater overall life satisfaction than those who do not.[2] Another study from the journal *Frontiers in Psychology*[3] found that people who incorporate spiritual practices into their lives can strengthen their mental health and psychological well-being. When we are connected to our soul, it can feel like we are in tune with God, the Universe, and everything in it, which gives us that satisfying feeling of oneness that we seek.

Reduced stress and anxiety. On top of the more spiritual benefits of communicating with your soul, there are some physiological benefits as well. Communicating with your soul through meditation (more on that later in the chapter) can help to reduce stress and anxiety. Purposefully relaxing your mind and focusing your attention away from external distractions enables you to enjoy a more peaceful connection with the world around you.

More clarity and better decision-making. Notice that when you make a decision from your mind, you will likely bounce back and forth between options, questioning your choices and doubting yourself. This can be an agonizing process that feels like it takes forever. But if you can take the time to ground, center, and connect with your soul and make a decision from there, you can *feel* the right answer almost immediately. For me, the answer that is in alignment with my soul gives me a warm feeling of rightness and calm, as opposed to the other choices that make me feel anxious, tight, off-center, nauseated, cold, or empty (fun!). It may be a different experience for you. Whatever the specifics are, when we check in with the body, *yes* often feels expansive, and *no* feels contracted. We're about to get into some tips and practices for connecting with the soul, but when it comes to making decisions and receiving clarity, I like to take a second to feel into the situation I'm in with my eyes closed and receive the answer or best course of action from there. Some people receive their answer as a voice in their head, an image, vision, dream, a knowing, or a sense in their gut that something is right or wrong. You and your soul speak your own little language, so take time to explore how the two of you communicate best.

Now, let's get into some ways to speak directly to your soul and hear its wisdom.

Soul Journaling

One of the most impactful practices I've learned for connecting with my soul directly is called *soul journaling*, and it came from a podcast guest, Elisa Romeo, author of the book *Meet Your Soul*. For the past twenty-four years, Elisa has been talking with her soul (who she calls Sophia) through her journal on a daily basis. Sometimes she's just checking in during these conversations, many days she's asking practical questions grounded in her daily life, and every now and then, she's shocked by what comes through. Elisa says that, for all of us, having this conversation in written form is important because it allows you to look back over time and view material affirmation that your soul always has all the answers. Of *course* your soul has all the answers and also knows how to deliver them in the way you can hear best, most clearly because your soul understands you better than anyone else.

Pass the Mic

Your soul is that inner perfect therapist-guru-mother that can heal every issue in our lives.

—Elisa Romeo, author of *Meet Your Soul*
ALMOST 30, EPISODE 390

Elisa's one caution about this practice is that it requires honesty with ourselves. If we are used to holding back, prioritizing others' needs above our own, and are unaware of our own feelings about a situation, we may be uncomfortable tuning in to that truth. There can be a discrepancy between what our soul says and what our ego wants, because the true self (soul) and the false self (ego) can have different agendas for our life. The truth that the soul has access to is from a higher, more expansive perspective, and based on more information than our human mind can comprehend. The soul also won't get caught up in the stories we tell ourselves and the drama of the 3D experience, so hearing or seeing the clarity of its voice on paper can be jarring at first. But the goal of this practice is to align your soul with your humanity, and to learn to distinguish between the voice of your ego and the voice of your soul in the process. Despite any discomfort you may experience along the way, I promise it is a worthwhile pursuit.

Journal: Connect with Your Soul

I've adapted this practice from Elisa and continue to soul journal a few days a week because it allows me to consistently remember the truth of who I am. It's been a life-changing way to hold my center and live my life from this place. Here's how to try it:

1. **Set your space.** This simply means that you are going to make sure your space feels supportive for your practice, and that will look different for everyone. You might light a candle or clear your environment by burning incense or palo santo or ringing a bell. Bring in plants or flowers to add more life. You might also want to make an offering, which could include flowers, herbs, or anything else you feel called or inspired by. For this particular practice, also make sure you have enough space to move a few feet in every direction, and that you have a journal and something to write with nearby. You'll also want a hydrating beverage, like water, tea, or coconut water, because you'll be moving some energy, and hydration can support this process.

2. **Set your intention.** Intention setting is a simple process that involves consciously directing your thoughts and energy toward a desired outcome or experience. By setting an intention you increase the likelihood of achieving it. Your intention can be spoken out loud or in your heart.

3. **Choose a song.** I've added this step to my soul journaling practice as a way to get myself out of my head and into my heart and body before journaling. If this sounds like something that might

be supportive for you, start by picking a song you love to move to. A song that not only makes you want to dance but that also evokes emotion. You can pick a few depending on how much time you have. Play the song(s) and allow yourself to be moved. Let go of what this movement should look like and let the feelings that want to be expressed come through physically. The movement should feel cathartic in nature.

4. **Find a comfortable seated position on the floor.** Once your music-inspired movement feels complete, either cue up meditation music that you love or turn the music off. Sit down on the floor so that you feel grounded, find length in your spine, and plug your sit bones into the earth. Imagine that there is a beautiful opening at the top of your head. Visualize energy running cyclically from the core of the Earth, up the left side of your spine all the way to the heavens through the top of your head, then back into your head and down the right side of your spine down and into the Earth. Give yourself at least seven to ten minutes in this meditative state.

5. **Greet your soul.** When it feels like the right time in your meditation, welcome your soul. Call her forward (you can say something as simple as, "Soul, I want to connect with you") and share your intention with her, again either out loud or in your heart. It may feel weird to just say "Hello," but your greeting really can be as casual as this. You can do nothing wrong here, because your soul knows you so intimately that, while words can be used, they're not necessary. Let yourself speak to her like a friend or someone you love; it doesn't need to be perfect, just whatever comes naturally. When it comes to your soul, you are loved unconditionally!

6. **Write in your journal.** At the top of a sheet of paper, address your soul by name, then write down your first question or anything you want to share with your soul.

7. **Write your soul's answer.** Take a deep breath and put pen to paper, allowing your soul to come forward and write through you.

Trust the process: don't doubt what's coming through. Your mind might want to interject, especially at first, but stay focused on your soul and ask as many questions as you'd like. If you're trying to distinguish between the mind and soul, know that the mind tends to get stuck in a loop of repetitive thoughts, and it might even communicate through criticism. The soul lovingly brings insight and wisdom to the surface that might surprise you at first, leaving you wondering, "How is this coming through me and onto the paper?" Don't stop writing until your soul feels complete.

8. **Receive your soul's wisdom.** Once you are finished writing, go back and read what your soul has to say. Trust what comes through, and notice how you feel. *Amazed? Shocked? Comforted? Seen and held?* Let yourself sit and marinate in the feeling of being connected with your soul. Try to capture it from a somatic perspective, so that you can remember how it feels to tap into your soul.

It might feel strange to write to your soul at first. You might even wonder if the process is working. But the more accustomed you get to directly communicating with your soul, the clearer her voice will become, and the more obvious her role in your life and the wisdom she has to share will become. Staying consistent and connecting with your soul regularly will help support you in developing a deeper relationship with your soul.

Feel All the Feels

Most of us lose our connection with our soul as we grow up. Once we become aware of what's expected of us and what others might think if we don't follow their prescribed rules of "acceptable" behavior, we tend to listen to societal influence rather than the whisper of our soul. In fact, many go from being total soul-pleasers to chronic people-pleasers in just a matter of years. We begin to outsource our intuition and imagination to figures we deem to be authorities or role models. We rarely allow ourselves to feel our Big Feelings all the way through anymore, because we've learned they'll be met with either punishment, shame, or, in some cases, even a threat.

Pass the Mic

We are a culture that worships happiness. We think we're supposed to be happy all the time, and if we're not happy, then everybody panics. When nobody talks about pain, you start to think that your pain means you're different and weird, and you start to hide or numb it. Then you miss the benefits of sitting with your pain. The point of life is to become over and over again, and to become more beautiful versions of ourselves. The fuel we use to become that is pain.

It's sitting with your anger. It's sitting with your fear and your doubt. It's not numbing yourself out of it, over and over again. It's not grabbing those red easy buttons. We all learned our easy buttons, and the tragedy of that is that when we transport ourselves out of our pain, we miss all our transformation. Because everything we need to become the people we're supposed to be next is inside the pain of now.

It's not about feeling happy. It's about feeling everything. I used to think that if I did feel my pain or my anger, I would be like a black hole from which I would never recover. That is just not true. You can feel all of it and survive. And also just this beautiful relationship you end up in with yourself when you become a woman who doesn't abandon herself. I have become a human being. I will abandon everyone else's expectations of me. Everybody's. Even Abby's.* Everybody's, before I will ever abandon myself again. That's the only failure for me now. The only failure I can think of is self-abandonment.

—Glennon Doyle, author of *Untamed*
ALMOST 30, EPISODE 325

*Abby Wambach is an Olympic gold medalist, FIFA World Cup champion, *New York Times* bestselling author, and Glennon's wife.

Think about it: How often were your feelings diminished based on the discomfort of an adult? "Oh, you're fine. Don't be upset—there's nothing to be upset about!" Or, on the other hand, how often were you distracted from your feelings by the promise of a cookie, or some new toy, or anything else to divert your attention? Sure, the adults in your life were well intentioned, but these kinds of reactions teach children that their feelings are not based in truth and should be questioned, minimized, or ignored. The denial of how you feel is so important to recognize and mend because one of the primary ways your soul communicates with you is through feelings and emotions. Your feelings might not always be convenient for those around you (or for you, for that matter!), but they hold important information about the state of your soul and how aligned with it you are. Consider your feelings a compass to help you find direction, clarity, and clues about your healing and fulfillment.

Your soul will always take the higher perspective. This means that sometimes your human experience or feelings might not match your soul's. Let's say you decide to blame someone or get angry at them for a situation you're involved in; your feelings may be different from the perspective of your soul. In this case, your soul could even be feeling appreciation, love, or joy for that person and the growth they are affording you by triggering your anger. The feelings you feel are always valid; however, it's important that you acknowledge them, process them, and allow them to move. Otherwise that distance between the lower feeling (anger, frustration, and resentment, for example) and your soul's truth of love and coherence can create tension within you.

In my life, I have learned that my ego can shoot for the small dream. But when I let go and allow my soul to guide me, life unfolds in ways that I never could have imagined. The same is true for and available to all of us. The ego limits our options and potential, whereas the soul expands them. The ego follows a plan, whereas the soul is guided by feelings and makes its own way. My soul has always been guiding me throughout the process, and it's wanted something different—something *more*—for me than my ego did. Something more aligned. Something that was bigger than a small-minded manifestation list I was ticking off in my notes app and that, whether I realized it or not, was driven by my sense of unworthiness.

One day when I was in the midst of one of the hardest periods of my life and it felt like my world was crumbling, I heard my soul say, clear as day, "Your humanness dislikes this, but I love it. We learn so much from contrast." Because it was so clear, this voice helped me remember that we often learn the most during times of suffering. The times in my life when I have felt tested the most have also been the times that have changed me the most. We tend to optimize so much for comfort, yet we learn so much in times of pain. I bet you can see this at work in your own life. Take a moment or two to think about some of the hardest times in your life: Did they make you better? Are you the person you are today because of the moments when you've been tested? By trusting your path, listening to your soul, and surrendering to what is, you can reduce the tension that you feel during times of suffering. Wisdom from the soul is usually crystallized through the experience of suffering. When things go well, we rarely stop to ask questions, but difficult situations force us out of our mindless state and offer up an opportunity to reflect on our experience and go inward to speak to the soul. The function of the soul is to indicate its desire, not impose it.

Unlike the mind, the soul is patient and gentle—she doesn't like to yell. Our minds can really get us worked up, repeating and looping anxious thoughts that sometimes aren't that helpful. The soul, however . . . she just keeps it cool. Much like your favorite teacher growing up, the soul is gentle, patient, and calm. She waits until everyone in the classroom is quiet before she speaks in her soft voice. In order to receive this teacher's guidance, you have to be settled, intentional, and listen intently. The information you glean from her is so much more valuable because you've earned it by forgoing the desire to keep chatting with your classmates, rustling in your chair, and working on homework. You're going to listen to whatever she has to say and act accordingly, because you trust, respect, and love her lessons.

Often, it's only through looking back that we can see how our soul has been at work in the background all along, nudging us toward a life of alignment, often while we're none the wiser. This is what I can say with confidence about our souls in the years, perhaps even decades, when we are still asleep to the power and truth of its guidance:

- *Your soul will guide you through your curiosities that are outside of the norm.* Sometimes this might lead to you feeling isolated or misunderstood, especially when you're a kid. Did you ever get strange looks from your classmates because of something you said, did, or even something you wore? Or did any of your interests as a child surprise your parents? Sometimes what the rest of the world considers unusual is just what our soul prefers. The unique aspects of your identity are likely signs of your soul already pointing the way toward your unique path.
- *Your soul will speak to you and guide you gently at first because she doesn't want to scare you away from your greatest good.* Have you ever had a gut feeling to take a different route on a walk or jog and then run into someone you know? Have you ever heard a song on the radio that felt like an answer to a question you'd been mulling over? The soul loves to speak through synchronicity. Natalie Miles, an intuitive spiritual guide and mentor who blew Lindsey and me away when she came on the show, talked about how there can be a temptation to run from what our soul wants because some of it involves making hard decisions, speaking our truth, and (as the inspirational poster of horses running in the wild that hung in my high school used to say) *blazing our own trail!* The soul doesn't always lead us down a path that makes sense or seems logical. But, when we are willing to overcome our fears and listen to what our soul wants us to hear, we can heal our pain and reduce our suffering rather than continuing to run from it. If we don't do the healing our soul is calling for, we'll often just continue to repeat the same patterns and stories over and over again.

Pass the Mic

I always say that the spirit will throw you little pebbles and if you're not listening to the pebbles, they'll throw larger rocks, and if you're not listening to the rocks, they're going to bring in that massive boulder that is going to make you stop and pause and change your life to get you back onto that light path that you're supposed to be going on.

—Natalie Miles, author of *You Are Intuitive*
ALMOST 30, EPISODE 127

- *Your soul doesn't need to be the loudest voice in the room.* The ego can get loud, and it's not the soul's style to overpower it in order to be heard. This means that you must first quiet the ego in order to hear the soul.
- *Your soul wants to connect with you.* Even if you're not completely sold yet, set your intention to reconnect with your soul, and she will find a way to let you know she's there.

As you think back on your relationship with your soul, let your mind wander to times when you heard or received clarity in a meditation, in the shower, while driving, or otherwise out of the blue. If you look for them, I'm willing to bet you'll find little clues scattered throughout your life that show you how your soul likes to speak to you and that demonstrate her unwavering support. She is just so, so hyped about your unfolding.

Waste Your Time

When you're in your twenties it can be so tempting to "do it all," to pack your schedule, try to do it all, and push yourself to capacity. In doing so, there's a danger in getting caught up in the addiction of *doing* instead of leaning into *being*. Sometimes the most radical thing you can do is to truly embrace and enjoy your life, to challenge the status quo of unworthiness and tap into the true knowing of your soul's worth.

Recently, my girlfriends and I went on a trip to Paris where we were immersed in a sparkling, vibrant, juicy Parisian summer. We spent our time wandering the cobblestoned streets, meandering around tiny vintage shops, eating buttery pastries, and pretending to understand fine art. This trip made me realize that I had forgotten how important travel is for my soul. When I'm on a trip, I am present, intentional, and my energy is light. In this state, I can practice listening to my intuition, that inner soul voice. Getting away like this always makes me realize how much of my daily life involves the small world of being on my phone, computer, and living online, looking at screens for connection and meaning, when real life is happening offline. I'm reminded that the world exists in the tiny towns that don't have Wi-Fi, where people slowly sip espresso and don't subscribe to the 24/7 news cycle or care about Instagram likes. It's made clear to me that I am easily able to connect with my soul whenever I have periods during which the productive part of me thinks I'm just wasting time.

What if what we previously saw as wasted time was the real way to live our lives and align with our soul? When I travel, I itch less for dopamine and excitement, and I feel more at peace. I smile at strangers and eat lots of carbs. I don't wear makeup, and I forget to look at my phone. I swim late at night and sleep in way past time for any sort of morning ritual. The only workout I do is dance. I sleep more and remember my dreams. I hear my own voice, and I listen to my soul. I see myself outside of my usual identities. Although the productive part of me can sometimes see travel as a waste of time, the wiser part of me knows that this is some of the most important time of all: when I can truly be in the moment, slip into a flow state, and commune with my soul. In this state, I understand clearly that the value of my life and soul is not dependent on any labels, job, or goal.

The soul is always there, but we can feel it the most easily when we rest, feel, and go slowly. It's easy to connect that way. For me, this happens through travel. For you, it might be another way. What if what we previously saw as a waste of time was actually the moment our soul didn't want us to miss? Continually living by our to-do list and schedule sucks the life out of us, and our soul wants more. Our soul wants us to live from what feels good, instead of what feels obligatory.

Five stars, would recommend wasting as much time as you can for your soul's sake! Don't just waste it willy-nilly, but waste it wisely, slowly, and with intention. Choose Friday night or Sunday morning (or both!) and waste your time like you have all the time in the world. Whip up your favorite dessert, go on luxurious dinner dates with friends, meander leisurely through parks, and talk to your pets in your finest baby voice. Stare at the stars! Even if it feels like you really *are* wasting your time at first, I bet you'll find it's what is most needed for connecting with your soul. Think of time wasted as the life you're creating. Live the novelty of the moment and notice how your soul responds. It's a gift to her, because your soul wants so much more than monotonously making plans, packing schedules, and living by minute-by-minute agendas. A normal life of checking boxes is not what she came here for.

Try Meditating (Again)

While I was writing this chapter, my soul tapped me on the shoulder and said to make sure to mention the OG way to connect, by getting quiet and practicing meditation. Sometimes I fear that people's eyes glaze over and they stop listening/reading when I bring up meditation, because the good old excuses start to come up: *But I can't meditate—I've tried!* Even aside from connecting with your soul, there are so many other incredible benefits to your overall well-being that come from meditation—or even just attempting to get quiet for a few minutes a day. If you have trouble meditating, I want to try to help you get through the sticky part and be with yourself.

No matter how much you've struggled with meditation before, now is the time to start. In addition to allowing you to regulate the nervous system, access source energy, and flood your body and brain with dopamine and serotonin, Emily Fletcher explains that meditation offers a prime opportunity to separate your own desires from those that were programmed into you by society. You can think of meditation as one of your biggest tools for navigating Saturn Return with finesse and seeing and learning all the things that Saturn wants you to.

Meditation has been the direct key for me to connect with my soul, and the one thing I always come back to when people ask about my spiritual path. It served as the soil for my budding spiritual practice and did more for me in that way than any psychedelic, tropical retreat, or conversation with a guru ever did. It's the quiet mind, the in-between, the patience, the calm, the nervous system relief that I so badly needed in my life. It helped me to separate from my thoughts and to finally figure out who I was outside of the reactions I had to my environment.

As someone who once had a hard time being with myself for longer than a few minutes at a time, I found it really hard to meditate. I was scared of what would come up, that my thoughts would consume me, and that if I sat for long enough I would hear the truth of what was really on my mind. You are not alone in feeling uncomfortable, but learning to sit with yourself is an essential part of life. We can only avoid ourselves for so long. Trust me, if I can do this, then so can you, my friend! It's not always meant to be easy, but if you commit, over time it will become one of the most important things you do for yourself.

Practice: Try Meditation (Again)

Here are a few basics to help you cultivate a meditation practice that will stick.

- Find a quiet place to sit, preferably where you won't be bothered by roommates, partners, kids, or pets—this time is for you.

- Wear comfortable clothes so that you can focus fully on the experience versus your jean waistband.
- Sit up straight with your spine erect, placing your hands gently on the tops of your knees or somewhere comfortable.
- Close your eyes (I like to imagine I'm drifting them closed).
- Start to notice your breath.
- Tune in to your senses: what you smell, taste, feel, and, yes, even hear. Allow the sounds of your environment not to cause you frustration, but to bring you closer to the present moment (the sound of nature can be really supportive, actually), which is the goal.
- When your mind wanders, let it. Allow the thoughts to come and go without attaching an emotion or feeling to them. The goal is to become the observer of your thoughts, not to conquer them. This is the practice that allows you to see your unconscious mind, which is important during Saturn Return (or any time in life when you want to get to know yourself better), because it helps you understand your current programming.
- Repeat this practice daily, or when it feels needed. Allow it to be imperfect and just what it is called: *practice*.

Coming Home Through Your Values

Just like all good relationships, your relationship with your soul is one that you have to prioritize, appreciate, and nurture on an ongoing basis. Even with that, there *will* be periods of disconnection throughout your life. For me, these are usually times when I feel angry, angsty, or "off."

Even during these times—*especially* during these times—know that the soul inside of you is always trying to capture your attention. No matter how far away you may feel from it, there is always a way back to your true home. I've found that when my values are clear, I can more readily connect with my soul.

During your Saturn Return, you are questioning the values that were given to you and discovering the values that exist at your core. These values are truly yours and will guide you in making better decisions, steer you along the right path, help you persevere through adversity, and, most important of all, keep you true to yourself and the desires of your soul.

In my experience, values are one of the few consistent things throughout life. Although I have changed, the seasons have changed, and my relationships have changed, my values have remained constant. When we know our values, we can also understand and respect the values of others because we can see them clearly, not to judge or condemn but to honor. Values are not something that can be compromised for any reason if you are to remain true to yourself. A firm set of values serves as a solid pillar and clear North Star. Values help prevent you from staying stuck or making decisions that aren't true to you because you're feeling swayed by emotions, fear, or other circumstances in life outside of yourself.

Clarifying and crystallizing your values helps the rest fall away, which makes the whole process of remembering who you are and living in alignment with that person so much simpler. I've found that when I remove anything that distracts me from the things I value, I'm able to see with clarity what *does* matter. The intentional promotion of my values is crystallized through this incredible process of purification.

Pass the Mic

For me, it's all about what my nervous system feels like based on how I run my life. Am I in line with my values? Am I doing what's important to me?

—Whitney Goodman, LMFT, author of *Toxic Positivity*
ALMOST 30, EPISODE 585

Practice: Clarify Your Values

Maybe you don't know what your values are, or maybe it feels like you need a little inspiration or some ways to support yourself in understanding what they are. Well, I got you.

- **Review your life.** What are your defining moments? These can be the times when you experienced the beautiful magic of what it means to be alive, like skinny dipping with friends at a lake house under the stars, laughing until you cry while running barefoot in the grass, or a moment when your strength was created through turbulence. What was at the core of these moments? The essence of these moments likely tells you something about your values. And, remember, sometimes we can create through contrast, to see what we do not want to experience, live, or embody as a way to further shed light on our authentic desire in life.
- **Consider what you admire the most about other people.** Think about the people who expand your life, and get specific about what it is you love about them. Who or what types of people do you find yourself drawn to? What do you notice about how they operate and move in their life, and how might you apply that to your own life?
- **Observe yourself and the decisions that you make for a week.** Why do you do what you do—what motivates you to make certain decisions or take on certain roles? Do these motivations feel like a true reflection of you, or are they driven by fear or an outside source? If they are the latter, what internal motivations would more accurately reflect how you actually feel and want to be? See how things shift when you start to be more intentional about honoring your true motivations and what direction they might be guiding you in.

- **Crystallize this information into values.** Notice what common themes have come up through this self-inquiry. What values are you operating according to that are your own? Which values have been inherited from others? The first list is your North Star; the second list belongs to someone else.
- **Put your values into practice.** Keep the list of your values with you to refer to when you're making difficult or confusing decisions. Notice how life shifts and you step into your truest self when you start making decisions based on your values.

One thing I've learned about getting clear on my own values and making decisions based on them is that, while I may not reach all my goals, I can always successfully maintain my values. When I act according to this inner compass, the right path seems to have a way of unfolding in front of me.

If You Get Lost Again

Remember that no matter how much you ignore her guidance, your soul is loyal and constant; she will be there when you decide to return. The return can happen in an instant.

If you need a little help, though, you'll want to identify clues about how your current life experience reflects things that make you happy (or don't), that make you feel like yourself (or not). Answer as honestly as possible without overthinking it. In fact, you might even want to let your inner child, that part of you that existed before everything else, take the wheel here. Your inner child encompasses the aspects of your personality from childhood, including your capacity for spontaneity, creativity, joy, and sensitivity. Like when you're scared to take a new step or feel inexplicably sad over a small thing, your inner child might be tugging on your sleeve, asking for attention and reassurance. It's a blend of your most unfiltered emotions and desires, serving both as your cheerleader and the ghost of childhood past needing a hug or a high-five. It embodies both the positive experiences and the unresolved trauma or needs from those years. Come back to that innocence, purity, playfulness, and joy, and have some fun with this! When you've finished, notice if there are any hidden signposts in your answers that lead you back to important parts of yourself you've forgotten.

- When have I felt my best? What was I doing? Who was I with?
- What scares me the most right now?
- What am I inspired by?
- Who am I inspired by?
- What brings me joy?
- What am I naturally really good at?
- What is the most important thing in my life right now?
- Who are the most important people in my life? Do these people have anything in common?
- What season of my life resulted in the most growth?
- What are some of my happiest memories?
- When did I feel most proud of myself?
- What in my life am I grateful for?

Allow these answers to remind you and revive you. *THERE* you are, always a soul connection away.

In our next chapter, we'll explore defining, cultivating, and expressing what spirituality means to you. But before we get there, a quick reminder: your relationship to spirituality—and really, all relationships in your life—starts with you. Your connection to your soul is the foundation for it all. Never forget that your soul has got you. She's working for you and pulling for you, just like we are.

Chapter 4

ARE YOU THERE, GOD? IT'S ME.

Lindsey

In seventh grade, I transferred from a local public school to an all-girls private Catholic school. My parents wanted me to have support and resources for my theater training, which this school provided, and they also wanted to place me in a more focused environment—*ahem*, no boys. When I transferred, my family was encouraged to formally convert to Catholicism, so we did, but it wasn't immediate, and I hadn't yet officially converted by the time the school year started. That first week of school I joined the rest of my classmates in the auditorium for a Mass to kick off the new year. I was feeling like the new girl, under a microscope as my classmates slowly sniffed me out. Was I cool and friendly or a threat? Was I weird or could I fit in nicely? (Honestly, all of the above when I think about it, *wink wink*, but I digress.)

The time came to approach the pseudo-altar in front of the auditorium stage for communion. I had observed how to receive the "body and blood of Christ" a bunch by that point, so I was pretty confident I had this, but I rehearsed in my head anyway. *Left hand face up on top of the right, use the right hand to grab the wafer placed in your left. Dip it in the wine? Stick out your tongue slightly and place the wafer on your tongue. Say "Amen." Or do you say "Amen" before you put it in your mouth? Then bow and walk away. Here goes nothing!* As I stood up to approach the altar with the rest of my row, I felt a hand on my shoulder, and Sister Lou Anne whispered in my ear, "You'll sit this out until you've converted." I felt my cheeks flush with embarrassment and, oddly, shame. I nodded and sat down, holding my knees in as my classmates passed, attempting to inconspicuously whisper to one another about why I wasn't included. Logically, I understood there were rules, but in my heart I didn't *really* understand. If I had the intent and desire to convert, or at the very least to learn more about Catholicism, why wouldn't I be able to participate in this part of the mass?

After that, I was placed on the sacrament superhighway and received my First Holy Communion and Confirmation in the same month, still unsure of what it all really signified. I remember feeling like I was "in" once I had those sacraments under my belt. But now what? I quickly came to understand that rules and memorization seemed to be a big focus of Catholicism, but I put very little effort into either of those things, because remembering the Stations of the Cross or a booklet of prayers to get to God didn't make sense to me. For years, I lip-synched some of the longer prayers and fumbled with my rosary. When I went to Confession, I made up things that seemed juicy enough to tell the priest. I just didn't understand why all this mattered when it came to building my connection with God. Most of the time I felt like I wasn't a good-enough Catholic because I hadn't perfected these things, so I just grew distant and indifferent.

In my eyes, the institution had created a chasm between me and God—both back then and today. I believe in my heart that God truly loves us and wants to be close to us, no matter what. He could care less that I was lip-synching prayers (He was probably laughing and loving it, to be honest) or that I ate a wafer a few weeks before I officially became Catholic. Though I understand how these practices and offerings can bring people closer to God, that wasn't the way that *I* felt close to Him.

From that point until my later twenties, I put the onus on myself. I didn't feel safe trusting my prayers and dreams to an institution with so many conditions I had to meet in order for God to love and guide me. I didn't feel worthy of blessings by God; after all, I had yet to master the Lord's Prayer. So, life became about me and me alone, just over here "figuring it out." At the time, I didn't understand that my soul had been speaking to me all along and would continue its gentle attempts to grab my attention until I became more familiar with her voice later in my twenties. She spoke softly through feelings, relationships, synchronicities, creativity, and any other way she could reach me and guide me.

As Krista just discussed, our soul is our copilot. Pretty cool, right? Comforting even. But how might you reconcile this idea of the soul with your own spirituality? I like to think of the soul as our personal spirituality tour guide who will provide direction, insight, gentle warnings, and much-needed reminders. I love a little etymology moment because often the original meaning of a word gets distorted over time to fit the social context. The etymology of the word *soul* is linked to the word "sea," which feels fitting because a connection with our soul will take us to depths in a way our mind cannot. Our soul will bring us to a vaster understanding of our personal multidimensionality, as well as the multidimensionality of our existence at large, which speaks to our *spirit*. I would have been LIT UP if I were to have learned about my soul in conjunction with spirituality in school. I don't think I would have felt as alone or lost as I did at certain points.

Prior to our Saturn Return, spirituality looked a lot like the religion we were raised in for both Krista and me. We share similar Catholic roots and experienced our own flavors of contradictions and confusion about it all. You might have a similar experience to mine and Krista's, where you were told how your relationship with God should look, sound, and feel, with no room to discover and build a relationship that's as unique as you are. Maybe you've had an experience with religion that is incredibly positive and supportive. You might have no experience with religion at all.

No matter where you fall along the spectrum, I can bet that you were not encouraged to create your own relationship to the spirit within you, just like I wasn't encouraged to create my own relationship to the spirit within me. Most of us were indoctrinated into behaving a certain way, engaging in certain activities, and even practicing a particular religion. None of this is inherently bad; it just lacks the consideration of what you, a unique soul that chose to come to this planet at this time, has on their agenda for this life. It's no wonder so many of us choose to disconnect from it all as we enter our late teens and twenties. This might look like rebellion to most, but I have a theory that it's really an innate urge to seek that which explains the unseen, that which explains the parts of us that are divinely designed, even though these beliefs might not be accepted by our families, friends, or society. It is a search for our own spiritual connection to Source, God, Creator, Universe—however you choose to label the Oneness.

Having a connection and a relationship with a higher form of consciousness is perhaps the secret sauce when navigating any period of change.

Oh! And speaking of labels, you might feel some type of way when the word "God" comes up. If so, I've been you. Up until my early thirties, I felt so weird saying "God" or talking about anything that would have exposed me spiritually. The words felt foreign in my mouth and, honestly, they didn't feel like a truthful expression of my beliefs at the time. In case you're two *Gods* away from skipping this chapter, I want to be super clear that this is not a chapter to convince you of anything related to your beliefs. It's not a chapter about why God has to be in your life in order to be spiritual or a Young Life pizza party to convince you Christianity is indeed *cool*. None of that. This *is* a chapter about reclaiming your own spirituality, reconnecting to what you understand as the unseen, and tending to the subtle energies of your heart rather than the domineering energies of your mind.

Still, there's no doubt that words hold charge—I get it! They hold memory and frequency that have the power to trigger an emotional and even physical reaction. Words can create a mental block when it comes to understanding and exploring and trusting, well, anything. So if the word "God" dredges up some sticky feelings, like resentment, confusion, fear, or the like, no need to force yourself to use the word. I want to liberate us all to choose our own words to represent this deeply meaningful aspect of our lives. I invite you to feel into what word best describes that which is greater than your human form, that expansive part of you and of everything. The ever-present, all-knowing, and all-loving consciousness. Some people call this "Source," "Universe," or "Spirit." Really, you can call it anything. Take a word for a test drive and practice using it in everyday life, both out loud and in your mind and heart. While it might feel a little foreign and silly at first, you may eventually find a word that fits perfectly with how you feel about what it represents and discover that it naturally flows when you want to reference your higher power. For the sake of consistency and clarity in this chapter, we'll use the word "God" to describe the original Creator, the entity of Oneness that lives in everything and can be experienced in any moment.

Spirituality and Your Saturn Return

Prior to my Saturn Return, I was muscling my way through my life, struggling to bear the weight of my dreams and desires, hoping my mind would come up with solutions and steps that I should take to get from here to there. I believed in the power of the Universe but was not convinced that it would find and help me. The Universe felt like luck that would bless me infrequently, which led me to believe that I wasn't part of the spiritually chosen. I wondered *why* a lot, unsure of how I found myself in situations and relationships and with feelings that weren't at all aligned with what I truly wanted to experience. Before my Saturn Return, I barely had a sense of how I played a part in creating my reality; it just felt like I was blindly getting things wrong in life but didn't have the awareness to take responsibility and heed the lesson or opportunity that comes with those missteps. Before my Saturn Return, I was spiritually malnourished, seeking guidance, love, and support in weird places. I saw my quest to find a soulmate as the mission that would allow me to become fully happy. My pursuit of acting became a mission to validate myself in a world where I felt pretty far outside the conventional professional box. I had no idea that what I was seeking had been placed within me when I was created. My spiritual journey turned out to be about remembering these sweet nuggets of truth. Yours might be similar . . . or it could look completely different. In the end, spirituality was the missing piece of so many parts of my life, just like it turns out to be for so many people.

Spiritual seeking tends to surface when you approach or start your

Saturn Return, when the rules of your teens and early twenties have dissolved, the real world has tossed you around a bit, and you find yourself on your own. The questions about who you are and what you are meant to do, who you are meant to be, who you will be with, where you should live, and more start to overwhelm you. You want answers because knowing feels safer than not knowing. But *needing* answers and *seeking* to understand more deeply (but maybe not completely) are two very different things.

Feel into the energy of "need" for a moment. There is a reaching, a belief in some sort of lack. A desperation. Needing holds us to a particular identity that most likely keeps us small and underexpressed. If you made room for expansive possibility beyond your need for particular answers, what might take shape in your life? You might be used to needing answers and operating accordingly, but I want to remind you of the power of instead leaning into possibility and into seeking. To seek is a natural part of who we are as human beings. As youngsters and teens, though, seeking might have been reprimanded or corrected; therefore this part of your nature may have become dormant. Now Saturn is ready to liberate that part of you. Remember: you are a soul with a body and not the other way around. So really, you've been "woo-woo" since the moment you incarnated, you've just forgotten. It's likely you have found this book at the point of realizing—or at least feeling—that you are much more than just a human body plugging along from milestone to milestone. How exciting to meet you here!

Pass the Mic

During your Saturn Return you will be challenged, encouraged to take responsibility, tested by the Universe, grow, and often feel as though you're having an existential crisis. When Saturn returns to that natal position, it's asking the question: *Who do you define yourself to be? Are you doing the work to be fully you?*

—Jennifer Freed, PhD, author of *A Map to Your Soul*
ALMOST 30, EPISODE 553

For most of us (and definitely for me!), the common denominator in seeking these answers is that they will require intense change. It hit me that this season is *the* opportunity to learn how to *work with* change. It is designed to be intense in order to erode the existing neural pathways that direct us away from change and create new ones that lead us toward a more fulfilling and confident way of living.

Whether it's in your face or more subtly making itself known, I *know* that you are experiencing that change right now, because *change is constant,* no matter how much you try to resist it. Your Saturn Return will magnify change in your life in order to get you in right relationship with it. How do you find your center, find calm and focus in order to dance with this planetary transit and rise to the occasion of its potent magic? *You nourish your spiritual life.* You connect with the spirit within you that is and always will be, that knows all and is loving and loyal the whole way through this journey you're on. Make no mistake: there are no hacks to bypass any of the messiness that comes during this period of change, but the depths to which you go to get honest and aligned are the heights that you will reach in your spiritual life. One cannot truly exist without the other. You'll likely find that the dust kicks up a bit in the one to two years leading up to your Saturn Return, giving you clues about where you will be called into deeper alignment. If you find yourself in this position, lean in, listen intently, and get curious about these clues.

To believe that you are so powerful that you can stop change is to completely undermine your soul's blueprint, the desire of your soul. It also denounces any faith in the natural evolution of who you are, whether you're consciously thinking about it that way or not. Believe it or not, your soul is champing at the bit to embrace change. She understands the precise alchemy necessary to know yourself more deeply. The unknown is the ultimate playground for the soul, a place to discover and explore. To the soul, the past is an experience that has informed where you are now, but by no means defines *who* you are or where you are going. In one of my favorite books, *A Happy Pocket Full of Money,* David Cameron Gikandi writes: "Sometimes we keep recreating the past, over and over, sustaining it out of fear of losing it. But new growth, new creation, lies only in the unknown."

What I know is that the heart often leads us into the unknown and asks us to trust how we feel along the way rather than depending on the mile markers that validate positive progress. I believe one of the bravest things you can do is listen to your heart. When you start to follow your heart, you will disrupt some patterns that you've built up over time in lieu of following your heart.

These patterns are designed to satisfy other people, and to avoid discomfort and change. They become the highway of confusion that you ride on the regular only to wonder why things aren't working out or bringing you happiness. This disruption of long-standing patterns might feel wildly unsafe at first, and could even rock your relationships and shake the foundation of how you've been living and working. But don't worry! You are coming back to who you really are, confronting who you are not, and actually answering the call of your soul. You are building the muscle of faith and belief that there is a plan for you and that your heart knows how to lead you there. At the end of the day, *that* is spirituality. Faith and belief that there are greater forces at work—and some part of that force is intrinsically connected with and lies within you, right there in your beating heart. This is a juicy part of your Saturn Return! Be aware and be prepared to remain focused and to stand by *you* at all costs.

The F Words

In the past, following my heart felt pretty scary. My choices were based on the *fear* of what might or might not happen, rather than faith in all that could possibly be and the desire within me. I'm sure that you, like me, are used to protecting yourself, fortifying this fortress of fear. That fear mutes your heart's own *yes* or *no* into something quite distorted. The fear might say, "Well, be careful, because what if *this* happens?" And "You know, you've never done that before, so how can you prove it's the right choice?" "What is so-and-so going to think?" "What would this mean for your reputation?" That fear is really sly, and slick enough to talk you out of something your heart actually wants to do. So how do we breathe more life into our faith rather than our fear? That is *the* spiritual practice.

The more you practice having faith, the greater the ease with which the life you're meant to live will take shape. This is not to say there won't be any bumps in the road, but you can be sure you're headed in the right direction! But sometimes *not* following your heart when it initially calls is the precise path you are choosing on a soul level to experience the contrast to what's really meant for you. This can be a painful, long, and confusing path if you're resistant to trusting in its purpose.

When I was a twenty-five-year-old dating in New York City, the idea of any relationship with my spiritual side had been trampled on long ago by my desperation for a romantic relationship. Trust me, the amount of time I spent on Tinder was unhealthy . . . and maybe even record-breaking. My type tended to be the emotionally-unavailable-but-physically-available-at-eleven-p.m. kind of guy. Yet, amid all this settling for less than I actually wanted and one-night stands, I met someone who saw me—like, really took all of me in—beginning first and foremost with my heart. *It was terrifying.* This guy felt like a level-up that I wasn't ready for.

On our first date, he took me to a super warm, welcoming, modern church in the city.

At first, I almost bailed because . . . CHURCH ON A FIRST DATE?! But I soothed that part of me that needed the jazzy, sexy first date and went anyway. The energy at the church was immaculate, and the music was so uplifting that I was brought to tears. And him? He would have gone to church whether we were on a date or not, so I knew he was being himself completely, not trying to impress me.

At the time, I didn't know who I was, and I didn't have a relationship with God. Instead of thinking about this, I was hoping that a boyfriend would solve my problems, fill the holes I thought I had, and set me on the right course. This guy and I didn't start dating after that day at the church, but we remained friends who always felt something deeply for each other. I was too afraid to admit that, though, so I kept him at a distance, and he eventually became tired of the dance I was doing around him. Meanwhile, I spent years and years continuing to chase guys who had no time for me and settling for mediocre connections. Finally, I got tired of waiting to be chosen by someone, and I began to choose myself. When you redirect your energy to *you* and become what you are desiring, your point of attraction changes. Choosing yourself means that self-abandonment is not an option. And in choosing yourself you get to see, experience, and appreciate why others are naturally attracted to you.

That's exactly what happened when that guy who *really* saw me came back into my life in 2019. Only now I could receive what he was offering to me, because I had chosen myself and experienced what he wanted me to see. That guy was Sean, and today we're married. I could have spared myself a lot of time and pain if I'd listened to my heart when it first spoke many years before, but I also believe that I needed to experience the contrast between those painful relationships in my twenties and the deep connection I have with my husband today.

This experience exemplifies so much for me when it comes to spirituality. I understand now that my heart *knew* the whole time. Not my physical, blood-pumping organ of a heart, but my "spiritual heart," as Michael Singer, author of *The Untethered Soul,* refers to it. To me, the spiritual heart feels like the doorway through which I've walked into my spiritual experiences and through which I keep my spiritual connection. The spiritual heart speaks through feeling, and this is what ultimately guided me to my husband. But I initially resisted the good feeling and let my mind convince me otherwise for years and years.

I eventually learned how to listen to my heart, but first I had to get to know my mind and the tactics it liked to deploy to keep me from trusting my heart, like fear, doubt, and overanalysis. The mind must be understood for what it is: the primal part of you that wants to keep you safe and comfortable but has no intention of bringing you into deeper communion with your spirit. The mind will always have something to say, but it doesn't have the ability to feel. The heart, on the other hand, is the way to your soul. It tunes you in to your personal soul radio. Your emotions, felt through the heart, connect you to the energetics of the unseen, the spirit of all that is, your true essence. From this place, you are able to receive guidance you can trust.

An open heart is our natural state, but if we allow the worry and worst-case scenario beliefs to crowd our being, the heart protects itself by closing. This is why I would feel my heart open around my not-yet-husband briefly but then slam it shut again. At the time, all this *feeling* in my heart was scary, because it was so much purer and truer than what my mind had to say about this potential connection. Spirituality is led by your heart, fed by your heart, and also feeds your heart. I wouldn't say that the heart and spirituality are one and the same, but the heart *is* a powerful spiritual mechanism working within you every second of every day. The question is whether you are listening and feeling from this place. Even if you are not ready to follow your heart, its GPS system will never turn off. It will always hum along in the background, loyally guiding you home to yourself, no matter how many detours you take along the way.

Spirit/God/Universe/Source/Whatever You Want to Call It can speak along so many different avenues and in so many different ways. Don't be fooled by the shiny spiritual objects, experiences, or even people. The most spiritual moments are often found in the mundane, and they're definitely not something that you have to be sold on, nor do they (necessarily) require any sort of formal ritual or place of worship. I often find God and feel most aligned with and a part of the Universe on the afternoons when Sean and I are reading our books in the same room, with the windows open, our comfiest sweats on, and dinner baking in the oven. In an instant, I'm reminded of how this moment is made possible by so many other moments of confusion, challenge, discomfort, and major highs and lows. And here we both are, content and at peace. It's a feeling of gratitude in my heart, a feeling that just feels so close to truth, to Source, to God. And in these moments, I'm reminded that that guiding omnipresence is always there for all of us to access.

What "Counts" as Spiritual?

So, what the heck *is* spirituality? What does it mean to be spiritual? At this point, the term "spiritual" is associated with everything from meditation to plant medicine ceremonies to rocking out in a New Age church to not wearing deodorant or a bra. Wear a red string around your wrist? You must be spiritual. Listen to mantra music? Spiritual! Some might roll their eyes—and I'll admit I've rolled mine on occasion—at the onslaught of various "spiritual" trends. But what I've come to realize is that as long as the intention is good and pure, it's beautiful to see so many communities, expressions, practices, and modalities that tend to the spirit. I love that the far-reaching labeling of spirituality has seemingly given people permission to consider what speaks to their spirit and allows their sense of connection to Source/God/Creator to feel like their own. Judging how this manifests for people individually feels—well, not so spiritual. The bottom line is that spirituality can mean so many different things. We're here to give you full permission to reclaim this word for yourself and make it uniquely yours. That might mean that, to you, spirituality is something that others don't even remotely associate with being spiritual—and that's okay.

One more etymology moment for this chapter: the word spirituality comes from the Latin word *spiritus,* which literally means breath, and thus signifies life. So, spirituality is the quality or condition of your breath, of your life. Today, there is a disproportionate focus on what outside of us can bring us to life—the promotion, the soulmate, the home or car, the perfect body. But we've got it backward. The quality of our life depends on our connection to and the honoring of our inner landscape, which includes our soul. Everything else is brought into form from there. Our soul is the forever part of us, it is the part that knows, it is one with whatever you believe is the Creator, it is the highest expression of who you are—it is who you *really* are.

Maybe when you hear people talk about chakras your response is chakra-who?! You might tune out, feel left out, roll your eyes, nod because you are well versed in the chakra system, or add "research chakras" to your to-do list. No matter what your response is, it's great, and it says absolutely *nothing* about your spirituality. Your spiritual path is an intuitive exploration, not a rite of passage or a mandate to do and learn certain things in order to be deemed spiritual. There is no spiritual hierarchy. You can do and learn the most and that's wonderful, but there is no destination. The path *is* the destination. There is no bumpin' spirituality club that you have to wait in line to get into. You are born *in;* maybe you just forgot that you have VIP access always and forever.

While I wouldn't say I was ever a club rat, I did feel that zing of acceptance and coolness every time I got into a hot spot, so I understand how this very human desire to feel special and accepted has found its way into spirituality. Standing in line, waiting to be chosen, passing time by comparing your outfit to that of every other girl in line, psychoanalyzing the bouncer, and moaning with regret that the heels you're wearing are actual torture devices is not much different than the feeling of standing in line waiting to meet your spiritual guru at an event, wondering whether you are more spiritually advanced than the others in line and practicing what you're going to say when you meet because, after all, what you say could persuade your guru to take you under their wing.

I can't define your spiritual experience for you, but I can ask you to think about this: imagine navigating your day today with the unwavering knowledge that there is a divine presence that orchestrates and holds you through each moment, each experience. And *you* are actually part of that divine presence too. Can you feel how many aspects of your life would be a completely different, more enjoyable experience if you knew this was true? How you connect with this divine presence, this breath of life, this part of you that is all-knowing and connected to all, has chosen a very unique curriculum in this life. Research published in the *Harvard Business Review* points to the fact that a sense of the vastness of the world and Universe comes from awe, and that makes us feel small. That's a good thing, because this perspective decreases our stress and mental chatter and, instead, shifts our attention to ideas, issues, and people outside of ourselves and improves creativity, collaboration, and energy.[4] It's hard not to feel a sense of awe and wonder when you view the world through this type of lens, and experiencing awe just plain old makes your life better.

The methods that will work for you to connect in this way will be different from those of others around you—maybe even people who you love deeply or are very close to. And that's okay because these methods are vehicles, not identities. They are varied, unique doors that ultimately lead to the same place. You will be tempted to become attached to the ways in which you experience your own divinity or believe that you *need* to do XYZ to be or achieve ABC. In those moments, try to remind yourself that the vehicle doesn't really matter; there are no *have-tos*. If something works for you and you're enjoying the experience of becoming yourself and feeling connected to yourself and the Universe, then BRAVO! *That's* what matters.

Pass the Mic

I remind people that sometimes it's not always the yoga classes and the hundred-dollar bottle of supplements or whatever, all the trendy things. Sometimes it's just going back to the basics. Sit next to an elder who knows how to pray, sit next to an elder who has a meaningful presence, and anyone who looks to have a meaningful presence.

—Lalah Delia, author of *Vibrate Higher Daily*
ALMOST 30, EPISODE 281

Anytime you feel yourself perceiving or building a spiritual hierarchy in your mind, knock it down immediately. In the spiritual context, hierarchies help us humans contextualize and gamify the pursuit of being spiritual. A spiritual hierarchy will say that one way of being is more spiritual than the other, that this practice or that ability gives you spiritual cred. The mind appreciates a system like this because it helps to make sense of it all. But it is of no use and can actually distort your spiritual journey. Release the idea that one method is better or "more spiritual" than another. Release any attachments to people or practices as the "only way." Get to know yourself through many, many vehicles, by walking through many, many doors. Allow your spirituality to be a bridge between your inner world and your outer world. Your connection to the Spirit within you will help you navigate discomfort, change, and pain with faith, grace, and confidence. Every rock bottom you experience will suddenly become a clearing and a launchpad to something greater, supported by, yes, your spiritual connectivity. Spirituality makes life meaningful. Rather than wondering, *Why, why, why?*, you will operate with an understanding of the undercurrent of the unseen. And by understanding, I don't mean that you can explain how this happens or what it is, but rather you know and trust that this is a law of the Universe, and you don't have to put forth so much force to make it all happen.

With all that in mind, your Saturn Return is a prime time to sample from the buffet of what calls you spiritually, relinquish the need to follow one way, and simply experience what calls to you and what does not. We all find and embrace spirituality in our own unique ways. Perhaps the most important thing to remember as you explore is that you are allowed to play. Spirituality can quickly become very serious. There are so many different ways to explore, most of which have nothing to do with organized religion. Heck, my most spiritual experiences have occurred in the most unexpected places.

Journal: Describe God

How would you describe God? What kind of energy is it: feminine, masculine, or neutral? How does God show love to you? How does God communicate with you? These are questions to reflect on. You might find that the answers feel very clear to you, or you might be scratching your head, realizing these are things you've never thought about before. Maybe you're wondering how you can answer questions like this, rather than being told who God is to you by someone else.

If the latter is the case, then I would like to invite you to pause and take a big, beautiful breath; in this moment, you have the opportunity to acknowledge a belief that is causing a block. There might be a part of you that is used to outsourcing your thoughts about a higher power to those who you deem more religious or spiritual, those who seem hierarchically closer to God. Or maybe there's a part of you that doesn't necessarily feel worthy of defining this experience with God for yourself. If that's the case, know that God wants to know himself through you, yes YOU, and through all living things, for that matter. So you are quite literally in a conversation and ever unfolding understanding with God in every moment, in every relationship, through every high and every low, every mundane and momentous milestone. How cool is that?

If the answers to these questions still feel foreign, begin by *living* these questions. Attune your awareness and your senses to this idea that God is within all, within you. Have fun observing or experiencing something and looking at it through the lens of God. For what purpose might God orchestrate this and allow for you to be a part of it? Trust the truth that comes through as you live these questions. Very soon you'll be living your life in this frequency of divine orchestration very naturally. You will begin to expect it and thus have a steadier and more expansive understanding of your life and the elements of it, rather than resisting it or trying to control every outcome.

It feels so nice to lean on the infinite intelligence of God and release some of the pressure you might be putting on yourself to figure life out. All of a sudden life becomes a collaboration with this infinite presence of love and guidance; never again will you feel truly alone.

Get Present

Creativity and flow bring us into the present moment, which is exactly where God speaks to us. Creativity isn't the only way God speaks, but it *is* one of the easier ways to get present, because we're usually so busy harping on the past or fixated on the future. The past and the future give your mind a whole lot to do, to regret, to plan, and to analyze. They are incredible pieces of your life that capitalism leverages for profit and dependency. There's a product or service for everything that you might want to fix or forget about from your past. There's also a product or service to "support" you in achieving your idealized future. But nothing and no one is going to give you the present except for you. The present moment just *is,* and it requires nothing of you except to be there fully. It rarely, if ever, requires you to buy something or seek outside of yourself to feel its potency. And it's super HARD for us humans to do, eh? Just being is difficult.

You can make this choice at any moment of any day. A good way to build this habit is by asking yourself *How do I want to feel today?* as part of your morning routine. (And if you feel yourself getting off track or moving into the past or future, you can pause and reflect on your answer to bring yourself back.) Asking the question is an opportunity to get clear about what you want and to then align your thoughts and choices accordingly. No, the present isn't necessarily going to be rainbows and butterflies all the time. In fact, it's your ability to be present for what is, no matter the positive or negative charge it elicits, that eventually brings the rainbows and butterflies.

Follow the Feeling

Raise your hand if you've been told that you're "too much" or "sooo emotional." Me too. I've come to learn that one of the ways God speaks to me is through my feelings. If only I had realized that earlier, I could have disregarded so many of those judgments about how I felt and the amount I felt and just kept it moving. A profound part of my spiritual journey has been learning to trust my feelings, which has been deeply freeing and transformative.

Your soul uses feelings and intuition to say, "Hey, you're on your path," or "Listen, let's pause, ground, and reassess." Just like your connection with God might have been outsourced to authority or institutions when you were young, your feelings were also encouraged to be outsourced. A child cries, and an adult might respond, "Don't cry, everything is all right," inadvertently dismissing that the child's feelings and intuition are valid and missing that they're pointing to something that needs attention. If you are someone with big feelings or even *any* feelings (which is each one of you reading this), know that your feelings and intuitive hits are more than valid; they are a direct phone line to God. When the call comes, you mustn't bury it or try to diminish its intensity; you must prioritize getting to know it better. The point is not to overanalyze your feelings but rather to feel them fully and ask God for more clarity if there is any to be had. This is a practice that might feel silly and awkward at first, but it's how you improve your connection to yourself, your feelings, and thus, God.

Pass the Mic

I love feelings. Our feelings are our friends. If we can learn to listen to them, let them voice whatever they have to say, then we can hear what insight the emotion has for our life. Anxiety is like that loyal friend that wakes us up in the middle of the night. It says, "Hey, something's not okay. Something's out of alignment. And I am going to be really loud and annoying until I get your attention." When we realize that our emotions are often just trying to get our attention and getting us to wake up, then we can understand whatever message they're trying to give us.

—Amber Rae, author of *Choose Wonder over Worry*
ALMOST 30, EPISODE 138

This is the perfect time to practice, because your Saturn Return has the power to bring up some of the most intense feelings you've ever felt—strong enough to make you question whether or not you're going nuts. But rest assured that the next iteration of your life, one that is even more expansive and fulfilling than you might have the capacity to dream, is on its way to you. These feelings of overwhelm or intensity match the bigness of what wants to be expressed through your life. While it might not be comfortable or familiar to let the full expression of these emotions come through, they have very potent messages and reminders for you. Next time you experience a feeling or intuitive hit that catches your attention, pause and ask God to guide you to more clarity. *What would you have me know about this feeling?* If it's an intuitive hit or knowing, practice following it without doubt or fear. You will build a record of trusting your feelings and connecting with God, a beautiful archive of proof that when you trust your intuition, you are speaking to God, and in speaking to God you are getting insight for your greatest and highest expression.

Whatever You're Doing Is Perfect

It feels fitting to end this chapter with a confession: my spiritual path continues to unfold before me and, to be honest, I felt a little bit of shame around that when I first started writing this chapter. *Shouldn't I have it more dialed in by now? Shouldn't I be able to prescribe some spiritual steps you can apply to your own enlightenment?* I thought that . . . and then I choked on my laughter. Like, *what?!* That's not why your soul picked up this book. Your soul guided you to these pages because she wants to start connecting with you more regularly and wants you to trust your own intuition and feelings because she sent them to you. Here's one thing I do know, though: your spiritual journey will be an exciting, ever-unfolding process, and one that's completely unique to you. Some seasons will have more spice and growth; others will be more gentle, soft, and healing. Both are golden threads woven into your spiritual path. Over time, I realized that the closeness I desired to have to the Creator in me and who created me was not just reserved for a designated time in a building, squished into a pew. It's time we liberate ourselves from any template provided by organized religion that feels expired and seize the opportunity to worship the beauty of what is at any time, in any place.

And one last thing: I've spoken to so many of you who wonder if you even *deserve* to be on a spiritual path, because there hasn't been One Big Moment of spiritual awakening. Someday you might have that experience . . . or you might not. Either way, know that you're doing it exactly right. Your soul, the sweet slice of God within you, has a plan, and whatever that plan is is perfect. I've personally let go of the need or expectation for my spiritual life to hit me over the head with profundity. Instead, spirituality has found its way into everything I do and every relationship that I have. It's really an awareness and reverence for what has been divinely designed (ev-er-y-thiiing) and honoring its role in my life. It is a practice. One that life will test over and over.

Body

One of the most consistent and ripe conversations among the *Almost 30* community is the discussion around our bodies. We've done podcasts and workshops, held sold-out live events, and shared endless amounts of content about body-related issues, and they always resonate deeply. Maybe it's because we all exist in bodies, or have all been affected by the experience of having a body in some way. Like death, bodies are one of the few universal experiences that unite us. There's no running or hiding from the physical body. For better or worse, it's what tethers us to life and the human experience. It is the home for our soul, which we just met in the previous chapter. Here we will come back to Earth and explore all the ways in which we've lost the connection with our body (and why) and learn to not only befriend, but to listen to and *love* our body, even as we age. First shifting our mindset around our physical state and then grounding into our body will help us unpack the way we view ourselves. By learning to change our mind, we can then employ tactical tools and practices to support a more loving relationship with our body.

Chapter 5

BEFRIEND YOUR BODY

Krista

At a young age, I learned that my body was something to improve and perfect at all costs, so it's not surprising that I used to be a fad-diet connoisseur: low-fat, low-carb, grapefruit, keto, the Master Cleanse—you name it, I've done them all. Throughout ninth grade, I ate a bowl of Special K for breakfast, lunch, and dinner, then topped my day off with a Special K bar for dessert. (By the way, a nutrient-rich diet of cereal flakes, sugar, and freeze-dried strawberries *should be illegal*. It's pretty wild to create and market a diet where most meals revolve around flake cereal.)

And, speaking of illegal, I've tried that too—or at least I've come close.

If you don't feel like we're BFFs yet, imagine me curling up next to you on the couch for a good, vulnerable share. When I was twenty-seven, I tried to source a thyroid medication that I heard Lady Gaga talk about in a documentary. She was shown in her doctor's office, looking overwhelmed and overworked, getting her prescriptions filled as she perched on the tissue paper–lined exam table. When she mentioned a thyroid medication, it piqued my interest. I had seen her shrink over the years (which seems like SOP for celebs), and I also knew that the thyroid was related to metabolism and somehow loosely related to weight, which correlated to weight *loss* in my brain. (This journey my thoughts took trying to find ways I could lose weight was always a fun one to track because you could feel the desperation and oftentimes delusion.) I'm guessing that Gaga had a prescription for a medical purpose, but some sketchy

Reddit threads helped me deduce that this medicine could also support weight loss, which was the real point here, right? I mean, why *else* would anyone take a pill if not for this most important purpose?

When you find yourself poring through Reddit threads to unearth information about the prescription pills celebrities are taking for weight loss, it's a pretty clear sign you're not on the right track. I thought that maybe *this* was the magic pill I'd been looking for, the key to my success, freedom, liberation, and happiness (this was pre-Ozempic days, mind you). Because of my single-minded goal of losing weight, I didn't think taking a prescription that wasn't actually prescribed to me was dangerous; I thought of it as a tool—a way for me to finally get what I wanted so that I could feel how I wanted to feel. Which was thin.

The perfect opportunity to get my hands on these pills presented itself when I was on my way back home from a retreat in Mexico. There I found a pharmacy in the airport where I could buy any prescription without a doctor's note. That weight loss I wanted so badly—and the new life that I was sure would come with it—clearly wasn't going to happen overnight without some assistance, and I didn't know when I would be in Mexico next, so this was my chance. And while I was at it, I might as well stock up, since my Google research had shown me that once I started taking this medication, I would have to continue doing so for the rest of my life.

I stuffed the bottles into my backpack and boarded my flight, wondering if I would have to fly to Mexico regularly to re-up. The idea of this sort of commitment gave me pause, but I was glad to have the option in case my weight started moving in the wrong direction. Back home, I must have held those pills in my hand at least twenty times, each time debating whether or not today was the day I was going to sign up for a lifetime with them (my fear of commitment may have helped keep me from taking the leap). But, in the end, I realized this was *not* the quick fix I was looking for and stepped back from the ledge. I had a ritual-like moment disposing of these pills, when I finally moved on from this destructive pattern of viewing my body as the enemy after some time in therapy and doing some healing work (which I'll share in this chapter).

Today, this story feels both tragic and almost comical; it was definitely the moment when I realized how far I would go in my quest for the "perfect" body. Before we get into it in this chapter, I want to acknowledge that the disordered ways in which we approach our body and food are so common and widespread that they can almost feel normal. I promise you, *they're not (not supposed to be, at least)*. Looking back, I now know that I most likely had an eating disorder, even though I was never diagnosed. But back then, it all felt status quo, especially since everyone around me had a similar relationship with their body.

For many years, I was convinced that by changing my body I would change my life. Once I shed the pounds that were holding me back, I would suddenly transform into a fully liberated woman who could say what she meant and do and wear what she wanted without thinking twice. I believed that my relationships would be easier, abundant love would arrive, and success would be mine because, the way I saw it, being successful meant being thin. And of *course* I believed that—I once heard a family member say, "You can do anything you want, but if you're fat, no one is looking at you." I was sure that once I wielded control of my body, opportunities for work and life would flow, and I would never second-guess myself again.

I treated my body as if it were the enemy, and the only acceptable outcome—shrinking—could be achieved through self-destruction. I held a deeply ingrained belief that self-hatred and torture were the best ways to change myself. Any natural change in the way my body looked throughout my teens and young adulthood was cause for panic and obsession. Food felt like a threat to my existence, to the state of control I wanted to have over my body and my life. Not only did I not accept or respect my body, but my appreciation for food and understanding of nourishment were completely distorted. Up until my late twenties, I struggled with disordered eating and negative self-talk. Looking back, I honestly think my goal weight wasn't a number at all; it was just being invisible.

So many of us—at least in the Western world—have a loaded experience with our body. Body-image issues seem to plague us, regardless of our success, accomplishments, and confidence in other areas of life. So, the good news is that you're certainly not in this alone! Most women I know have stories about their body, shame around their body, and want to change their body.

Pass the Mic

Body doubt is the one thing that some of the most accomplished women in the world still struggle with. It's part of our greatest journey. So often women create a prison of not-enough-ness in our mind.

It's the one thing that I haven't fully flipped and solved in my own life. I figured out how to build a billion-dollar company, I figured out how to believe my rosacea is beautiful, I figured out how to believe God exists. This is the one thing where I feel like I'm still in a prison, and I'm determined to break free of it.

—Jamie Kern Lima, founder of
IT Cosmetics and author of *Worthy*
ALMOST 30, EPISODE 429

These stories and the shame and desire for change that come with them can get even louder and more intense as you approach your thirties because your body *is* changing (as it has done up to this point and will continue to do throughout your entire life), though maybe not in the ways you want. You might even be stuck in a cycle of trying to force your body *not* to change. But the truth is that as you move into your thirties, biological changes are happening, and your body shape naturally changes as you age, whether you like it or not. The good news, however, is that this period is an opportunity to rewrite the story of your relationship to your body so that you can navigate these changes in a healthy way. If you respect your body as the luxurious temple it is, you will feel healthy, and even radiant, through all this! My hope is that you even find yourself befriending your body as you drop into the truth of who you are during your Saturn Return. But if instead you bully your body, choose to restrict calories, overdo workouts, and compare yourself to the girls on your (or your boyfriend's) IG Explore page—this journey will be challenging for you.

Trust me. I *get* it. It was for me.

As I get older, I realize that true happiness is not about changing my circumstances, but about changing the eyes through which I *view* my circumstances. Saturn Return provided the prime petri dish for me to review the ways in which I was with myself and my body . . . and for that I am so thankful. If you can relate to any of this on any level, I'm excited to share some of what I've learned through my own experience, as well as what I've since learned from experts on the show in hope that it will help you get to a place where you love your body and recognize it for the beautiful gift it is.

Saturn Return and Your Body

If you know your relationship with your body can use some tending, your Saturn Return is going to offer you a pretty baller entry point. What if you saw Saturn Return as the opportunity of a lifetime to rewrite the story you tell yourself about your body? What if you used the time to acknowledge, understand, and process the negative ways that you view your appearance? During this period, your body wants to reclaim its role and responsibility as your wisdom system. You might have spent the better part of the last twenty-six-plus years of your life looking outside of yourself for answers, guidance, inspiration, and truth, but now Saturn is here to suggest that you get serious about collaborating with your internal guidance system—and your body plays a major, if not paramount, role in this system. A solid connection with your body will support optimal health throughout your entire lifetime. Allowing this relationship with your body to work as it's meant to will quell your doubts and fears, draw you into the present, and allow you to feel more empowered.

Like any other good relationship, having respect for and trust in your body is essential to create a strong foundation. Sadly, most of us aren't taught this. If it feels foreign to you to respect or trust your body or if you don't know where to start, that's okay! Like all relationships, this is one that you'll build and strengthen over time.

Journal: Your Body and You

Before we go any further, I'd like to invite you to think through where your relationship with your body currently stands and how you got here over time. By doing this, you are creating a new awareness, which means that the process of reconnection has already begun.

- When you see your body in the mirror, are you more focused on what there is to fix or what there is to appreciate?
- When you see yourself in the mirror, what thoughts or beliefs narrate your experience?
- What patterns of behavior do you exhibit that confirm these beliefs are true?
- Are you willing to release these beliefs and create new ones?
- What is your reaction to particular sensations within and signals from your body? Do you doubt them? Fear them? Get curious about them? Create space to understand them?
- Can you recall a moment or time in your life when your relationship with your body changed to what it is now?
- What does your body *really* need right now?

Your answers to these questions serve as information about where you are now and perhaps offer some clues about how your connection to your body might be strengthened. It is the first step in recognizing the treasure trove of information your body truly offers: everything you are experiencing in relation to your body is a manifestation of what you are holding on to and believe about the past.

Your Saturn Return is inviting you to be present, which requires an awareness of what got you here and (if necessary) forgiveness of yourself and of the people who played a role in getting you to this place. So much of what feels stuck, frustrating, and immovable within you can be set free, and from that point you can begin building a conscious relationship with your body.

In order to do this, my friend, you have to open your mind to the possibility and belief that you can actually change the narrative. As you read this chapter, I'm going to ask you to let the doubtful part of you take the day off, and let's speak instead to the part of you that believes this *is* possible, that you *can* change your story. And let me also say that if I can do this, you can too.

Your Body Story

I knew after the prescription escapade in Mexico and how I generally felt about my body during this time that Saturn's message was loud and clear: the time had come for me to deal with my body image once and for all. Saturn's arrival in my life called me to acknowledge, understand, and process my negative beliefs about my body so that they wouldn't consume me anymore. I have to be honest: this wasn't always a fun process, but it was no worse than living with the narrative that had been lurking in the background for my whole life.

During my Saturn Return, I finally started to tune in to that background noise and to unpack where I got the idea of what a body should look like. Some of these ideas were shaped by the size 00 characters on TV shows like *Friends*, popular teen movies where anyone overweight was ostracized, and culture in general. I also realized that some of my fears about my body were passed down to me from my mother. I don't think I'm unusual in this way; most of us take on cultural and familial programming as it relates to our bodies.

I invite you to think about how your parents saw their own bodies, each other's bodies, and other people's bodies, because their beliefs most likely established the foundation for your own. Before you take a look at these beliefs, remember that you want to do so from a neutral, centered place, because your parents' perspectives were informed by and inherited from those who came before them. We cannot heal from a place of resentment. We *can* heal ourselves and generations to come from a place of compassion, self-love, and awareness. I get it: it can be easy to blame our parents or caregivers for who we are today and the challenges we face. Instead, call in compassion for the younger version of you who was privy to their thoughts, feelings, and behaviors at an incredibly formative and impressionable time in your life. You might have taken them on as your own truth without even realizing what was happening. Remind your younger self that her caregivers were most likely doing their best with what they knew, but that adult you will do better.

Journal: Inherited Body Beliefs

As you seek to uncover some familial messages you may have inherited about your body, ask yourself:

- What kind of language did my parents use when observing and discussing bodies?
- What was important to them as it relates to their bodies (and the bodies of others), or what did they focus on most?
- Do I see any of my own language, behaviors, or beliefs overlapping with those of my parents?
- How can I re-parent that part of me and begin to use language and employ practices that create new beliefs connected to the truth of who I am now?
- What messages did I see on television or in the media about bodies and weight?

In addition to our parental influences, each culture has different philosophies, beliefs, and practices about how to treat and be in a body. Most of us are exposed to a mixed bag of positive and negative cultural influences. For example, perhaps you have inherited a reverence for your body shape but a hyperobsession with maintaining a certain standard of beauty. These cultural issues are so ingrained that a lot of times we don't even consciously realize they exist. As you start to examine your own connection with your body, consider how your feelings about or behavior around your body may have been influenced by cultural roots.

Then, of course, there's social media. Oh, social media. It's probably no surprise that the images you see and beliefs you digest online may very well also be affecting your ability to connect with your body. As we all know, there is no shortage of body conversation and distortion on social media. It has become the first place we go to for answers. Social media has played a major role in rewarding the perfect and polished, the airbrushed and hourglass-figured. It has sent our feeling of not-enoughness skyrocketing, and even monetized them by targeting us with ads for products and services to fix whatever it is about ourselves we're comparing to others. Make a concerted effort to notice any self-talk that arises as you scroll, and if it's unkind or judgmental that's a cue to log off or unfollow. Remember that you are in control of your own algorithm, and that algorithm can set the tone for your life. Choose wisely and intentionally.

The Games We Play

Right in the thick of my Saturn Return, when I was still feeling pretty uncomfortable and embarrassed about my body, *Almost 30* hosted one of our very first events. The topic was body love, and more than two hundred women of every shape and size, height, weight, race, and style were in attendance that day. The house where we were hosting the event was packed, and we definitely violated some codes and pissed off some neighbors, but we didn't care—Lindsey and I were just so excited to connect with our community IRL. Sitting on the floor together, we all discussed the way we felt about our bodies and how we had fought with them over the years.

After feeling alone in my struggles with my body for so long, hearing my own experience reflected back to me through these amazing, kind, lovely, cool, and powerful women was *wild*. I felt so seen, so heard, and so liberated by hearing their sometimes tear-jerking and other times hilarious stories. I also felt deeply sad. As I sat there, I started to wonder, *What are we doing?* It suddenly dawned on me how much of our brain space was being taken up by fretting about, feeling shameful of, and trying to control our bodies. It was clear to me that these incredible women had so much more to offer the world than how they looked (which, by the way, was beautiful). And if I could see that in them, I figured it was probably true for me too. Think of what would be possible if only we could shift our focus and change our stories about our bodies. *How could we get that energy back?*

And then I had what felt like a novel idea: *What if we just . . . stopped having these fears?*

I GET IT. It's easier said than done. But if we were able to accept that we change, evolve, and grow as humans in almost every other way, how does it make sense that we don't expect the same for our physical selves? The time we spend hating our bodies, wanting to be a different size, and wanting to look "better" is such an energy suck, and it's an important story we need to work on rewriting. Imagine the brain space and energy we would reclaim if our relationship with our body was neutral acceptance (at the very least). Dinner, made. To-do list, completed. Cancer, cured. World peace, solved. We would run the WORLD.

I have good news for us, and it involves science. Your body image is actually highly malleable (which means it can change and evolve), and it's rooted in your brain's integration of multisensory stimuli, because your brain is literally entwined with your body via your nervous system. As Helen Payne, PhD, of the University of Hertfordshire writes, "Neuropsychology tells us that our thoughts are governed by our emotions which are, in turn, grounded in our bodies, emotions being part of self-regulation (homeostasis)."[5] All this means that, for as much as you might like to separate your mind from your body, it's impossible. Think about that for a minute: *Your body hears everything your brain says, and you can change your body's chemistry based on your beliefs.* Your body is listening intently for whatever it hears—your kindness, your love, or your criticism. Your body knows if you are constantly bullying, shaming, blaming, or trying to force it into a particular size or shape. With this in mind, it can be helpful to review your thoughts and think about what you're actually telling your body. Would you say the same things out loud or to your friends? Would you have any friends if you talked to them the way you talk to (or think about) your body? If not, it's probably a sign that your body would be best served by a mindset refresh and some loving kindness.

I don't know about you, but for too long, my body was receiving the very clear message that there were things to fix. My inner dialogue was sometimes cruel, and the message was usually that I was somehow *not right;* that I was too big, that my arms were too thick, that my waist was too wide. Mostly, I told my body that I needed to shrink all areas of myself. No matter what I looked like, I always believed there was a lot more shaping, sculpting, and molding to be done ASAP. And once my inner critic finished critiquing my body, it moved to the next obvious villain in my story: the food lineup. What could I control? All for my own good, of course. I constantly thought about counting calories, controlling my intake, and burning off what I did allow myself to eat through workouts. I also spent a lot of time strategizing outfits I could feel comfortable in because I never felt good in my own skin, no matter how I tried to control my body or behaviors.

I don't think I'm alone in this. If you're like me, you are a person with body issues who is working hard to change that body. You are someone who "needs" to lose weight and be thin. In other words, the message you're giving yourself is that *you are someone who has something inherently wrong with them.* This idea and fixation becomes your identity and purpose. You take that belief with you everywhere you go, every minute of every day.

When put like this, it sounds awful, right? Of *course* you don't want to identify as someone who feels broken and needs fixing! But that's probably not how you're seeing it. Instead, your desire to constantly change your body (a goal that will never be achieved, because the goalposts keep shifting) may actually make you feel motivated. Sure, you're being motivated by shame or guilt, but they will help you get the job done! The planning, strategizing, counting, scheduling, and efforting it takes to achieve this goal provides something to focus on. Incessantly. Because winning is not a part of this game; it's meant to keep you chasing. I promise you that until you change your mindset, there's no way to play and win this game because the problem isn't your body; it's how you view and feel about your body that's the problem. Having said that, some of us are goal oriented; if that's you, consider how it might feel to shift those goals away from changing your body and instead changing your *mind*. How would it feel to set goals that involve practices that will move you toward feeling better in your own skin and healthier than ever as you enter this brand-new decade?

In addition to changing your conversation with yourself, you can also change your conversations with the other people in your life. When Sarah Landry (who you might know best as @thebirdspapaya on Instagram) visited us, she shared one of the more meaningful conversations she heard as a child. When her sister had a jaw surgery that resulted in her mouth being wired shut, Sarah says, "I remember there being a huge conversation about how she was going to lose all this weight. After the surgery, her face looked completely different, and her body looked different. I watched and witnessed as compliments came in like wild."[6] Sarah says that, at the time, she didn't even acknowledge the disordered eating the people around her were engaging in because it was so normal to want to be thin.

We're actually *taught* that talking badly about ourselves is a way of connecting and bonding; entire relationships are focused on this self-shaming behavior. But what if we connected around other things? What if we moved our conversations toward things we could feel, sense, and perceive rather than just those things we see? What if we spent that time sharing and supporting one another in goals that have nothing to do with shrinking or otherwise "improving" our bodies?

When you change the focus of your conversations, not only will you shift your focus and positively impact the messaging you're sending to your own body, but you're also doing the same for the person you're speaking with. And think about it: if we change these conversations one by one, woman by woman, at some point the entire conversation will have to shift for society in general. We're stopping the cycle, because when we feel ashamed of our bodies, we're teaching other girls and women that they should too.

Pass the Mic

I always thought that I had a dysfunctional relationship with food. But through really understanding myself and my habits and the things I was resorting to, I realized that I had a dysfunctional relationship with *myself* and the food was the vehicle. I was really beating myself down.

I can honestly tell you with everything inside of me that I have such a liberated relationship with food now that is so freeing. I want to give hope for anyone living in that cycle because it's a really tough place to live. When I actually learned how to love myself, I started to really see who I was: the beauty of my soul, of my heart, and of what I'm meant to be doing. And it changed the way that I treated myself. I no longer wanted to hurt myself or talk badly to myself. It really started with looking at myself in the mirror and catching myself every single time I would go back to that negative way of thinking or being or talking about myself. I would remember that it is an old story that is in the past, and I have rewritten that story, and am going to focus on the things that I love, that I'm grateful for.

—Melissa Wood-Tepperberg,
founder of Melissa Wood Health
ALMOST 30, EPISODE 623

I can and do hold space for honesty around the journey so many of us go on with our bodies and sense of self, but I think there comes a point when it's healthy to remove ourselves from the cycle of continually discussing our story about our bodies. So many of the issues I experienced were exacerbated by being in community with people who constantly live for the way they look and prioritize the appearance of their body over the experience of their soul. Yes, I still speak about food, body, and diet (obviously), but now it's from the vantage point that we are all so much more than just the way we look.

And that's how I finally healed my body issues—by breaking this constant quest and conversation about changing anything about my body and, instead, focusing on changing my mind. My great hope for you during your Saturn Return is that you can stop trying to be anything other than who you are. This includes what you look like and the body that you're in. My hope is that you can begin to imagine a world in which you don't diet or count calories or talk badly about your body to yourself or anyone else. I hope you begin to live in a world where you're not at war with your body or trying to "fix" yourself every day. And I also hope that you're patient with yourself in the process. Don't expect that the way you view your body or think about food will change all at once or that you have to be perfect at it. But you can start by imagining what it might feel like to love—I mean, truly *love*—your body. You can be aware when you slip into habituated behaviors. You can focus on changing the way you see yourself and think about food and taking care of your body. And you can begin to recognize that people don't love you because of how you look; they love you because of who you are.

In the next section, I'll share some practices to help you begin to shift your mindset about your body and to emphasize overall health rather than weight loss. But the most important thing here is that you can change your story during this period of transformation. And once your story changes, so does everything else.

Changing Your Mind, Befriending Your Body

We know that loving and accepting our bodies is an important goal to have. But how exactly do you get there in a true, authentic, and honest way? How do you build a relationship and a deep connection with your physical body? How do you embody all that you are more often? How can your body be the key to unlock what you are sensing energetically?

Let's get tactical about how you can practice this connection in your everyday life.

Body Language

In the beginning of my body journey, I felt so angry at my body for how it looked and how I felt in it. The only conversations I wanted to have with it involved judgment, criticism, and anger. Basically, I was bullying myself, and it didn't get me anywhere. The first few times I heard my body speaking to me, it was through the loud messages it sent to let me know it was suffering. Initially, I could only hear its cries for help or desire for rest, but as I became more attuned to my body's sensations and experience, we dropped into a true communication. Over time, I was able to get clear and quiet enough to hear my body's more subtle language when it was happy, and when it felt pleasure and joy. From this point on, my body's language helped me make decisions, know who to trust, where to go, and allowed me to connect with my soul.

Practice: Listen to Your Body

You can experience this too. Your body is built to communicate with you; it just takes some practice. I recommend that you start by engaging in a daily conversation with your body. Even if you've neglected your body for years and years, time has no bearing when it comes to how willing your body is to collaborate with you. If you make a conscious effort to connect with it, your body will reciprocate by patiently working with you.

The key is to start subtly and consistently. To begin, try this every day for a week and see how you feel:

1. Set a peaceful alarm for morning, noon, and nighttime as a reminder to check in with your body. You can label your alarms

on your phone, so give this one a name that speaks to you. Mine is called "Tune-In Time!!" (The exclamation points do something for me.)

2. When the alarm goes off, stop what you're doing and close your eyes (if you can do so safely). Lay your hands on your body, wherever they intuitively want to go.

3. Take five slow, deep inhales through your nose, filling up the lower belly first, then the chest; exhale out of your mouth. After that, return to a measured breath, in through and out of your nose.

4. Say hello to your body. You don't have to do this out loud—but you can if you want! Ask your body how it's feeling and if there is anything that deserves your attention right now.

5. Notice what your body tells you: a sensation in your body might intensify or you might experience a replay of a body memory from earlier in the day that you missed the first time. Maybe the sensations you felt in the wake of that impromptu chat with your boss this morning will come up again, affirming the importance of that moment. You might realize you feel unsettled (which is a cue to tap into *why*—chances are you'll find the answer is right there once you notice the sensation and ask the question). Maybe you'll realize you're thirsty or craving a certain food. Acknowledge whatever sensations arise, and thank your body for its intelligence.

In addition to creating a friendly, open dialogue with your body to learn about what you're hungry for, when your period is starting, and if the Mexican food you ate last night was a bad idea, it's safe to say that your broader health depends on a strong connection with your body. How many times have you heard stories of people who felt the warning signs of a health challenge well before its diagnosis? I'd argue that our bodies are sending us messages even before *that* about what we're putting in them, the activities we're engaging in, the stress we are putting ourselves through, and so on. If we're not regularly tuning in to our body, we will miss the sensations and signals that it's sending to us. Over time, these signals intensify, but even then, most people would rather not face health issues head-on because it feels ominous. When you *are* connected to your body, you can catch those signals earlier on and address any issues that need your attention as quickly as possible, which increases your chances of addressing a minor situation before it becomes a more significant one. Knowledge is power, baby.

Pass the Mic

I don't stand in front of a mirror and like to pick myself apart anymore. And if something doesn't fit me, I don't blame my body. I blame the thing.

Before, I was like so many women who refuse to record the Instagram story. Or show the picture or sign up for the job or get on the dating app or whatever that is because of what they believe about their body.

How much of our lives, how much time have we focused on what we hate about ourself? What we want to change, why we aren't enough, why we don't work. We are wasting our lives focusing on things that really don't disqualify ourselves from our dreams. I want women to stop waiting for their body to be perfect and stop trying to separate their mind and soul from their body.

—Jenna Kutcher, author of *How Are You, Really?*
ALMOST 30, EPISODE 528

A connection with your body also allows you to experience your own divinity on the daily. How often do you allow yourself to observe and be in awe of your body? As you read this, your four-chambered heart is beating a steady rhythm while its arteries and veins circulate blood to every organ in your body, and then back to the heart. This heart works without you having to think a single thought to make it happen. Come on! This is AWE-WORTHY. Saturn wants you to return to the miracle that is your natural state of being in your body. So, when your body starts to set off alarm bells during your Saturn Return, know that those bells are a direct call from the Creator in you to come closer, to listen intently, and to begin creating and living a life that is more embodied, a life in which you actually feel *alive*.

Find a New System of Measurement

It's so easy to become focused on numbers—the number of calories you ate today, the number on the scale, the size you wear. But really, what are those numbers actually telling you? I know that I've had entire days of my life overshadowed by a certain number I didn't like on the scale; days that were full of so many other experiences, connections, and accomplishments, all tainted because of that one inconsequential number. I used these numbers as a form of judgment against myself, as a gauge of what I was worthy of on that particular day.

Jessica Sepel, author and founder of health and wellness brand JSHealth, vividly remembers the day she broke up with her scale, which she used as a way of determining her self-worth. Following a little breakdown on the scale, Jess's husband decided to take matters into his own hands. "That's it," he told her. "I'm not letting you do this to yourself anymore." As the two of them walked the scale down to the dumpster and tossed it in, Jess remembers that it felt almost like a ceremony. She hasn't weighed herself since.[7]

Today, Jess encourages her clients to step away from their scale for the first three months of their journey to a better body image. This gives them the time and space to feel more liberated and free in their relationship with food and their body, with the goal that they are no longer governed by a number. The thing about numbers is that they reduce a whole story, a whole life, a whole human, into a few digits. As if that can even begin to represent all the things that are happening in a body and a life, and as if we gain any real, meaningful information from it.

Remember this the next time you step on a scale or feel bad about yourself because a certain size of jeans doesn't fit: these are just numbers, and *you are more than a number.* Shift your focus instead to the number of connections you've experienced this week, the number of times you've smiled, the number of times you've made progress on something that matters to you. These are numbers that actually matter.

I know other people who, like Jess, have decided to banish the scale from their lives altogether, and it has worked well for them. If this works for you, absolutely give your scale a break. Me? Well, the scale and I have an on-and-off-again relationship that's been toxic at times. But what I've learned in my journey is that it's a good practice for me to train my brain that the numbers on the scale should not impact my day one way or the other. So, instead of getting rid of the scale, I changed my relationship to it. However you do it, the important thing here is to detach your worth from a number. Because it's not the "thing" but the stories we tell ourselves about it that can send us into a tailspin.

Savor the Meal for Sweet Results

I'm pretty convinced that some of us who struggle with body issues don't slow down when we eat because we don't feel like we deserve food. At least that was the case for me, even though I didn't consciously realize it when I was scarfing down meals, almost like I was hiding this terrible sin of nourishing my body. And forget about snacks and dessert: I felt like I was somehow a bad person if I stopped for long enough to enjoy a cookie. It felt like if I actually paid attention to, really tasted, and enjoyed the food in front of me, the calories would somehow double.

Of course, other factors can influence this habit of speeding through meals too. For example, those of us who grew up in homes where things were tough might have rushed through mealtime to hurry up and get out of an uncomfortable situation, like Mom and Dad stonewalling each other again. Or perhaps you're just not used to stopping the constant stream of YouTube clips, scrolling through social media, answering emails, or tending to Slack, so you continue to fixate on your screen rather than your food.

Whatever the reason, most of us don't sit enough with our food, which is incredible when you think about it, because it's this combination of cells we consume daily that ultimately creates both our reality and our body structure. It's a pretty important life function. You are what you eat, and many of us don't even look at our food long enough to know what we are eating.

~~~~~~

Practice: Mindful Eating

If you fall into this category of not being truly present while you eat, I challenge you to focus on shifting that habit.

1. **Start by seeing if you can eat one meal a day with no distractions.** This means no phone, no laptop, or other device, just you and the experience of being in the present moment as you nourish your body. *Go with Your Gut* author and podcast guest Robyn Youkilis recommends taking a deep breath before you eat to relax your body, which also helps with digestion. Once you start to eat, she stresses the importance of chewing your food completely to slow down the process.[8]

2. **Allow your five senses to enjoy the full-body experience that each meal offers.** Be with your feelings and the conversations that happen around the table as you eat. Notice the smell and texture of the food as you eat. Check in with the sights, smells, tastes, sounds, and textures of the meal.

3. **Consider creating a ritual around your meal.** I make my breakfast a ritual, because I find there is less opportunity for distraction in the morning. Whatever meal you choose, take your time preparing your food in silence, maybe even pray over it before you eat or bless it if that resonates, and visualize this amazing meal in front of you as a key to the life of your dreams— that with each bite you eat, you receive blessings, nourishment, joy, happiness, and fulfillment. Romanticize your life, one meal at a time.

4. **Notice how your experience changes.** It's incredible what a difference eating with presence makes. Take a moment after your meal to tune in to your experience. Do you feel more satisfied? Does it feel like you're digesting your food any differently? Did you feel a greater sense of mental clarity and peace as you ate? How about after? If you tune in to the way you're feeling, you'll notice that your body is sharing information with you about what it does and doesn't need.

Pass the Mic

We need to return to a more loving way of eating, but also acknowledging that, yes, we are still very wounded and traumatized. We've learned that food is one place that we can find comfort, we can find escape, we can find these things. But the only way to not have that relationship with food is by loving the part of us that needs that, and not wronging it or trying to force our way out of it.

Because when we are using our bodies as emotional dumping grounds for food or anything else, it is holding us back. However, the only way to evolve into something more loving is by loving our way through it.

—Peta Kelly, author of *Earth Is Hiring* and
Honeycomb Substack
ALMOST 30, EPISODE 459

Rework Your Workouts

Much like I find it important to slow down while eating, it's also import-ant to slow down workouts. When I used to do high-intensity interval training (HIIT) and cycling classes all the time, I felt like I left my body as it was moving. I don't think I'm the only person who does this. As I looked around the gym, it seemed to me as if everyone was sleepwalking from one station to the next as we alternated our workouts throughout the class. I mean, we women have basically been training for war the last few years, pushing our physical limits like military personnel multiple times a week, going to intense boot camps, and even working out in the dark. What's the goal here? To look good and stay healthy? Or to go into BATTLE?!

Don't get me wrong, I love a good class and thrive in group energy, but when I really think about it, the slower I work out, the more I can connect my mind, body, and soul together, the more I get out of it. Moving more slowly and intentionally also offers some real, tangible benefits, like promoting recovery and reducing the chance of injury, improving form, and offering a more sustainable exercise routine. For many years we supported thousands of women through an online membership platform. As a part of this experience, once a month, Lindsey would gather with dozens of our members on Zoom for a morning workout. The intention of this practice was to come into connection with our bodies. She designed this part of the Almost 30 Membership based on her own practice: a few days a week, she ditches her structured fitness class and instead ecstatically dances and moves to a playlist she loves. She took the group through their entire body, moving in a way that was a complete expression and release. The hips, for example, moved in big circles, taking up space and allowing the group to feel into their femininity, while simultaneously releasing all the emotion that gets stuck there.

One of the many things I loved about the Almost 30 community was that they always showed up ready to get vulnerable—which is truly half the work. In one of these sessions, one of our regulars, Devon, shared that she had purposely done her workout session in front of a full-length mirror. This was a big deal because it had been months since she'd let herself really *see* her body. That morning she got emotional as she watched herself move freely and fluidly and witnessed the relief and joy on her face. Until that morning, Devon had been afraid to look at parts of herself she felt judgmental of, like her thighs and stomach. What she saw that morning was a reflection of how she felt within . . .

and she felt beautiful. The simple act of moving freely created a connection between Devon and her body, and reminded her of who she really was: a beautiful woman who didn't need to contort herself to look how she thought she should look. Instead, she could love and accept the woman she saw in the mirror. Even though she was on a virtual call with a few dozen of her Almost 30 friends, Devon was able to create a similar space for herself to feel comfortable, safe, and free to fully witness her spirit and body in concert. This moment brought through new observations and emotions to replace the expired stories she'd been telling herself about her body for so long.

When talking it out isn't enough, movement invites you to activate the many layers of an experience and imprinting.

Practice: Reconnect Through Movement

With that in mind, I'd love to share the movement practice that Devon and others experienced with Lindsey that day. It's annoyingly simple and so easy to implement on a daily basis that I can barely find an excuse not to do it, and I bet the same will be true for you. I'm hoping that you too will feel lighter, more grounded, more openhearted (yet discerning), and more grateful for what presently is and what is to come through your relationship with your body.

1. Curate a playlist of your #favoritesongsofalltime—songs that literally MOVE you!
2. Designate a consistent time every day to spend fifteen minutes or so dedicated to moving.
3. Press play on that playlist.
4. Move ecstatically, with no judgment and no structure. Just organic, soul-led movement. There are no rules here. If it helps, close your eyes and take any mirrors out of the room so you can do it without judgment or fear!

In addition to moving intuitively, slowing down, checking in, and listening to your body, practices like progressive muscle relaxation, mindfulness-based stress reduction, biofeedback, and yoga all strengthen the body–mind connection. If going from intense to slow flow isn't your jam, try switching out just a few of your more intense classes or workouts, or adding some slow movement into your routine in addition to your regular workout program.

This might mean going for a walk rather than a run or a session at the gym; it could mean a low-impact workout, like swimming or rebounding (jumping on a trampoline); or resistance work, like Pilates, yoga, or weight lifting. Believe it or not, you get all the same benefits when you move in a gentler, slower way, *and* you prevent stress on your joints, which can come from many of the faster, more high-impact workouts. It's not about any workout being "good" or "bad," but being able to stay present for whatever it is that you're doing so that you can connect with your body while you're moving it.

Get Outside of Your Routine (Literally)

If you aren't spending time staring at the blue sky, with your feet in the grass, and hugging a tree every once in a while, then what are you even doing with your life?

Now I have to admit that during my late twenties I was so hungry for success and to find my purpose that I thought of nature as more of an accessory than a necessity. I didn't realize how powerful it was from a health and wellness perspective, and that connecting with it is easy, free, and beneficial for your mind, body, and soul. Nature and outside spaces can even make you feel safe and are an antidote for stress. Among other scientific evidence and studies, researchers point to what I think many of us can feel, which is that being in nature can increase our happiness and improve our mood, sense of meaning, and overall well-being.[9] Sometimes the best things in life are free, eh?

I love to spend at least an hour outside every day, and once a week I try to make a point of spending as long as five or six hours in the great outdoors. I know that talking about time allotments might make this start to sound like a chore, but hear me out: not only is being outside incredible for your body, mind, and spirit, but it's also easy. Think about how many of your fondest memories involve the outdoors. Hiking a trail, walking through gorgeous tree-lined neighborhood streets, lying in the warm grass, working out with friends in the park, enjoying a leisurely meal on a patio, or a day on the beach—all these simple activities tend to create a memorable experience. Oftentimes outdoor activities evoke happy memories because we tend to be so present when we're out in nature, and because they offer such a relaxed, multisensory experience. With so much engagement of our senses we naturally shift our focus from our thoughts to the present moment.

Hot-girl walk, anyone? I highly recommend getting your daily steps in with friends because it's a great opportunity to catch up and connect, while simultaneously moving your body and getting in some vitamin D. Most of my hangs are done while moving, and it's the best way to multi-task. According to a recent study published in the *Journal of Happiness Studies,* even if you aren't able to spend a significant amount of time outside every day, it's a person's overall sense of *connectedness* to nature that matters. In this study, author Alison Pritchard, PhD, says that people who feel more connected to nature experience a specific type of content-ment that involves feeling like their life has a meaningful purpose.[10] If you're not in the mood to move, that's okay too. You still reap a ton of benefits just by being outside, even if it's to sit back and enjoy a meal or read a book. I know this might not be possible for those who live in colder or urban areas, but I hope you can still find creative ways to break out of the normal, screen-addled routine of modern life and bring your-self back to what's real and true.

Mealtime Mantra

Believe it or not, mantras do work! In its traditional Hindu and Buddhist form, a mantra is a word or sound repeated to assist with concentration while meditating. In Western culture, mantras are more frequently practiced as a statement or slogan that's repeated frequently to instill a thought or shift a mindset. Either way, mantras have been proven to offer many health benefits. Mantras can help generate a relaxation response, providing a sense of calm. They can distract you from distressing emotions like fear or anxiety, and reduce stress or the sensation of burnout.[11] This means that, in addition to helping you rewrite your story, mantras can also assist with how you actually digest your food, because stress suppresses digestion since it shifts your body's resources to trigger fight-or-flight.

In the morning, before a meal, or whenever I find myself going down the road of restriction, I make a point of turning to mantras to switch my mindset. Incorporating them into prayers before I eat a meal is one of my favorite ways to do this, because it allows a moment of intention, clarity, and clearing to connect with both my body and the meal in front of me. This direct intention manifests itself as a magnetic and electric frequency that feels as if it almost changes the vibration of the matter in front of me, makes my salads taste fresher, my sandwiches taste more savory, and generally makes my dining process more interesting. I like to use simple ones like: *I love food and food loves me* or *I listen to my body when it speaks to me.* You might prefer getting a little more detailed with something like: *I trust my body and its intelligence to digest everything I eat perfectly.* Most important is that the message resonates with you.

I've found that my mantras have evolved over time as I have become more and more comfortable in my body. I try not to make them so far out there that I don't believe them. For example, starting with *I love my body; it's perfect* wouldn't have worked for me when I was so far from that place. I would have felt inauthentic and disheartened. Instead, I recommend focusing on statements that feel true, attainable, and applicable—

even if they feel like a bit of a stretch from where you stand right now. Maybe you can start with *I am healthy today, and that is enough* or *I appreciate what my body does for me.* Once you feel like a mantra or truth has been integrated into your cells, find a new one and move on, slow and steady, toward the truth.

Name Your Shame

Shame is such a slippery, unpleasant, often unconscious emotion. It may never go away entirely, but we can have a better relationship with it. Shame is prevalent in civilizations where there is a perceived cultural "good" and "bad." And we certainly all receive a ton of messaging that good and bad applies to certain foods and the way we look. In these judgments about food and body it's usually either implied or stated outright that what is "good" is also "attractive" and that thin is "good," while fat is "bad." So, if you find yourself veering off that prescribed path, it makes sense that you might feel as if you're somehow "bad" because you're not adhering to the societal narrative. Shame tends to go way deeper than thinking, "I ate 'bad' today and will take note of how I feel right now so that I can eat more mindfully in the future." Instead, we might go so far as to think that we're a *bad person* because we ate something that's "off-limits." We can turn one action into an entire value judgment on our worth.

Once I made the conscious effort to confront my feelings of shame, I could then start my healing process and acknowledge that, although I had been in a bad relationship with my body and food, I wasn't a bad person. Once I acknowledged this truth, I was able to clearly see the patterns I had been repeating and make progress in being compassionate with the parts of me that felt bad about myself. Through examination, you too can become aware of the causes of your shame and how it impacts your behavior. And, I promise you, shame *is* affecting your behavior, because shame sits at the very core of our belief system, and we build behaviors based upon it. Geneen Roth—who has written extensively about the connection between compulsive eating behaviors and a spiritual disconnect—says it best in her book *Women, Food, and God*: "For some reason, we are truly convinced that if we criticize ourselves, the criticism will lead to change. If we are harsh, we believe we will end up being kind. If we shame ourselves, we believe we will end up loving ourselves. It has never been true, not for a moment, that shame leads to love. Only love leads to love."

When you become aware of shame and its triggers, you can then work toward reconstructing your thinking so that you can be kinder to yourself. One of my favorite tools for doing this is talking to myself the way I would talk to a good friend or loved one. As I have gotten older, I've realized that the body is where life happens. It is our home and our best friend, and this friend has been through it all. Think about the kindness and patience you would extend to your BFF and ask yourself why you don't deserve to extend that same care and compassion to yourself. Then practice doing just that.

Untangling It All

While all these practices helped me get to a place where I shifted my focus and felt better about myself and my body, it wasn't until I realized that my soul is not somewhere *out there* but exists *within me* that my perception about my body really changed. Once I understood this, I began to realize how miraculous my body really was. Until that point, I tortured and fought with my body, thinking it was what needed to change. I ultimately came to realize that I felt like something was wrong or missing because it was: my connection to my soul and all the sweetness of being that comes with that.

Today I see my body as my friend and someone who has been with me through everything. I understand that it is always trying to find balance and equilibrium so that it can do right by me. I know that my body is always looking for my approval and acceptance, so I try to offer that. When I finally released myself from the prison I had locked myself in for all those years and instead saw my body as a form created by generations before me and by God, it felt like exhaling a deep sigh of relief. As if, all this time, my body had been waiting to be seen, acknowledged, and understood. When you are able to look at it like this—or whatever your version of this is—it's easy to understand that the value of your life and soul are not dependent on a number or goal.

I've come a long way with body image and feel so much better in my own skin now. But I'd also be lying if I said I always feel full and complete body acceptance—and I know I'm not alone in that. In the moments when I do feel the urge to change myself, when I start to pick apart my body, or fall into those old patterns of shame, I try to take a deep breath and remind myself of what I've learned, which is this: we complicate things that are meant to be simple, including the things that sustain us. Really, it's this easy: Tired? *Rest.* Hungry? *Eat.* Sad? *Laugh with your friends.* Overwhelmed? *Do less.* Feeling alone? *Connect with someone.*

We need these reminders, because it can be so easy to drop back into the stories we've always been told and that we've gone on to tell ourselves. But, remember: Saturn Return is all about becoming aware of and (if you want to) adjusting the habits and stories that you've identified with up to this point. It's hard to think of any other area of life that is as rife with damaging habits and stories as a woman's body image.

Is it true that you've spent a lot of your life doing so much more because you want to weigh less? It's exhausting, I know. But what I've learned is this: when you are well fed, both internally and externally, you can finally become free. You can tune in to your body, which is impossible when you're spending so much time fixated on your body in the wrong way, your days strictly scheduled with the latest wellness routine and biohack.

I recognize now how my brain really thought it had put one over on my body. Not to say that the two aren't intricately connected (because they are), but rather that the body has incredible wisdom and intelligence that the brain benefits from receiving. Our body is like an antenna, receiving messages, transmuting, and translating energy all the time, helping to process (or hold) emotions. The body is connected to the seen and unseen. Rarely do quick fixes work because they don't take into account the complexity of causes and effects occurring within the body at any given moment. It has quite a lot to do and transmute on the daily.

So really, our responsibility as a conscious being with a body is to tune in to the physical cues and messages our body sends us with the intention of understanding rather than controlling. It's important that we create a relationship with the body that's characterized by consistent tune-ins, reverence practices, and deep awareness of what the body knows about our past, present, and future.

Your body is an extension of your soul. It is a vessel for your unique being. It is an intelligent presence that speaks to you. It is a teacher that shares essential information about your health, growth, and well-being. It is a dear friend who is seeking—and deserves—your love, respect, acceptance, and care. It is your home in this incarnation. Just like every other aspect of your life, your body will change and evolve. So will your relationship with your body. Your Saturn Return is an invitation to embrace that evolution and deepen that relationship. I hope you'll say *yes* to that invitation, and that you'll experience the possibilities that unfold when you embrace your body for all that it is, all that it does, and all the magic that it provides you.

Chapter 6

THE POWER OF NOURISHMENT

Lindsey

When I was living in Los Angeles, a friend asked me to go on an impromptu walk one Sunday afternoon saying that she desperately needed it. As a girl who knows the healing power of a good walk-and-talk, I happily obliged. I was waiting at a bench on the Venice boardwalk when I heard the distant scuff and drag of shoes making their way in my direction. I peered over my shoulder and saw my friend wearing her largest sunglasses, an oversize sweatshirt, a high messy bun, knee-high socks, and what looked like fuzzy slippers. She was gripping a venti iced coffee in one hand, a Celsius energy drink in the other, and had a boardwalk burrito tucked under her arm (you know, the kind of burrito whose contents may or may not include real food).

My friend and I hugged, and then she launched into a saga about the previous night. It involved an adventurous escapade following around a guy she had a crush on, and more and more drinks as the night went on in hope that she would eventually feel loose and comfortable enough to talk to him (and, hopefully, go home with him). She ended up meeting up with him after a flurry of *where are you?* texts exchanged around eleven p.m. By the look of what I now recognized as a dude's sweatshirt, she had ultimately stayed the night.

My friend's anxiety was running the show that morning as she spiraled about how she had acted, what the guy must have thought, and whether or not he'd text her later. Sound familiar? I'm raising my hand! That was me, I was she! It was only about a year before this meetup with my friend that I had consciously cut back on my drinking when I got intentional about both how I was treating my body and how I was showing up when it came to dating. I'd chosen to make these changes because my anxiety had reached an all-time high. By process of elimination—which involved reducing alcohol, caffeine, inflammatory oils (such as corn, safflower, soy, sunflower, and vegetable), and processed foods—I realized that the root cause of this anxiety was what I had been putting in my belly.

When I saw my friend's enormous caffeine arsenal that morning, coupled with the dehydration she had to be experiencing from all the alcohol (not to mention the alcohol itself still running through her system), I knew that so much of how she was feeling could have been avoided by making different nourishment choices. Her Sunday Scaries were really a by-product of compounded poor and unconscious nourishment choices, which disrupt all systems of the body. *No judgment.* Trust me, I've been there and done that, and I went there and did that for *years.* I had to experience the contrast of unconscious and conscious living to truly understand what my body needs (and doesn't need) to feel really good, connected, and *alive.*

Your navigation system is a beautifully complex orchestration of your body, mind, and spirit, and when it's fueled by proper nourishment of every kind—including what you put in, on, and around your physical and energetic body—all its instruments will play together harmoniously to create a life experience that feels good, connected, and centered. Even when circumstances challenge your joy and peace—as they will throughout life and *certainly* throughout your Saturn Return—a properly nourished system ensures a rock-solid homeostasis that serves as a bug-free GPS back to what is true. Not to mention how supportive these choices are to the physical changes that come as you move into your thirties and beyond.

There's so much to say about nourishment—it really is a whole book in and of itself. We'll narrow our focus here to the parts of nourishment that I see as being most related to Saturn Return: recognizing which of the ways in which you're currently nourishing yourself are and aren't working, and what you can adjust from there to best serve this unique organism that is your body. The intention of this chapter is to bring you back to an intuitive way of nourishing yourself, where you trust the messages from your body and trust that which is closest to Mother Earth. Take what speaks to you, and leave what doesn't. That's important, because both the *way* in which we nourish ourselves and the intention that we infuse our choices with are equally important. In fact, sometimes the intention is *more* important than the choice itself. You might order a healthy salad on your lunch break with the intention of giving your body what it needs to feel really energized for the rest of the day, or you could eat a salad with the intention of canceling out the few slices of pizza you had before. In my experience, the body will metabolize these same salads differently based on intention. So notice your *why* when you nourish yourself. Your body is listening.

Saturn Return and All Systems Coming Online

Saturn Return requires all systems of your physical, emotional, and energetic body to come online. Your body was divinely designed to work in harmony across all systems and to be able to experience the world through all your senses—especially your intuitive sense. In order to do that properly, you must consciously nourish your body. What you put into it has a direct impact not only on your physical state but also on your mind, energy, and spirit. You are a soul with a body, and nurturing the vessel within which your soul resides allows it to communicate with you much more clearly and directly. I don't know about you, but I'm pretty sure my soul had a tough time getting my attention when I was four shots of Smirnoff deep, dipping soft pretzel nibs into a vat of melted cheese during a typical Friday night pregame in college.

If you're anything like me, your body was extremely resilient for a period of time in your late teens and early twenties, no matter what you did or didn't put into it. I really put my body through the wringer during those years. My daily meals were imbalanced and sparse, inspired by my desire to "watch what I ate," and then easily influenced by drunken hunger late at night. Still, I was able to bounce back from a hangover relatively quickly. (Or maybe it's that I was okay with feeling just okay back then.) Only years later was I able to make the connection between what I put in my body and how I felt on a physical, emotional, and mental level.

I noticed that my physical and energetic systems naturally sought harmony during my Saturn Return, and I have spoken to many people who had the same experience. The process of understanding how certain foods, drinks, and other substances affect your body, and then developing habits based on this information, won't happen overnight. In fact, it's more likely to be an ongoing process that will continue for the rest of your life. Before you read any further, please understand that the changes recommended in this chapter are not the destination. Instead, you can think of them as the beginning of a long-term conversation between you, your body, and your intuition. Becoming attuned to your entire system—physical, mental, and emotional—and then adjusting your choices based on that information is an ongoing process that will offer you insight on a moment-to-moment basis. Your responsibility is to get still and quiet enough to listen.

We will not be using the words "good" or "bad" to describe anything in this chapter, nor is it my intention to tell you what to consume. Your body, mind, and spirit work together like an orchestra, so please know that what works for one person might not work for you. My goal is to point you toward the songs your body might be playing that will be telling of the harmony or dissonance within the systems of your body.

Tuning In to the Subtle Body

According to an article in *The Wall Street Journal* about the ways in which our brain continues to evolve throughout our twenties, the rates of depression, anxiety, and other mental health issues are higher in our teens and twenties than in any other decade except the eighties. There's speculation that this is because of all the change and uncertainty during these years.[12] Often, your mental health and ability to deal with the stress of all these transitions will be even more severely diminished if your nourishment is out of whack—if you're eating processed foods more than whole foods, messing with your hormones via birth control pills, or if you're overdoing it on the caffeine or alcohol. When Ara Katz, the co-founder of Seed Health, visited us on the pod, she put this in no uncertain terms: "The most critical thing for a healthy microbiome and for health in general is nutrition and diet."[13] There is even an emerging field around this called nutritional psychiatry, as scientific research about the gut-microbiome connection continues to grow, illuminating for us all the effects of the food–mood and gut–brain connection.

In addition to changes in and a new focus on your physical body, there's also a shift in your subtle body. According to the *Bhagavad Gita,* the subtle body is one of the three bodies recognized in Hindu and yogic philosophy, and it's a combination of the various energetic layers that make up a human being beyond their physicality: mind, intellect, and ego. This subtle body controls the physical, and it's how you experience pleasure and pain. As you transition into your thirties, your subtle body starts communicating with you more frequently and becomes increasingly sensitive as you tune in to your own reactions, responses, and sense of self. You may not be able to see your subtle body, but it's vitally important, because the subtle body directs the physical body. This means that when you evaluate how you're nourishing yourself, you're really looking much more deeply than just the fact that you have a habit of eating double-stuffed Oreos late at night. Instead, you're looking at what ingredients are in the cookie and whether or not they work harmoniously with your body. How close to being from the earth are these ingredients? How were they sourced? What messaging is being used to sell these cookies? (Yes, even that matters.) What is your intention when you eat the cookies?

I know, I know. HOW ANNOYING AND UNREALISTIC. It might seem tedious or even overwhelming to think through these types of questions before eating a cookie, but as you more deeply understand your personal nourishment requirements, this type of evaluation will happen naturally and in the course of mere seconds. Now that you're listening, your subtle body will start speaking up about what feels resonant and what does not, and you won't have to consciously think through all this.

Instead, you will become linked to the *yes* or *no* that immediately presents itself as you make nourishment choices.

Here's the thing, though: once you're listening to your subtle body, you may find that you don't really want to hear some of the things it has to say, because it requires change. For example, perhaps you can no longer share that bottle of wine with your friend at dinner, head to the club to socialize and listen to loud music, or pick up that late-night slice of pizza when the drunken hunger starts to set in. But fear not, my friend! Thanks to Saturn Return, you are changing on every level, and this is all part of that evolution and growth. To support this expansion, your body is letting you know how it would like to be nourished to sustain you. Your body is also waking you up to the fact that what you might have been told through messaging, marketing, and your upbringing about what to put in your body might not be in alignment with your expansion, especially during your Saturn Return but also beyond.

Pass the Mic

We've lost that connection. We've lost sight of the fact that when you feel a certain way or something happens in your body, that's a message. Your body is super wise; it knows way more than your brain. People need to learn to listen to it.

—Jessie Inchauspé, author of *The Glucose Goddess Method*
ALMOST 30, EPISODE 579

So, no, this new sensitivity you're feeling during your Saturn Return isn't in your head. Like a compass, it's there to help direct you along your path. This might show up as overwhelming new sensations in your body or a sudden aversion to activities or food that you've been partaking in for a while, and have had no adverse reaction to up to this point. But now maybe you're suddenly aware that these same things are resulting in chronic pain, rashes, headaches, and fatigue, among other symptoms. It might be tempting to keep doing what you've always done despite your body's messages, but chances are that your body will begin to communicate rather loudly if it's ignored. The task in this chapter is to listen to the messages your body is sending you and be more thoughtful about what you put into your body in response. This is simple enough, yes, but also know that it *can* be challenging. You're building a new muscle here.

This part of your awakening might be a bit shocking—and even frustrating—at first. Ignorance can be bliss, but in this specific scenario ignorance is more likely to be a block. At the same time, you *are* still in a period of peak physical health, and, for most, the chronic illness and disease that some people suffer from won't start for a while. Now is the time to heed those messages from your body and to adjust as necessary to enjoy the healthiest lifespan possible.[14]

This chapter isn't meant to incite fear but to inspire making healthy choices that will pay off both now and in the years to come. It's meant to open up your aperture of awareness when it comes to what you put in your body. When you acknowledge both the subtle and not-so-subtle ways your light is dimmed and your body systems are compromised by certain foods and beverages, you will find it hard to forget or ignore. And once you know how good you *can* feel, you will want to feel that way as often and as much as possible.

Let's take a look at some of the factors that might be impacting how good you currently do or do not feel.

Pass the Mic

What you do as a teenager is showing up in your twenties; what you do in your twenties is showing up in your thirties. So don't wait till you get sick. If you are living a toxic lifestyle now, it's not going to be fully activated by the time you're thirty. And then it magnifies by the time you're forty and fifty, and it just gets worse.

—Queen Afua, author of *Sacred Woman*
ALMOST 30, EPISODE 532

Making an Educated Choice

Clearly, food is a central topic in this chapter, and we'll get to that part. But one of the first things to think about as a woman undergoing a transformational physical and biological time of life is birth control. During my Saturn Return, I went off the pill and transitioned to tracking my cycle naturally, and I felt more like myself than I had in more than a decade. I also know it's a topic that women are hungry to learn more about, because it's one of the most popular discussions on both the podcast and within our community at large, so it feels important to discuss here.

Pass the Mic

When you give birth control to a grown-up woman, what you're doing is shutting down her ovaries. Her ovaries aren't maturing an egg follicle, which is what's responsible for the release of estrogen. And it's not releasing an egg and then creating empty egg follicle, which is what releases progesterone. Instead, you're supplanting that with synthetic hormones.

So, every day you take this pill, it gives you a dose of synthetics, and that keeps your own ovaries from producing your own levels of sex hormones. When you do this with an adult woman, it means it's going to change the hormonal message that her brain is receiving. Sex hormones impact the activities of billions of cells in the body at once, many of which are in the brain. There, they play a role in influencing attraction, sexual motivation, stress, hunger, eating patterns, emotion regulation, friendships, aggression, mood, learning, and more. This means that being on the birth control pill makes women a different version of themselves than when they are off of it.

—Sarah E. Hill, PhD, author of
This Is Your Brain on Birth Control
ALMOST 30, EPISODE 577

First of all, it should go without saying that you should have informed consent when it comes to anything you put in or on your body. That's relevant here because so many women who are or have been on birth control aren't informed of the full spectrum of side effects when they start taking it.

It sounds shocking, but it's true: altering your hormones can have a very impactful cascade effect on your entire body, mind, and spirit, and that's exactly what birth control pills do. Also important to know is that these tweaks to a woman's normal hormonal environment can result in sexual dysfunction; this doesn't refer to just the desire for sex, but also how much effort a woman puts into her appearance and how motivated she is to be around potential partners in general. Emerging research is also beginning to point to the fact that there is a possible link between birth control pill use in adolescent girls and an increased risk of developing major depressive disorder over the course of their lifetime, even after they stop taking the pill.[15]

WHOA. I never thought to ask about the effects of being on the pill. I assumed that because a doctor was prescribing it, it was A-okay. And honestly, I was just delighted about the pill's promise to combat my teenage acne and prevent pregnancy since I was having sex with my high school sweetheart. To me, it just felt like birth control was a rite of passage as a woman, and I had no idea about the changes that might occur physically, emotionally, and neurologically as a result. I know I'm not alone in this; I don't think most of us were clearly informed—or even particularly curious—about the impact of birth control on our body; we just assumed that taking the pill was part of being a woman. As you enter further into your adult life and have a better understanding of how your body works and what does or doesn't work for you, and as you may be beginning to more seriously consider whether or not you want to have children, it is the perfect time to reevaluate and ask questions about your birth control choices.

Not surprisingly, there are no black-and-white answers when it comes to oral contraceptives. They are highly effective at preventing pregnancy and can also have some incredibly positive effects on your well-being. For example, oral contraceptives can be highly effective and a saving grace for women managing conditions like endometriosis, PCOS, and hormone imbalances. But it is important to note, as with any medication, they may not be without risks. For some individuals, prolonged use has been associated with potential negative side effects, including cardiovascular issues, metabolic changes, and mental health concerns like depression and anxiety.[17] It's essential for anyone considering or currently using birth control to work closely with a healthcare provider to weigh the benefits and risks based on their unique health profile.

There are no right or wrong answers here, just information to have and things to notice in your body.

Journal: Birth Control and Your Body

Here are some things to ask yourself when it comes to how your body reacts to the birth control pill.

- Why did I originally use hormonal birth control?
- Are there alternative ways to address my original need?
- How have I been feeling physically, mentally, and emotionally since starting hormonal birth control?
- What changes, both positive and negative, have I experienced since starting hormonal birth control?
- Is it possible that I could feel better than I do now?

Reflecting on these questions can provide you with information and further questions that you can bring to your doctor. In addition to your OB/GYN or general practitioner, you might also want to invite in the expertise of a naturopath or holistic practitioner who specializes in hormone health as a way to balance Eastern and Western approaches.

Food for Thought

Before we touch on what you eat, let's rethink *how* you eat, how you can reconnect with your food, and what kind of energy you're putting into your food.

> ## *Pass the Mic*
>
> Modern society is suffering from disconnection syndrome. We are disconnected from the messages of our DNA. We are disconnected from the attempts of our gut bacteria to influence our health in a positive way. We are disconnected from the prefrontal cortex that allows us to be those things that we could be. We're disconnected from our families, our communities, other countries, and we're disconnected from the planet. So, in a very broad sense, we need to reconnect. We need to reconnect to our genome. We need to understand that our food choices, our lifestyle choices, have a powerful effect on which genes are expressed at any given moment.
>
> —David Perlmutter, MD,
> board-certified neurologist, author of *Grain Brain*
> ALMOST 30, EPISODE 202

I've come to realize that, when it comes to food, reconnecting actually isn't that complicated; it just takes intention plus action. Let's start here: *How often do you prepare your own food?* There's no right or wrong answer here, just an opportunity to take an honest look at how you might be able to connect with your food more thoughtfully for a more nourishing experience.

Studies have shown that people who cook at home are more likely to eat a healthy diet, consume fewer calories, and thus be less susceptible to obesity or type 2 diabetes.[18]

Practice: Connect with Your Food

Preparing and connecting with your food creates a harmony between the food and your body well before you even eat it. This can look however you want it to, but here are some suggestions:

- **Take your time grocery shopping . . . and take pride in the process as you do it.** Look at all these fresh, colorful foods you're able to provide for yourself (and maybe those you love too)! At a time when quick and convenient usually wins, use your grocery shopping as a way to slow down, plan your meals thoughtfully, tune in to what you are truly craving, and give a bit of gratitude for the ability to choose your own food!
- **Wash and organize your produce as soon as you bring it home.** Your refrigerator will look pretty, and your future self will thank you when you can grab that still-fresh goodness. I also just love treating my food with love and care. Nothing I hate more than finding a dirty, overripe zucchini in my veggie drawer! Poor thing.
- **Seek out local farmers' markets.** There's so much to be said for meeting the people who are growing and raising the food you're eating, and their foods also potentially offer a more affordable option than their big-store counterparts. Even though foods at markets such as these might not be labeled organic, free-range, and so on, you can talk to the sellers about their growing practices—most of which are optimal.
- **Carve out time to cook.** So often, cooking feels like a rushed item to check off your to-do list. See if you can, instead, use it as a relaxing time or moving meditation as you slow down to prepare the ingredients you'll need for your meal. As you cook, take pride in knowing exactly what's going into the food you're about to eat, including the energy and intention.

Perhaps most important of all when it comes to what and how you eat is how your food makes you feel. There's plenty of guidance out there to point out different nutritional paths, but the real goal here is to find out what works for you and your body, to detach from any labels you may have previously put on your eating habits as you do so, and instead to notice how the food you're ingesting is impacting you on a holistic level. If you just listen, your body will let you know what you do and don't need.

Not only do I encourage you to think about what you're eating, but also *why* you're eating. For example, I think we've all had a good comfort-eating sesh before, and *that's okay*. But the next time you find yourself in this position, stop for a moment to think about what you really need and how the food you're eating is going to impact you. Is it *actually* going to comfort you, or is it going to do something else? Often the food we think about as comfort foods aren't really doing what we think they're doing at all.

Pass the Mic

In my early days, comfort food was junk food. It was fried chicken. It was cakes and pies with sugar and egg whites in it. That was comfortable because that's what my mother gave me as a child.

But true comfort food is healthy. Comfy is whole foods. Comfort is foods that grow out of nature. Just like when we go to a park and sit out in the grass and the sun is shining, don't we feel so comforted and embraced by nature? Well, when we eat the foods that come out of the soil like that, when they come out of the earth and we take them in, our body's in comfort. Our heart is healthier. Our blood is cleaner. Our minds are clearer. That's comfort. To be sick is not comfortable. Comfort is things and circumstances that support me, that nurture me, and love me.

—Queen Afua, author of *Sacred Woman*
ALMOST 30, EPISODE 532

As we've discussed, this process of determining what does and doesn't work for you will become intuitive and almost instantaneous as you attune with your body over time. But checking in with yourself can take some conscious effort at first. To become more mindful about how what you eat is impacting you and of any adjustments you might want to make, try the following exercise.

Practice: Post-Meal Check-In

After you eat, find a quiet space and take a few deep breaths into your belly to drop into your body. As you breathe, focus on any sensations you are feeling in your body, particularly in your stomach. Once you have checked in, think through or journal the following questions:

- What is my dominant feeling in this moment?
- What sensations do I feel and where?
- Do I feel how I want to feel after eating?
- If not, what might I try to do differently in the future?

See what patterns you notice over time to identify what does and doesn't work for you. In addition to noticing foods that do and don't feel nourishing in your body, also be aware of how food sourcing, preparation, and your state of mind may be impacting your experience so that you can adjust as necessary.

Eat from the Earth

We've lost our connection to Mother Earth and our food supply, as well as to our own bodies, when it comes to what we need for nourishment on all levels—not only physically but also mentally and emotionally. With this, we are missing out on the incredibly positive impacts the right foods can have on our holistic health.

Pass the Mic

We feel better when we eat in certain ways, but very few people make that connection. We often think about how we eat in connection to our waistline or a number on the scale, but we're not connecting it to mental health. There's so much power at the end of our fork, and we can control it. It's such an autonomous process.

—Uma Naidoo, MD, author of
This Is Your Brain on Food
ALMOST 30, EPISODE 564

Because this process of eating to feel better is highly individualized, where do we even begin to figure out what we should and should not be eating to best support ourselves? The truth of the matter is that optimal nutrition choices are different from one person to the next based on genetics, age and life stage, health conditions, activity level, metabolism, cultural background, and allergies and intolerances. But there are a few universal truths, and one of those is that ultra-processed foods do not support a healthy microbiome (which, again, impacts our physical, mental, and emotional health). Processed foods often lose nutritional value and gain unhealthy additives, preservatives, and refined ingredients in the manufacturing process. What makes that Cool Ranch Dorito taste so good? *Mm-hmm,* those additives keep you coming back for more, baby.

This, combined with all the other hurdles we face in our food sourcing today, means that it's important to be super intentional not only about what we're eating but also where it's coming from and how it's being grown. As a rule of thumb, I try to stay as close to the earth as possible when making my food choices. In other words, I tend to eat whole foods, like fruits, vegetables, nuts, eggs, meat, and fish. This philosophy has acted as a guide and helped me streamline my diet. Also, it's applicable across the board, whether you're plant-based, pescatarian, a carnivore, or, really, an omnivore.

Staying close to the earth means that you can easily identify what plant or animal the ingredients of a food are derived from. That's it: if you can do this, then you are close to the earth. Farm-to-table is a common phrase used to describe this type of food. But that's only the first qualifier; also, there should ideally be very little to no meddling with the ingredients or final product during its journey from the ecosystem to your plate.

Our food should be as fresh as possible when we ingest it, because the fresher the food is, the more nutrients it offers. This means that it should have gone through as little transportation and intervention as possible. Plants and grains should not be exposed to pesticides or herbicides and should be certified organic when possible. If not organic, properly wash the food before eating. If you're eating meat and other animal products, it's important to understand the quality of life the animal had when it was alive and the means by which the product was made. You are ingesting what the animal ingested, both literally and energetically.

When you do find yourself buying packaged foods, be sure to look at the ingredient list, not what the front of the package says about the food. Food companies are well aware of the general trend toward organic, healthier food choices and use that as a marketing strategy. Courtney Swan, an integrated nutritionist and host of the *Realfoodology* podcast, gave us great advice to think of the front of food packaging as a billboard. They're meant to sell you on the product, not provide real information about what's actually in it. Let ingredient lists be your guide: look for ones that you immediately recognize as food, and as few ingredients per package as possible.[19]

There are two other major components of this that I want to mention, which are the importance of protein intake and the limiting of added sugars. I think we can all agree that the negative impacts of added sugar are widely recognized. For this one, it is important to check the label for added or excessive amounts of sugar. Consuming too much sugar can affect you physically, mentally, and emotionally. It puts you at risk for chronic diseases like type 2 diabetes, heart disease, and certain cancers, as well as cognitive decline that can manifest as depression, anxiety, or a neurological degeneration such as Alzheimer's. Emotionally, you might experience mood swings, irritability, and other mood disorders. In my experience, the temporary sugar high and comfort are not worth the health risks long term! Let's also acknowledge that some of my favorite food joys are desserts. Oh, you too?! Okay, cool. No need to ruin your life by nixing desserts altogether. A good rule of thumb is to be mindful of the amount of sugar in 80 percent of your foods. The other 20 percent? Truly enjoy it without guilt.

Interestingly, I've noticed that I've been able to reduce my sugar intake over time by increasing the amount of protein I consume on a daily basis. So how much protein should you be consuming? Well, it depends on your body composition and other factors. Dr. Gabrielle Lyon, the author of *Forever Strong,* joined us on the pod, and was quick to note that the average woman in America consumes 60 grams of protein a day, which is generally not enough. Based on all the systems in the body that require protein to work properly—like your neurological system and gut microbiome, plus the constant protein turnover happening all the time—she recommends at least 100 grams of protein per day. To be honest, it took a while for me to get into the habit of incorporating this practice. But now I crave protein and make sure that things like nuts, seeds, legumes, bone broth, meat, or fish are incorporated into every meal I eat. I've never felt healthier, more energized, or stronger.

There's a lot to consider when you make your food choices—I get it! While the information out there is aplenty, it can be overwhelming to filter through it all and find what works for you. So give yourself time and grace to build these healthier habits when it comes to your food. With some time and practice, you will find food sources, recipes, and combinations that you and your body love. You will understand the cravings of your body better over time. You will become more attuned to what makes you feel *really good* on every level and what does not. It will get easier and, soon enough, it will become a way of life.

Is This Anxiety or My Coffee?

Anxiety is something that many of us have to grapple with—especially in our twenties. But it's also surprising how much of that anxiety can be related to nutritional choices. Those choices might be exacerbating your anxiety, or they could be causing it altogether. And there are two main culprits that you might want to consider using in moderation: caffeine and alcohol.

CAFFEINE

I know, I know! I love my morning coffee just as much as you do. And your girl loved an energy drink in her day too. For so many of us, coffee is comforting and ritualistic, a promising burst of energy and excitement to a perhaps otherwise sluggish start. An energy drink pre-workout or even to kick off a night out gives us the jolt we tend to crave.

Consider the fact that it takes up to ten hours for your body to clear caffeine out of your system, and that drinking caffeine throughout the day may very well mean that your body barely has a window to process the caffeine.[20] *Oh, that's why I can't fall asleep?* As a result, your central nervous system is in a constant state of stimulation, and the caffeine in your system negatively impacts anxiety and sleep, decreases cerebral blood flow, and increases cortisol and adrenaline.[21] Not to mention the fact that caffeine is dehydrating. It goes without saying that soda and energy drinks—the latter of which consist of caffeine, sugar, and added stimulants—bring with them all these issues and more. Studies have pointed to the fact that energy drinks, in particular, are associated with increased heart rate and blood pressure, gastrointestinal upset, headaches, and dental erosion.[22]

Another thing to be aware of is that caffeine is habit-forming. No, you won't become addicted to it in the way that you can to other substances, but you *can* build up a tolerance and find that you have to up your daily dosage over time or start to feel withdrawal symptoms, such as fatigue, headaches, irritability, and difficulty concentrating. This means it's worth considering the role caffeine plays in your life and whether you are drinking it based on choice or necessity.

If you experience any of these symptoms, looking at your relationship with caffeinated beverages is a good place to start. But even if you're *not* experiencing any of these symptoms, the threshold of thirty is an important time to audit your caffeine habit, because caffeine can raise your heart rate and breathing rate, which activates your sympathetic nervous system's fight-or-flight response. This is a time in life when you want to remain as centered as possible, which requires that you remain in that rest-and-digest parasympathetic state to the greatest extent possible. This is critical because, as Dr. Nicole LePera explained to us, the state of our nervous system impacts, well, everything. Included on that list is our emotional resilience, how we tolerate emotions, and how grounded we are in the world around us. Simply put, she says, "It really governs our day-to-day life."[23] Of course, many factors affect our nervous system, but caffeine is a good place to start, because we can monitor and control it more easily than we can most aspects of life.

THE BUZZ OF SOBER CURIOSITY

I'll admit it: if I see a dirty martini with a bleu cheese–stuffed olive on the menu, I'm in. Mainly for the bleu cheese. But I digress. For the most part, I've reached a point in my relationship with alcohol that places my desire to feel good at the top of my priority list, which has changed the amount of alcohol I consume and the intention that I bring to those moments. As you embark on your thirties, it's a perfect opportunity to reevaluate how you want to incorporate alcohol into your life as both your body and priorities begin to shift.

Like me, you have probably had your fair share of mornings when you've woken up, head pounding to the beat of Avicii, mouth drier than the Sahara, swearing off alcohol . . . until the next weekend rolls around. Ah, the cycle of social drinking. If you find yourself riding a similar merry-go-round and want to feel better, allow me to introduce you to a growing movement that's all about reevaluating your relationship with alcohol, without the pressure of abstaining completely. It's called *sober curiosity*. This approach is about mindfulness and intentionality, remaining in honest conversation with yourself about why you choose to drink and how much is too much.

But there are even more reasons to try out a sober curious lifestyle, and those reasons are different for each of us. Most of us will come to understand these personal reasons on our own, and often we come to those realizations during this Saturn Return season when we're transitioning and looking at things a bit differently than we were before. Maybe you don't like the way you interact with people when you've had one too many. You might hate the way you feel the next day. Those high bar tabs might be keeping you from doing and investing in other things you'd like to do. You could be moving into a phase of life that just doesn't accommodate drunken nights. Perhaps alcohol has been a dulling agent to the real feelings that lie beneath, an escape, a way to numb, a calming habit, a social lubricant, or what feels like a pass to social acceptance.

Have a lot of grace for yourself as you uncover your true *why* for drinking alcohol (more on that in a minute) and recalibrate your relationship with it to be a bit more measured, centered, and healthy. In the typical, very impressionable college and post-grad experience, the pressure to drink is great. Hold compassion and understanding for the fact that you had to move through your relationship with alcohol exactly as you have up to this point in order to arrive right here, where you are today.

As you think about all this and utilize Saturn Return as an opportunity to redefine your relationship with alcohol, let's focus first on intention. Intention is the missing piece for most of us when it comes to how we do and don't nourish ourselves, and that's particularly true with alcohol. How many times have you asked yourself *why* you're imbibing? If the answer is *never* or *rarely,* that's okay. But why not start building the habit now? This is not to recommend that you don't drink, full stop, but that you be clear and specific about why you're drinking. I find it helpful to set an intention before I drink to help me embody my why, and you might do the same to build the habit of gaining clarity about and setting parameters around your alcohol consumption in any given situation. For example: "My intention is to enjoy this beautiful glass of wine, take in its complexities with every sip (as I pretend to know more about wine than I do), and allow it to make what I'm eating even yummier. And I intend to feel really well rested and energized tomorrow morning."

There's a big difference between having a glass of wine with a nice dinner and mindlessly drinking a vodka soda or three to soothe or forget about the day, because the *intention* between the two scenarios is completely different. In my experience, setting an intention allows me to be more conscious and my consumption tends to be on the more conservative side as a result. Plus, the clarity of intention allows my body to relax and trust the night ahead. Personally, I've noticed that being in a relaxed state allows me to metabolize my alcohol better. And according to the University of Notre Dame,[24] stress emotions such as depression, anxiety, and anger can cause a change in the enzymes in the stomach, affecting how the body processes alcohol. So basically, approaching drinking from a place of calm, regulation, and intention can improve how your body reacts to the alcohol itself.

When you start drinking without an intention, it's easy to lose sight of how you want to feel both now and later, which can make you especially vulnerable to heightened emotions while drinking. Before you know it, you're four cocktails deep, haven't eaten, and are well on your way to a compromised physical state that will last through and ruin the following day. So what do you say? Cheers to being in right relationship with alcohol, to feeling better physically, mentally, and emotionally *every* weekend. And cheers to knowing that you don't need alcohol to have a great time, to be fun and funny, or to be liked. Alcohol can be a part of your experience, but it no longer needs to control the experience.

Small Changes Matter

If you would have told me at age twenty-seven that I would feel the best I've ever felt at thirty-six, I would have looked at you cross-eyed. HUH?! Not to mention the fact that I feel more beautiful and embodied than ever. The foundation for how I feel these days is how I nourish my body. Everything else is important, but the emotional, mental, and energetic aspects of myself cannot properly integrate if my body is not capable of supporting those processes.

So while you might feel a bit overwhelmed after reading this chapter, know that your gradual exploration and implementation of anything that calls to you here will make a big difference. Simply infusing your food with love and intention, for example, which costs nothing and takes mere seconds, can have a profound effect on how you feel. If at any point, you notice that trying to incorporate what we've recommended causes you stress, drop it and reset, because stress likely overrides any benefit. When you're ready to start again, start small and keep a written reflection of how you feel with each change you make, taking note of what's working and what is not. Trust the wisdom of your body as you experiment with more conscious ways of nourishing yourself. Your body knows—even if you're questioning.

Career

Contrary to the fantasies that might be playing out in your head, if it's tough going in your work life at the moment, the right move probably isn't quitting it all and moving to a cabin in the woods or flipping off your boss as you slo-mo walk out of the office. Instead, it's getting to the root of what's *really* driving you to burnout (which might very well be different from what you assume it is), making sure that your finances aren't forcing you to make career decisions that you wouldn't otherwise, finding what truly motivates you, and getting clear on your intention—which is exactly what we're going to focus on in this section of the book.

You are not what you do, and you do not have just one purpose—yet it's an honorable desire to find purpose, and most of us *do* need to find a career for the sake of our livelihood. So, how do you balance this dichotomy? Your human self knows that making money and earning a living is important, that life feels better when you're working toward a clear goal. Meanwhile, your soul knows how expansive, multifaceted, and infinite you are. Whatever your current situation is, if you're feeling unsatisfied or uncertain of your purpose or career path, know that more and more women are intuitively feeling like something is off with the way they've been taught to approach these arenas. We hope to open up a window of possibility if you're feeling burnt out or overwhelmed, and to ensure you walk away from these pages feeling confident in knowing yourself enough to let your inherent gifts shine.

Chapter 7

FEELING THE BURNOUT

Krista

In 2019, Lindsey and I went on our second world tour. It was a wild time in our lives; while on the road, we also had full-time jobs and used all our PTO to plan and execute these events in cities we had never been to up to that point. Being onstage with your best friend, meeting people who love what you do, and literally watching your dream business grow in front of your eyes sounds pretty freaking glorious, and in so many ways it was one of the most fun periods of our lives. Meeting people where they were, both physically and emotionally, solidified for me that what we do at *Almost 30* was part of my purpose and also taught me a lot about where we women are as a collective today.

And, at the same time, Lindsey and I were dying inside, even as we wore our burnout like a badge of honor. All the love and energy from our audience could only go so far when we were pushing ourselves beyond every limit imaginable. It was just the two of us and our intern, Chloe (who later became our first employee and worked for us for four years), scheduling, marketing, organizing, executing, hosting, and running more than twenty-five events everywhere from Chicago to London to Sydney. Each stop was different because we curated our content based on the location to ensure we were speaking about relevant topics.

I will never forget the medicine we received at our Washington, DC, show, which took place about two years into both *Almost 30* and Lindsey's and my Saturn Return. As we faced the kind eyes of more than 150 women in the crowd (most of whom had come to the event straight from work), something came over Lindsey and me. Without discussing it with each other first, we began the event by asking the audience:

"How many of you are burnt out?"

It's hard to say whether we were channeling the audience's energy or just being way too honest and projecting based on our own exhaustion from juggling travel and an eighty-hour workweek. Thinking back on it kind of makes me laugh. Can you imagine how you would feel if you walked into an event expecting the Black Eyed Peas' "I Gotta Feeling" pumping to segue into a motivational speech about hustling for everything on your vision board and, instead, got hit with a shot of truth serum to start the evening? What can I say? It's the way that we roll, and what happened as a result has stuck with me to this day.

As the question hung in the air, I lifted my hand in encouragement to those who wanted to step out of their own burnout closet. And then, one by one, every single person in the audience lifted their hand in solidarity. Some raised their hands meekly and with a sort of trepidation, almost as if they were fearful of admitting to burnout; others seemed somewhat ambivalent about it, like, *Yeah, but who's* not *burnt out?*; and others looked like they wanted to wave both of their hands in the air like a propeller. The looks on these women's faces were heartbreaking, as if they'd just realized how they were *actually* feeling. They looked tired, defeated, broken down, and downright depressed as they glanced around the room and acknowledged how pervasive this feeling was. There was also a hint of resignation—like they were all trapped and couldn't do anything about the pace at which we were all running on this hamster wheel, seeking something we would never quite catch up to.

Over the course of the next few hours, it was beautiful to see a cascade of unfurrowing brows, loosening jaws, and unclenching fists—as if something clicked not only in all our minds but also in our bodies.

I know so many successful women: brilliant, driven, powerful, badass females. But a well-rested, relaxed woman? That's much harder to find. Many of us are ambitious, driven, fierce—and burnt out. This term that we hear so often is a state of physical, emotional, and mental exhaustion that sets in when we feel overwhelmed and unable to meet the demands of our life. Burnout is so prevalent in this day and age that it's even been designated as an Internationally Classified Disease (ICD) by the World Health Organization. This is important to be aware of because during this transition to a new decade, your opportunity and potential to burn out is on the rise—particularly for women. Research shows that the average age of burnout is thirty-two,[25] and that women are more burnt out than men for a variety of reasons, including working harder for less recognition and pay, statistically taking on the lion's share of childcare, and also the increasingly acknowledged mental load that comes from all this.[26]

While there may be periods when you go through stress and feel overcome by the challenges in life, the experience of burnout is different (it's like your eyebrows: they're cousins, not twins). Stress can come and go depending on the day, but burnout is constant. And, after a while, it's almost like we learn to live with it, to accept it as part of adult life—which, to be clear, shouldn't be the case. I encourage you to take a moment now to sit quietly, check in, and notice if you are experiencing symptoms of burnout.

These include:

- anxiety
- bad moods
- depression
- exhaustion
- frequent sickness
- insomnia
- physical pain

If this list feels like a diary entry, take a deep breath and know that you're not alone. Recognizing your current state is important, because to heal or change your trajectory, you must first be honest with yourself. When you're living in an unconscious state, you can—and, let's be honest, probably *will*—run yourself into the ground. But with time, attention, and some loving kindness, you can change your path to one of more rest, ease, and calm. Know that I'm with you: I've been there, and I feel thankful for the tools, resources, and awareness that have helped me, and more important, that can help *you* get in the right relationship with yourself so that you don't live a life of glorifying or normalizing burnout.

Saturn Return and Burnout

The reevaluation that comes with Saturn Return very much includes taking a look at what you have been told about work ethic and hard work. Concepts like *the work is never done, hustle,* and *grind* have been drilled into us from a young age. Most of us are taught that the harder we work, the more successful we will be. We're even told that to have a life we love, hard work, long hours, and pushing beyond our limits is necessary.

Maybe you're like me and feel like you have to "get it right" in life—like it's some sort of win-or-lose proposition. If you have this mindset to begin with, Saturn Return can compound it, because this tends to be a time of so much pressure piled on top of the pressure you already feel and put on yourself on a day-to-day basis. NBD to casually unpack your entire life's programming while you're at it, right? It can feel like you're being pulled in a million different directions, yet also somehow running in place, making seemingly no progress despite the great efforts you're putting forth on multiple fronts. All this can easily send you careening down the burnout path with your pedal to the metal, wheels spinning, and no end in sight.

All this is exacerbated by the fact that, whether we're consciously aware of it or not, we live in a society that tells us that capitalistic hard work is the true definition of success. It's the American dream, baby! We've been told that time is money, and hard work is the only surefire way to not only success but survival.

It's easy to slip into a fear-based, work-hard-at all-costs type of mindset. And because Saturn is the taskmaster planet, it's easy to imagine that Saturn Return is asking us to work even harder, to put in even more than we already are. But we shouldn't interpret Saturn like this. As we've established, many people are actually already very responsible and hard-working before their Saturn Return—and this isn't the kind of success Saturn wants for everyone, anyway. If necessary, Saturn will use this as an opportunity to strip away all the burnout-inducing programming to pare you down to your most authentic self and set you on a road that will actually fulfill you. It will potentially shine a light on where you're working too hard and overextending yourself. Of course, others *will* have the opposite experience and find that Saturn wants them to do some hustling and grinding, or to be more responsible. Whatever your scenario, Saturn is here to shift it ALL up so that you're aligned with your highest good, whatever that may be. For many of us, that can involve recognizing burnout so that we're forced to take a step back from hard work and focus instead on cultivating a more disciplined approach around rest. This includes, first, getting to the root cause of burnout, which usually extends beyond work; we're looking to the deepest cause and the core reason why we're pushing ourselves so hard in the first place.

Pass the Mic

When burnout happens, we have to remember that it is an overwhelming feeling that affects us emotionally, physically, and behaviorally. I think a lot of people think, "If I can just streamline or get a better handle on my to-do list, I won't be burnt out anymore." When burnout happens, it's a sign that your life is not in alignment in a way that works for you.

—Whitney Goodman, LMFT, author of *Toxic Positivity*
ALMOST 30, EPISODE 585

Know that if you find yourself feeling burnt out, Saturn is showing you that there's a better way of being. There is a better way to build a life, achieve your goals, and work. You can find balance between striving and self-acceptance. There *is* a way of being that allows you to enjoy the process.

We're discussing this topic in the career section, but please know that while burnout is often most apparent in your work life, it's generally a deeper issue than that. And until you tame your burnout, chances are that any other career-related decisions ultimately won't get you where you want to go.

Hustling at a Cost

Before we dive any further into burnout, we have to acknowledge the culture that we exist within and how it promotes burnout. This is important to recognize because, when it seems that everyone around you is also burnt out (and perhaps even glorifying it), it's easy to figure this is just the way things are supposed to be. What we are collectively experiencing, though, is not the way other parts of the world live. There *is* another way, and it doesn't have to involve going off the grid. It *does* involve cultivating awareness about the system you're operating in, though, or it's all too easy to unconsciously get swept up in the *go, go, go, do, do, do* current.

I wouldn't say that capitalism is all bad. It allows people to achieve their dreams and potential. But it's also a system that can be highly stressful and exhausting, and can take a toll on both our mental and physical health. It leads to burnout as the result of working long hours, never taking time for yourself, and feeling like you can't catch a break. It's the result of our constant quest for success. And the forces of capitalism and consumerism extend beyond the workplace too, instilling in each of us a general sense of not-enoughness that also leads to burnout. This system promotes short-term gains at any cost, while disregarding the long-term consequences on people and societies.

Burnout is all-pervasive. Way beyond work, it makes us disregard the wisdom of our bodies, our mental health, and our happiness. When we're striving and seeking to make our way in the world—all the while not having clear boundaries or tuning in to our bodies to check in with our well-being—it can be a recipe for disaster.

The stress that comes with burnout is like your party playlist. You only want that playlist turned on when you're in need of a boost or want to exert intense physical energy. Listening to it at all hours of the day will most likely leave you feeling either tired or insane. Similarly, stress is good in doses and in situations where you need that extra boost, but it can wreak havoc on your body and mind when it's constant—and if that goes on for long enough, stress can literally be lethal. When people are under stress, their bodies undergo changes that include producing higher-than-normal levels of stress hormones such as cortisol, adrenaline, epinephrine, and norepinephrine. These stress hormones can interrupt your body's natural processes and put you at a higher risk for a host of issues, like anxiety, depression, digestive issues, headaches, muscle tension, cardiac issues, and sleep and weight issues.[27] Stress can also literally alter the structure of your brain, resulting in worsened memory, cognition, and mood disorders; impair your immune system, making you more susceptible to illness and disease; diminish cardiovascular health; and adversely impact GI health and the functional physiology of your intestine, resulting in things such as decreased digestion and GI inflammation.[28]

Let's sit with that for a moment. This stressful, overtaxed way that so many of us have become so accustomed to living is actually potentially causing our body very real, very serious physical damage. Sure, you may not feel the full impact of it now—but at some point, you probably will. If nothing else convinces you that living in a burned-out state is no way to be, let this be it.

Pass the Mic

I had that millennial mindset where I'm like, "Nah, I can do it. I can pull all-nighters." Then I started to feel crappy. I realized, I don't know if I want to be in the position where I sacrifice my body for success anymore, because my body helps me get up in the morning and walk up the stairs.

I unsubscribe from the idea that I have to sacrifice my body to be successful. I think I can actually be healthy *and* be successful. We're not told that enough.

—Lilly Singh, author of *Be a Triangle*
ALMOST 30, EPISODE 512

In the following chapters, we'll look at some real ways to shift how you look at your professional career that will help you transition out of burnout mode (if that's what you need), but even that won't change the fact that you live in a world that promotes this way of living. So most important is learning to recognize the signs of stress and burnout and understanding how you can manage your stress in a productive way.

Regardless of the messages society sends, the ultimate goal is to live a life that includes the least amount of stress possible. But the reality is that there are times in your life when you will feel stressed, and since stress compounds, it's important to have tools to recognize that stress when it appears, do what you can to alleviate it, and to hopefully avoid burnout or chronic stress in the long run.

Be honest with yourself about how and where you've been pushing your boundaries. This honesty can help you ground yourself into the truth of where you are and what is happening, which represents the first step in healing. Even before you start changing patterns that aren't serving you, there is liberation in being honest and acknowledging the truth of how you feel.

Get enough sleep. We tend to skimp on sleep when we're rushing around and pushing ourselves. Sleep is so important for your body to rest and recover. In fact, getting quality sleep for the appropriate amount of time (at least seven hours, according to the American Academy of Sleep Medicine) may be one of the most important things you can do for your stress levels, overall development, health, and happiness—especially as you support yourself through Saturn Return.

Unplug from the phone. The biggest misconception I see in our community is the belief that spending time on the phone is relaxing. The truth is, you aren't actually resting at all when you're on the phone, because you're in a continuous cycle of stimulation. When you scroll, your body can't drop into the rest-and-digest state; instead, it remains in fight-or-flight for as long as you continue to consume. Now, don't get it twisted: I love a good scroll at the end of the day, but I know that it's better for my physical and emotional state to take intentional time off my device.

If it feels overwhelming to just put the phone down, start by putting your phone down at least two times a day in fifteen-minute increments. Instead, use that time to rest without a screen—whatever that looks like for you. Once you're comfortable with that, you can set hours during which you turn off your phone (I turn mine off between eight p.m. and eight a.m. each day), and you might even incorporate a three-day digital fast a few times per year.

Take your paid time off (PTO). Like, ALL of it. Don't wait for things to "slow down" because the work will never end. Some companies now offer "unlimited PTO" (aka we say we want you to take time off, but will judge you if you do), and while it's a struggle to actually log off in environments like this, you are *legally* entitled to do so. Remember, no matter what your colleagues are or are not doing, you're not breaking any laws by going on vacation; you're being a human being who deserves—and *requires*—some vitamin D and rest. Not to mention the fact that it will make you more productive in the long run. If you're a freelance worker or contractor, plan out your quarter or year and let your clients know when you're taking time off. For both employees and gig economy folks, I suggest four weeks at the very least, but ideally we would be more European about it all and move toward six to eight weeks off per year to get a better balance in life and be more human being than human doing. To put some numbers behind it, if you were to take off four weeks (twenty days of the 261 weekdays per year) that's still only 13 percent of your year, which means you'll spend 87 percent of the other days working.

Give yourself five *nos* to use per week. Designate five *nos* that you have to put to use each week—whether it's saying no to working later, no to the project you really don't have bandwidth for, or no to that dinner out that you're dreading at the end of a long day. Use them when you're being asked to go to happy hour or to a HIIT workout that really just makes you feel exhausted rather than strong. These sacred nos are designed to create more space in your life, so be sure to use all of them.

Pass the Mic

I used to have this thought that if I stop pedaling so fast and pushing so hard, it's all gonna be taken away. And I can tell you, at least from my experience, it's not true. I've given myself permission to just really feel into what's a true yes and what's not, and to also question my own assumptions about running a business. We're supposed to work five days a week. It's supposed to look like this. You're supposed to have X many weeks of vacation.

But what does downshifting look like? I'm interested in experimenting in a major way, and I'm interested in facing those fears of irrelevance.

—Marie Forleo, author of *Everything Is Figureoutable*
ALMOST 30, EPISODE 593

The Burnout Traps of Your Late Twenties

Let's talk through some of the common themes that underline burnout and how you can support yourself as you begin to shift them as necessary.

COMPARISON

President Teddy Roosevelt said it best: "Comparison is the thief of joy." You know those moments when you're sitting there minding your own business, enjoying your life, and all of a sudden you hear about a friend—or even a stranger—living their best life, in the sexiest relationship, feeling good in their body sporting the dopest clothes, living out their purpose, with one hundred million friends following their every move? Then, right after you learn how easy life has been for them and their micro goldendoodle, you find yourself swept up into the comparison loop. The loop that feels like nothing you do is ever good enough, like everyone else is luckier than you. The one that focuses intensely on what is good about everyone else's life, and what's *not* good about yours. Most of us compare almost every aspect of our lives, from how we look to how much money we make to the quality of our relationships—and Saturn Return will only amplify that. Really, we can compare ourselves against any measure, whether it's tangible or intangible. We can even see our happiness as relative to that of others.

This comparison-focused and scarcity-based mindset makes it challenging to be truly happy, because it can sometimes seem that every person you meet is doing better than you are in at least one respect. This can then lead to the desire to chase, hustle, and do, in an effort to keep up with the Joneses and prove that you are worthy based on what you have and what you do. The goal is to instead focus on your own life, to become aware of the comparative lens, and to then consider and prioritize your unique path and journey. To admire your gifts and experience without thinking about them in relation to others.

Pass the Mic

When I was twenty-seven or twenty-eight, I didn't feel good about myself. I was comparing myself to everybody that I knew. I felt miserable. I felt empty. I didn't have any purpose. I needed to start doing the work. What that meant for me is going to therapy more seriously, and not just venting about my day, but being like, "These are the things that I want to change about myself. These are the things I want to work on." And journaling, and reading the books, and doing all that. It's been therapy, continuing to do the work of being self-aware, and realizing, "Okay, this is affecting me." You have to train yourself. Your brain is a muscle as much as anything else.

—Tinx, author of *The Shift*
ALMOST 30, EPISODE 615

Comparison is hard to avoid altogether, but I found that it somehow eased all the feelings that come with it once I recognized that comparison is *normal*. In fact, our brains actually prefer it. At the end of the day, our brains are simply computing devices that provide information for interpretation.

One of the reasons that could explain why our brain loves social comparisons is because it provides a faster and easier way for us to make judgments and decisions. Comparison requires the brain to focus on a small subset of information (this versus that, black or white) as opposed to contemplating nuance, exploring complexity, and doing an exhaustive search of our brain's entire knowledge base to find a more holistic answer. Social comparisons enable us to reserve scarce cognitive resources by keeping the energy exertion low. Comparison makes your brain's job easier—but that doesn't mean it can't send you into a tailspin. When we go into this comparison vortex, we end up driving ourselves even harder, when the truth is we're trying to achieve the unachievable. When comparison is serving as momentum to achieve our goals or find success, much like an espresso shot in the morning, it will never generate the energy we're hoping for; all it does is create a swift undercurrent that leads straight on out to the sea of burnout.

Here are some ways to support yourself and reduce your reaction to comparison.

Reframe Your Feed

Remember that social media is a highlight reel, and that you are quite possibly comparing your current IRL situation to someone else's curated image or best day. When we are online, it's natural to drop into a comparison vortex and unconsciously drive ourselves even harder. This comparison, which is fueled by a subconscious drive of not-enoughness, can cause us to spin our wheels and seek to become something other than who we are, which can be exhausting if left unchecked.

Pass the Mic

What I'm seeing in this generation is a real desire to reconnect. I think the disconnection brought on by our modern society has become so pervasive that finally there's pushback.

I would recognize and portray the importance of re-establishing connections with your friends, understanding that social media and likes on posts aren't important and that when you're doing that, you're judging yourself based upon the responses from others. When you're looking at everybody else's posts, remember those aren't reality. Nobody posts themselves having a crummy day and looking ugly. We only tend to see the best. And the ads that pop up on social media are targeting you. You know that. We all know that. But they're very pernicious, aren't they? Your brain is being manipulated and degraded to make you connect to your fear center as opposed to your empathy and compassion center.

—David Perlmutter, MD,
board-certified neurologist, author of *Grain Brain*
ALMOST 30, EPISODE 202

Be the Hype Woman

You know that friend who you can always count on to be your cheerleader and ultimate hype girl? The one who will gas you up even in your cringiest moments? Be *that* support system for yourself. Speak to yourself as if you were your own friend: with kindness, love, compassion, and empathy. Find the things you love about yourself and your life, know that you'll never be like anyone else, and recognize that you are truly one of one. And that's a beautiful thing.

And while you're at it, hype your friends up too! Yes, it's normal to feel a tinge of envy even when it comes to those we love, but how would it feel to convert that comparison into celebration? It's a quick way to shift out of the scarcity mindset and show yourself that you're comfortable with success, because you know it's on its way to you too.

Practice Gratitude

Gratitude is soul nourishment. It's a way for you to be with and love yourself and your life. Gratitude will help you feel more positive, relish the magical experiences, and build stronger relationships. When we are burnt out, we are negative, cynical, and exhausted, but with gratitude we notice what is true. It allows us to broaden. Some of the ways our podcast guests have taught us to practice gratitude include keeping a gratitude journal and having conversations that center around thankfulness frequently. Notice how your attention and mindset naturally shift to gratitude once you start making a regular practice of being consciously thankful for the people, events, and experiences in your life.

Reframe Your Jealousy

I know it might not feel like it, but know that it's okay if you feel yourself morphing into a green-eyed monster. We've all been there, and there's a way to support yourself in reframing the experience to be a positive one. True story: envy is actually a really powerful tool and can be turned to your advantage. The energetics of envy are such that it often arises when we see in another something that we are capable of achieving or having ourselves. This means that when you are feeling envious of someone, it's actually your soul showing you a person with the elements of what you desire or as a way to see where you are not living authentically. That person you're feeling jealous of is orbiting around you to help you unblock whatever may be preventing you from having your unique version of what they have. I don't know about you, but I feel a lot of comfort and inspiration because of this.

Pass the Mic

First, let me explain something about jealousy: it is impossible to be jealous of people who have something that you don't want. Here's the mistake we make with jealousy: we put a lid on our desire. Our insecurity makes us say, "I can't have what those people have." What I want you to start to do is, anytime you feel jealous from now on, stop and go, "Oh, interesting! I'm jealous. What is that jealousy trying to tell me?"

Jealousy is a directional signal. I used to be super-jealous of my girlfriends who were able to renovate their houses and could go on fancy vacations. The truth is, my jealousy had nothing to do with the kitchen. I had to unpack exactly what I was jealous of, and in those years I was jealous that I wasn't pursuing my ambition. I finally realized that all these things I was jealous of were the benefits of somebody working really hard at something. I now had a bridge to cross the divide between where I was, stewing in jealousy, and pop the lid off my desire, which was to have financial freedom and abundance in my life. Now I could get to work on making that happen.

When you don't follow your jealousy toward the things that you want, it will haunt your ass. You need to wake up, unpack it, flip it into inspiration, and start taking action in the direction of that thing.

—Mel Robbins, author of *The High 5 Habit*
ALMOST 30, EPISODE 460

Now that you know comparison can be a guide to what you want in your life, you can be in a better relationship with your comparative nature. Like the other broader burnout-related themes we'll discuss in this chapter, the goal isn't so much to get rid of comparison, but to recognize and understand, then support yourself through it while simultaneously increasing your self-love.

PERFECTIONISM

Perfectionism is a vicious cycle; it's impossible to be perfect, so we're always on the hamster wheel seeking to reach a destination that doesn't even exist. Despite the greater collective awareness of perfectionism and all the issues that stem from it, it's actually on the rise. "As many as two in five kids and adolescents are perfectionists," says Katie Rasmussen, who researches child development and perfectionism at West Virginia University. "We're starting to talk about how it's heading toward an epidemic and public health issue."[29] What's really wild is that the rise in perfectionism doesn't mean that everyone is overachieving, receiving all the accolades, and has a perfectly organized makeup drawer; it actually means we're getting sadder, sicker, and stunting our potential growth. Similarly to comparison, when we find ourselves chasing something that doesn't even exist (perfectionism or someone else's perceived perfect life), we're burning ourselves out.

So how does perfectionism relate to burnout? Well, imagine how exhausting it must be to pretend to be something you're not for your whole life. Not only does it take energy to put on a perfect face, overachieve, and curate everything in your life, but it also takes a lot of energy to incessantly hold yourself back from being the *real you*. Attempting to prove yourself in this way requires you to spin your wheels, push yourself beyond your limits, and worse, strive to be something you're not in order to be loved. You may push your body beyond what it feels good doing just to look a certain way. Or push yourself to work past hours that allow enough time to rest just to prove that you're a high achiever. And that's just the beginning: tendencies toward perfectionism have been linked to depression and anxiety, eating disorders, PTSD, fatigue, insomnia, and in some cases, suicide. It's a serious issue, and a big contributor to burnout, especially during our twenties when we're in a phase where we deeply care about what others think of us.

Even if you're not quite at the full-blown perfectionist level, your inner critic who unconsciously controls your little Sims self can chastise you for an unlimited number of elements in your life, including work, relationships, body, money, cleanliness, and, well, pretty much anything.

Here are some ways to support yourself and reduce perfectionism.

Recognize Your Tendency Toward Perfectionism

Bear with me here: it took me a long time to recognize my own perfectionist tendencies because I thought of myself as imperfect. So how could I possibly be a perfectionist when I am so flawed? I was so embedded in my perfectionist ways that I couldn't see that I was always reaching for more, or better. Finally, I realized that perfectionism isn't about your output, achievements, or even behaviors, but how you *speak* to yourself. Notice if you are constantly putting yourself and your efforts down, think that nothing you do is ever enough, or don't recognize the many wonderful qualities you innately have and the things you *have* accomplished in life. Notice all the ways in which you might think you're not enough. Think about how you might respond to a friend who is and does the things you do. If there's a disconnect there, chances are that you have perfectionist tendencies. Just notice that to begin, place your hand over your heart, and imagine what it might feel like to give yourself the same kind of compassion and credit you would offer a friend.

Focus on Your Self-Talk

Now that you've recognized the way you speak to yourself, make a conscious effort to be aware of your reactions to yourself in the moment. When do you find yourself pushing too hard? Do you make a habit of expecting too much of yourself or holding yourself to unrealistic standards that you wouldn't hold a friend or loved one to? The next time that flagellating taskmaster of an inner voice comes up, stop it in its tracks and see how you can shift that voice to offer more recognition, more kindness, and more compassion.

Seek Therapy If You Feel Called to It

Breaking perfectionist patterns can require a lot of undoing. One of the best ways to support yourself in breaking through perfectionism is with psychotherapy techniques. (One of my favorites is called Internal Family Systems, which helps us heal by acknowledging the various parts of ourselves—such as the inner critic, perfectionist, or people pleaser—and fostering compassion and curiosity toward each part.) By bringing tender, loving awareness to the perfectionist part of yourself (that, by the way, really just wants to keep you safe, loved, and protected), you will be able to see your perfectionism through a different lens. Once you've gotten to know and understand your perfectionist tendencies, you might even find yourself developing a relationship with this part of yourself, communicating with her, and acknowledging her presence when she speaks up.

I promise that you will feel such a wave of relief once you get to know and love your inner perfectionist. You'll be able to move in the world with more confidence, trust, ease, and grace. In the end, you'll be able to release the tight grip you have on yourself to be something you're not. While you are perfect in all the ways that matter just as you are, we are also *all* flawed and human—so know that you're in good company. Why be perfect when you can be real?

CARING ABOUT WHAT OTHERS THINK

To varying degrees, we *all* care what others think about us. Like Lindsey explained in chapter 2, caring about other people's opinions and wanting to be liked is a survival mechanism as old as humanity itself.

Today, there's more pressure than ever before to belong, because in addition to our own internal drive, how much we do or do not belong is also on display for others to see in ways that it wasn't up to this point in human history. Social media quite literally serves as a public record that's broadcast out to the world, quantifying how many friends we have and how much they "like" us. (The fact that I didn't grow up with social media is on my gratitude list most days.)

But even if you take social media out of the equation, we're taught long before we ever log on that we should act a certain way, dress a certain way, buy certain products, and adhere to certain ideologies if we want to be liked and accepted. Your Saturn Return is an ideal time for you to review, evaluate, and explore all these messages.

This shared experience of wanting to be liked and to fit in can cause a lot of stress and even propel us into a state of inauthenticity that can eventually lead to burnout. When we care too much about what others think, and allow that to steer our life, it can get pretty exhausting. With 8 billion or so people in the world, there are a lot of opinions and perspectives out there. Like the ancient Chinese philosopher Lao Tzu says, "Care about people's approval and you will always be their prisoner."

Pass the Mic

All these behaviors that we pick up—like perfectionism, avoidance, and anxiety—are all survival strategies. They're so we can create some sense of safety, but often it's just the illusion of safety. Gabor Maté has this great line where he says, "A lot of what we call our personality is just our adaptive strategies." He said that you have two needs as a human: one is authenticity and self-expression, and the other one is belonging. But if authenticity and self-expression threaten belonging, belonging wins.

—Mark Groves, founder of Create the Love
ALMOST 30, EPISODE 496

For all the reasons it's natural to care what people think about you, it's also problematic, because you're attaching yourself to an outcome that you have absolutely no control over. The belief that you have any ownership of or control over people's opinions about you is just inaccurate, and if you spend too much time focusing on it, you'll only be left feeling crazy and burnt out. The reality is that what other people think about you is none of your business. (And life is much better when you allow yourself to think that way!)

You're probably thinking, "If it were only that easy!"—which I understand, because the truth is we can't just stop caring what people think. It's important to be honest in your journey, because if you really do care what other people think, telling yourself that you shouldn't care or should stop caring isn't going to make that actually happen— and you'll probably just end up feeling like you've failed. Understand that there's a difference between caring what other people think and letting your entire self-image ride on their opinions. It's normal to feel happy when we're praised and defensive when we're insulted, but it isn't healthy when an insult sends you into a tailspin of self-doubt or self-loathing that lasts for days—or even weeks—on end. If you find yourself on the latter end of the spectrum (or anywhere close to that) here are some ways to support yourself and create a better relationship with caring what people think.

Meet Your Needs First

When you're taking care of yourself and your own needs, you're bringing your focus back to yourself rather than another person and also habituating and shifting to a state of self-compassion and love rather than self-loathing. Make a habit of regularly checking in with yourself and asking "What do I need right now?" This should happen all the time, but especially when you're feeling wounded by someone else's opinion.

Shift Your Attention from What Someone Says to How You Feel

You're building toward a mindset shift here, where it's no longer about avoiding disapproval but about sitting with the feeling of being disapproved of as it arises within your body. Once you realize that it can't and won't kill you, you'll even be okay with the discomfort. From experience,

I can say that there is an unparalleled inner peace just waiting for you as a direct result of understanding that you can trust yourself to be able and willing to experience and feel anything.

Get Comfortable Being Disapproved Of

I know that the DGAF attitude is easier said than done, but it's important to develop a willingness to be disapproved of. Like everything else we're talking about here, it just requires some intentional effort and practice. The next time you feel like someone disapproves of you, take a deep breath and remember that your reaction is just your brain traveling the same ol' neural pathways it always has in its attempts to keep you safe. Rather than attempting to escape or "correct" the situation, instead take a moment to sit with yourself, acknowledge your hurt, and send yourself some unconditional love. Practice this enough, and you'll find that *your* approval is what ultimately really matters. And with that . . .

Validate Yourself

People assume that validation is the same thing as praise or encouragement. It actually isn't. Validation is confirming that something is logically or factually sound. It's the recognition and acceptance that your feelings and thoughts are true and real to you, regardless of logic or whether they make sense to anyone else. It's normal to want external validation, but some of us seek it to an unhealthy level. External validation should be in *addition* to self-validation, not in place of it. Instead, we need to learn how to validate ourselves. For example, say you just got out of a meeting with your boss and felt like their feedback wasn't all that great. Instead of calling all your friends in hope of a reminder that you're good at your job, spend time remembering that you're not what you do, and that feedback is just a part of life and a chance to do better. By remembering that *your* opinion is the most important, you can give yourself the chance to be your own BFF prior to getting that bonus boost from your work wife via Gchat when you tell her what happened.

Recognize How Critical You Are of Others

This is where it gets real, my friend. Of course you know how you feel when someone criticizes you, but it can be easy to overlook how others feel when you are critical of them. The next time you go to that place, stop for a moment and ask what is motivating you. Many of us become critical of others when we feel insecure, jealous, want to be right, or are just plain ol' bored. What we criticize in others can reveal our own insecurities and how we feel about ourselves. How does this work? Criticism of others is often a defense mechanism to avoid confronting our own perceived shortcomings (after all, it takes WAY less energy to focus on someone else than to actually make change ourselves). Our minds and bodies constantly seek to protect us from discomfort, so *projecting* our insecurities, fears, guilt, or embarrassment onto others gives us an external focus, which is less likely to cause any real distress on our own account. Pretty wild, right? Check in with how you view and judge others, not only to get a window into how you see yourself but also to release some fear about judgment that's directed toward you.

Consider the Source

While we want to focus mainly on bringing your attention back to you, sometimes it can help to take the person's insecurities and character into consideration, as well. Could they feel threatened by you in some way? Is this the way they treat all people? Perhaps they lack certain social skills and feel the only way they will be heard is by being rude or aggressive in their language, or by bullying to get their way. Are they projecting some sort of fear, jealousy, or a suppressed aspect of themselves onto you? So often, others' opinions of us have more to do with them than they actually do with you.

One of the strangest things about the ways in which we consider other people's opinions is that we place so much weight on them—even if it's coming from a person you don't respect. Imagine giving up all that energy and brain space for someone who you might not even want to have coffee with. And yet, we all do it. Think of all that unnecessary energy just waiting for you to reclaim it!

Balancing Striving and Self-Acceptance

When I first moved to Los Angeles, I saw a lot of people around me achieving a lot of things, generally succeeding in life, and looking gorgeous and glowing in the process. I wanted that life. I wanted to have it all. During this period, I really started to work toward my goals. I added in morning routines, night routines, lists, rituals, diets, online learning—in every way possible, I was doing the most. Lindsey and I say TTH, which is short form for trying too hard, and lemme tell you—if TTH was a sorority, I would've been the president.

> ### *Pass the Mic*
>
> Taking breaks is actually bending time. I can rest and expand at the same time. My most powerful counsel these days is to treat yourself like a five-year-old. They need breaks. You need naps. You need to eat at the same time every day. And you need to get good sleep. That's self-love. And every mystic has been talking about that for thousands of years.
>
> —Danielle LaPorte, author of *How to Be Loving*
> ALMOST 30, EPISODE 612

In the process of really going for it, I was also really burning myself out. I was doing everything in the hope of being more happy, more healthy, and less stressed, but my list of things to do had become so long that everything I was doing in the name of self-improvement was stressing me out more than it was helping me. All the self-care had become too much, and it was defeating the purpose. I was striving to be more, be better, be all these things, and hurting myself in the process.

But there *is* a way for us to find a happy medium and to nurture and become more accepting of ourselves without burning out along the way. Here are some ways to support yourself in finding greater self-acceptance without becoming complacent.

SCHEDULE TIME FOR BOTH
STRIVING AND SELF-ACCEPTANCE

It's unsexy but effective. By adding time in your calendar for self-acceptance (i.e., just *being*, whether it's in nature, at home, resting, or otherwise finding pleasure in your life), you can ensure that you are creating space for being as well as doing. On the flip side, making time for yourself to focus on personal development and growth can help satisfy that part of you that desires growth, change, and evolution.

CELEBRATE THE SMALL WINS

Actually, you *should* sweat the small stuff. Don't just give yourself a pat when you make big, milestone achievements; just as important is acknowledging the small steps in the right direction. This not only builds your confidence and creates a positive reward association but it can also help you create momentum and love yourself along the way. These small win celebrations can be so small they seem laughable. For example, you had a hard conversation with someone you loved, so you took time out of your day to play with your pets and talk to them in a baby voice instead of logging more time on your laptop.

BE OKAY WITH WHAT IS

I am someone who says, "This can be better," in response to just about everything. If you relate, make an intentional effort to not only see things for what they are but to also *be okay* with what they are. These are two very different things.

BE MOVED BY POSITIVITY, NOT NEGATIVITY

One more time for the people in the back: no amount of self-hate will eventually make you love yourself. You must be motivated by self-love, positive reinforcement, and acceptance in order to make real, deep, and lasting change. The next time you find yourself falling into negative self-talk or behaviors, take a beat and see how you can apply some love and compassion to yourself in the situation at hand.

ACCEPT WHERE YOU ARE
TO GET A NEW EXPERIENCE

Here's a news flash: you're not perfect, and there's always room to grow. But before you can do that, you must accept where you are and what you're experiencing in the moment, while also putting steps to improve in place. This is the fundamental dilemma, the fundamental paradox of human existence, the continual push-pull of being a human. We seek growth, and yet we must accept where we are while moving toward it. All parts of us need to be embraced, preferably with a playful and accepting attitude. When you feel like the journey, the spiritual path, the practice of presence, or even self-love is too much work, know it's just your inner voice telling you it's time to relax and play. When you feel like you're slipping into an unconscious and unexamined life, into old patterns that are stagnant and that foster the status quo, it's time to delve deeper into practice.

I know that this journey to self-love and self-acceptance is not conceptually challenging, but in my experience loving oneself is the biggest challenge of all. Even within our quick-fix, hack-for-everything culture, this is a process that cannot be hacked. If you're into self-development and growth, know that embracing imperfection is not giving up—it's the actual work.

Pulling Up from Burnout

It may not seem like it at this moment, when you're binging Netflix (because it's the only way to turn off your brain after finishing your nine-to-five and wrapping up the to-dos for your side hustle), but it's a good thing that Saturn is giving you this chance to pull up and reevaluate your why, to challenge yourself to rethink why you're doing all this striving. There are a lot of traps when it comes to burnout, but if you can reconnect, re-ground, and recenter, you can come back to a place where you can make better choices and set yourself up to feel more spacious and energized as you enter into the journey of finding (or remembering that) you are here for a purpose and that you are here on purpose—even if you don't always feel like it. An in-depth exploration of the big p-word is coming atcha in chapter 9.

Chapter 8

WHY DIDN'T I LEARN THIS? THE MONEY CHAPTER

Lindsey

When confronted with financial woes, it can feel like your mood, confidence, and sense of self seem to shift on a dime (no pun intended). I spent years of my life feeling this sense of instability. I didn't get it then, but now I know that this is because money (or lack thereof) is a powerful part of our life experience and even our identity.

Flashback to during my Saturn Return. I had spent most of my energy during that time being blissfully unaware of how much money I did or didn't have to my name—whether it was how to get more of it, or the fact that I didn't want to look at my balance and see the result of months of hiding from my financial situation. At the time, I was working as a fit model—a job where I was quite literally paid to be a human mannequin while watching grown adults fight over the color of a button and the cut of an armhole. The job was lifeless, but the paychecks were sizable, so I stuck it out despite feeling unfulfilled. Even at that, the money I made dissolved quickly between rent, bills, and the frivolous lifestyle of a twenty-seven-year-old living in New York City. My bank account was like a sieve, money draining from it with every move I made. It felt like each time I left the house I had to pay $50. I just couldn't keep it, or better yet, give my money a place and a purpose. I preferred to maintain my lifestyle and live in denial rather than getting honest and changing my spending habits.

Every time I picked up the phone to look at my mobile banking app I went into a state of fear. I didn't want to see a number that would inevitably make me feel like a failure—especially a red number with a negative sign in front of it, which I saw often enough. I didn't want to see a slew of overdraft fees laughing at me in the right-hand column and a robot chatbot in the corner mocking me, asking if I'd like to talk to a debt specialist. Mind your business, AI chatbot.

I couldn't handle receiving another "insufficient funds" email notification; each time my nervous system would light up like an electric fence, activated with every inbox ping. Eventually, I knew I had to sign in, so there I was, hiding under my covers after my roommates had gone to bed, eyes closed, as the accounts loaded. I opened one eye and saw two negative numbers, one next to my checking and another next to my savings. I cringed and felt my chest tighten. Rent was due in a few days, and I knew it would be at least another week until I got a check for the fit modeling jobs I'd done the month prior. Not only was I anxious, but I was angry too. Why was I never taught about finance by my parents or teachers? How did I miss out on understanding anything about this fundamental piece of being an adult? As usual, I was quick to blame and sulk as my money story ran through my head. I felt as though everyone had it figured out, and meanwhile I was silently drowning, struggling to get my finances together.

What I know now is that this is a common struggle. A report from Annuity.org found that 23 percent of people between the ages of eighteen and twenty-nine have credit card debt more than ninety days overdue. Many don't feel their retirement savings are on track, and most feel unprepared for financial emergencies and long-term financial planning. It's not common to talk about these things. It can feel as though you are the only one who hasn't gotten it together in the money department. As these statistics show, the truth is that you're not alone.

How we feel about our money often colors how we feel about, well, everything. It's the purple marker that bleeds in your white leather purse (that was a sad day). But it doesn't have to be! You deserve to feel comfortable and in control of your money. You deserve to navigate your career without the ghost of money haunting you, subconsciously influencing your every decision. Whether you feel tempted to say yes to a miserable job that pays well or you are fearful of mismanaging your money once you make it, it's time to banish those ghosts, honey. Together, we'll do a little digging into that proverbial purse to find the cap and put it on that marker, to stop the bleed and protect our sanity. We'll build an awareness about the experiences that shaped our relationship with money during this timely transit, which will explain the purpose of this dissonance and cultivate some healthy habits that you can begin to practice to create a foundation for a relationship with money that you'll want to brag about. Best of all, the discipline, mindset, and skills you will develop from being good with your money will create a launchpad for a flourishing career—a career in which you can make your decisions based around what you want and feel called to do, rather than what you *have* to do to pay the bills and keep your checking account out of the red. *This* is where personal growth and professional development are intertwined.

We included this chapter in the book not to teach you how to be rich monetarily. Instead, our intention is to give you the insight and tools to find confidence, stability, and peace around money. More important, we hope this book as a whole will help you cultivate a richness within that will sustain you regardless of the numbers in your bank account.

Saturn and Money

Your Saturn Return will demand that you get right with your money *and* that you untangle yourself from the grip and power that money has over you. That's why, in this chapter, we want to offer some tactical ways to give your money a place in your life where it can feel safe and respected, so that it can step into its own power rather than having power over you. We will also reframe wealth (*hint hint,* it's not all about money, honey).

This cosmic checkpoint is not to be taken lightly. It can set you on a trajectory of financial stability and wellness for the rest of your life. Not only are the stars pointing to a new way of relating to money, but your brain development supports this shift as well. We've mentioned this before and will continue to happily talk about the prefrontal cortex until the cows come home—*moo*—because it's just so wildly validating. If you remember, the prefrontal cortex is responsible for decision-making, impulse control, and foreseeing the consequences of our actions. It's also one of the last areas of the brain to fully develop. This biological milestone potentially enhances your capacity for financial planning and spending impulse control. With a more developed prefrontal cortex, you're better equipped to make decisions that align with long-term financial health, rather than succumbing to instant gratification. So, while it might feel like your money sitch is dire, developmentally speaking this is *the* moment to change your relationship with and habits around money forever.

Trust me, *I was you*. At the peak of my Saturn Return, you could find your girl buying expensive, ridiculous outfits for weekend nights out (never EVER repeat an outfit!!!!). These one-hit wonders were bought with money I didn't have—thank you, credit! These outfits were worn to dinners that cost me a minimum of a hundred dollars. My expensive shoes were run ragged at a club where drinks cost as much as my dinner. My emotional shopping trumped my logic every day of the week. My need to escape my financial reality drove me to spend, spend, spend more than I could afford on a social life that was not life-giving. Thankfully, I turned a new corner during my Saturn Return and learned to pause when I noticed my emotions driving every swipe of my credit card(s). But this took awareness, discipline, and practice, the adult superpowers that come online thanks to the maturation around this time of the cortical region known as the pre-frontal cortex that makes us uniquely human.

During your Saturn Return, changes in your money mindset and behavior might look like:

- **Graduating from impulsive spending to mindful investing.** You might notice that your impulsive spending habits, formed in your early twenties, are unsustainable. Saturn Return could manifest as a sudden realization that instead of new shoes for every event you need a savings plan or retirement account, which marks a shift toward long-term financial planning. At a higher level, your Saturn Return is also supporting you when it comes to crystallizing your value system, which will impact the way you spend and save your money.

- **Facing financial reality.** This period should highlight the need to get honest with yourself about where you are financially. Honesty is the first step to healing! Maybe you have to tackle debt you've accumulated from student loans or credit cards, or maybe you need to start a savings account. Sometimes just the realization of a lack of clarity in your finances, or that your debts are impeding your future goal for home ownership or travel, can motivate a strategic approach to financial freedom.
- **Career reevaluation.** This transition often prompts a deep reevaluation of career choices (as we will delve into shortly) and their alignment with your personal values and financial aspirations. The desire for a more fulfilling or lucrative career can lead to significant changes, such as pursuing additional education or starting a business.
- **Realizing that your parents' money story is not yours . . . and deciding to write your own.** Whether you're aware of it or not, what you saw and heard about the stability or instability of your household's financial situation when you were growing up has an incredible impact on how you relate to money today. If you decide that story is not serving you, your energy is best spent learning and practicing new ways of relating, rather than blaming your parents/caregivers for imprinting a money mindset that has kept you from having a healthy relationship with money . . . until now.

No matter how your financial lessons present themselves during Saturn Return, the goal is to reclaim power and responsibility. No one is coming to save you and, honestly, thank goodness! As tempting as it is to think about being saved by someone, a savior would only prolong your complicated relationship with money. In fact, if you have a go-to safety net that you draw from during moments of financial instability (say, a person or your savings), I *highly* encourage you to resist that route. This is *the* time to understand clearly and fully the role money has played in your life up until this point, and to finally make a different choice, a choice that places you and your finances in a collaborative relationship.

Pass the Mic

Money is a neutral tool. It reflects the consciousness of the person using it.

—Natalia Benson, CEO and astrologer
ALMOST 30, EPISODE 507

If you are feeling completely overwhelmed, frozen, and just a few pages away from treating yourself to the $400 pair of wide-leg jeans with the big cuff at the bottom that makes your butt defy gravity, stay with me. *I* bought, and wore only once, those jeans, and I can tell you that they won't solve your money problems. Sure, you might get a few compliments, but ultimately those jeans will only sink you farther into the hole that you're digging for yourself. I promise you, there *is* a way out of that hole, and there is most certainly a vibrant existence waiting for you alongside the money that you make.

Before we get into the nitty-gritty of smarter money management, come with us for a tour of the unseen aspects of money and abundance—the energy that informs your experience of money.

The Energetics of Money and Abundance

One big mistake a lot of people make when working to improve their finances is thinking that an adopted habit or two will magically fix their relationship with money. That's why we're starting with energetics: it sets the foundation for everything you do financially. A habit is hollow without intention, and tuning in to the energetics of what is true here will clarify your intentions really quickly. Diving into financial tactics before you understand the energetics of money is like trying to bake a cake without knowing the difference between flour and powdered sugar. Sure, you can meticulously follow the recipe—preheat the oven, grease the pan, even crack the eggs with one hand like a fancy-ass TV chef—but if you're not aware of what your ingredients actually do, you might end up with a dessert that looks right but tastes like you've just sweetened your spaghetti.

Mastering your finances contributes to a sense of security and abundance, which energetically aligns you with confidence and positivity. In the workplace, this confidence can be palpable; it allows you to negotiate better, stand firm in your worth, and take calculated risks that can lead to career advancement. THAT'S RIGHT! When you're not constantly stressed about money, you can focus your energy on creativity, innovation, and productivity, which are key to both professional growth and building a career you actually love. This energetic shift toward abundance and confidence attracts opportunities and people who can propel your career forward. It might feel like magic, but it's all energy, baby.

Because our brains do the bulk of their development before the age of seven, it's no surprise research has found that our outlook on money is primarily established by that point. But that doesn't mean we can't shift our money mindset. Like everything, it is a practice. Once upon a time, a financial tale was written for you. Like so many of the stories you've inherited, this story too was carefully crafted from family experiences, societal influences, and cultural patterns. Even though the money story you learned during your childhood may not be representative of your present values, it has likely guided your entire financial life. Fortunately, you are not bound by the narrative of your past.

Money Diaries

From a young age we learn that money is a marker of success, that money can solve lots of problems, that money makes us happy, that money is what we'll make when we work really hard, and so on. None of these statements are inherently false.

We humans are sneaky, though. Our subconscious will often insert an "only" in there based on our childhood experience with money and wealth. "I will make money *only* when I work hard." "*Only* money will make me happy." "*Only* money will solve my problems." When money becomes the primary focus in your career, relationships, inner world, or anywhere else it can influence, it's imperative that you get honest and touch base with the experiences that wrote your money story so that you can begin to write a new one based on your present reality.

Journal: The Origins of Your Money Mindset

You can start by reflecting on the conversations about money that took place in your home. Ask yourself:

- What emotions did these discussions evoke? Fear? Anxiety? Hope? Confidence?
- Was the lack of money always a concern?
- Was the distribution of money always a point of contention?
- Was money always a topic of discussion? Never a topic of discussion?

Understanding the emotional landscape of your financial upbringing, noticing the common themes, and being aware of any strong emotional charges attached to those early experiences is key to recognizing the beliefs and patterns that may be limiting your relationship with money today.

Next, reflect on habits with money in your childhood home, community, and any other space that was an integral part of your younger years.

- What did your parents tend to spend a lot of money on? What did they spend very little money on?
- Were there more financially stable times of year? Why?
- Did your parents have differing relationships with money?
- What did your local community value when it came to money? Living modestly? Showing off their money?
- Was there ever competition for money? Was there a belief that there is not enough for everyone?
- What did the TV shows or movies you consumed teach you about money, if anything?
- Were you ever jealous of someone for how much money they had? Describe the feeling in detail.

When you reflect on your answers to these questions, what immediate parallels can you identify between what you learned as a kid and your financial life today? It might be hard to come to terms with the perpetuation of unhealthy habits or patterns. It might make you want to pause this process for good and slip into blissful denial of it all. After all, none of this was your fault. You were born into many of these circumstances. If you feel like this, remember that none of the thoughts and feelings that might be coming up are bad—they're just information! We're almost there, so don't quit now. Relief and liberation are just around the corner.

Limiting Beliefs and Credit Card Limits

Without being consciously aware of it, you play thought patterns over and over based on all these experiences. The patterns feel like home, which means it's usually not obvious that they must change in order for you to experience a peaceful, empowering, and authentic relationship with your finances.

I entered adulthood believing that I had to work hard to have enough money to feel comfortable. In my twenties, I usually had more than one job. I worked upward of forty hours a week, always on my feet, until the wee hours of the morning. I made quite a bit of cash, which reinforced this idea that I only had enough money because I worked hard and for long hours. Our culture drives the belief that money is earned through hard work, which isn't always the case. There are many ways in which you can find more ease and joy in earning money, like by investing wisely or setting up various streams of recurring revenue. It *is* possible, and it is up to you to prove that to yourself. Do you know anyone who earns money with very little effort? Or perhaps they front-loaded their effort, and now they create wealth with ease? Study their approach, or better yet, talk to them about it, if possible.

Any patterns and beliefs you're holding on to must be identified and shifted if they're holding you back or making you unhappy, and *now* is the time to do it. Your life is a physical and energetic manifestation of your thoughts. So, if your relationship with money is on the rocks, it's important to pinpoint the thoughts and beliefs that have created the state that relationship is in. If you grew up in a household where money brought stress and chaos, for example, you might have a fear of money. That fear of money might be creating insecurity about managing your money, or it might be capping your potential at work.

Pass the Mic

I'm not going to let someone else, especially some distant agency or some stupid bank, tell me who I am—I decide! And that's my wish for everybody. You decide. You decide your rich life.

—Ramit Sethi, author of *I Will Teach You to Be Rich*
ALMOST 30, EPISODE 448

Journal: Your Limiting Beliefs About Money

Let's uncover the truth about your current wealth mindset by bringing any limiting beliefs you might have about money into the light. Start by writing down *all* the beliefs you have about money. Then identify the beliefs that do not support your conscious dreams and desires.

These limiting beliefs might include:

- You don't have enough money.
- You'll never be able to afford that.
- Wanting money is greedy.
- You don't need money because you are spiritual.
- You're not good with money.
- The more you give away, the less you will have for yourself.
- The only way to earn money is through hard work and sacrifice.
- Dealing with money is such a hassle.
- You need to get to a point where you don't have to worry about money.

How did that feel? I was so resistant to this part of the process. When it came to money and my issues, I just didn't want to look. So seeing my limiting beliefs written down was sobering. "*Those* beliefs have been running my bank account?" I thought. "*No wonder I'm in this position.*"

So what do you do with those beliefs that you now know are wreaking havoc?

ACKNOWLEDGE AND ACCEPT YOUR CURRENT BELIEFS

Recognize that these beliefs were likely formed through past experiences and may have served a purpose at some point. Forgive the version of you who wholeheartedly believed something so untrue because it was the safer thing to do. Accepting these beliefs and forgiving yourself are crucial to moving forward.

UNDERSTAND THE IMPACT

Reflect on how these limiting beliefs have shaped your financial behavior. This could be in any number of ways, including undervaluing your services, fear of investing, or avoiding financial planning altogether.

CHALLENGE YOUR BELIEFS

Question the validity of your limiting beliefs. Are they universally true, or are they perceptions based on specific experiences? Gather evidence that contradicts these beliefs to weaken their hold over you. For example, if one of your beliefs is that you can never hold on to your money, acknowledge any instances when you saved enough money to invest in, let's say, a vacation or an online course that you were interested in.

REFRAME YOUR BELIEFS

Turn each limiting belief into an empowering one. For example, if you believe "I'll never be good with money," reframe it to "I am capable of learning and becoming proficient with my finances."

The truth is that these beliefs you are working to reframe have been habituated over the years. Therefore, you will apply this process more than once—and, most likely, many times. This practice isn't about stopping those old beliefs from arising but about identifying and rewriting them in a way that feels more authentic to who you are today and who you want to be in the future. Soon enough, this process will become automatic, but in the meantime, practice patience and consistency!

The Ghosts of Your Financial Past

I didn't have my own credit card until I was out of college—I just used my debit card everywhere I went. This kept my spending in check because I couldn't spend what I didn't have, but it didn't allow me to build credit for my future. With very little understanding of how credit worked, I got a credit card at age twenty-four and began using it. On everything. By the end of the first month, I had spent more than I made, and thus began a cycle of accruing debt that I couldn't pay off in full and being charged a ton of interest in the process. This went on for more than a year. I felt so upset and ashamed of the financial hole I had dug for myself. The experience scarred me and taught me that I couldn't trust myself with credit. Instead of fixing my bad habits right away and understanding how I could gradually pay off my debt, I rode the merry-go-round of deficit for a while because the solution seemed so out of reach.

I suggest you take time to identify any specific incidents from your past that caused you to make a decision—and take on additional limiting beliefs—about money. Negative emotions from past events often can hinder your efforts to earn, receive, and keep more money. Releasing these negative emotions will help to cultivate a positive money consciousness.

This release will look different for all of us, but here's how I did it: I felt all the emotions I'd been holding on to that were associated with my past money missteps. Fully. I used my meditation practice before bed to call in that version of me who experienced particular incidents with money that cemented some pretty heavy money stories. I replayed these situations in my mind's eye and, rather than focusing on what I would have done differently or how dumb a decision I had made was, I found compassion for that girl. I allowed myself to feel fully what I had avoided feeling back then. The morning after a session like this, I woke up feeling ready to start believing something new and more true about my relationship with money.

A New Financial Mindset

Once you have taken stock of your current wealth mindset and any experiences in your past that might be holding you back, you can think about the financial processes and rituals you *do* want to adopt.

Excuse the phone analogy (because who needs to be on or talk about their phone more?), but I'm using it anyway because I know you've run a phone update recently, and it's a good way to think about what we're about to discuss. Just as a smartphone operates on a system of pre-installed software that dictates how it functions, your mind operates on a network of beliefs and thought patterns established over your lifetime. When you decide to update your mindset and belief system, it's akin to downloading a new software update that promises better performance and new features for your phone. The initial installation of this update (the introduction of new practices and rituals) can be exciting and promising, but it doesn't end there. For these changes to effectively take root and not get overridden by the old system's default settings, you need to regularly run these new applications. This means consistently engaging in your chosen practices and rituals, much like how you'd regularly use new features on your smartphone to integrate them into your daily routine.

Over time, just as consistent use of new software and features gradually makes them indispensable parts of your smartphone usage, regularly engaging in these practices and rituals integrates these new beliefs and mindsets into your life. They become your mental default settings, altering how you perceive and interact with the world around you. This transformation doesn't happen overnight. However, with consistent use and openness to this new operating system, the updates become a seamless part of your phone's (or in this case, your life's) functionality, leading to improved performance and, ultimately, a more fulfilling user experience.

Our practices might look different from the ones you adopt, but here are some of our favorites. Feel free to incorporate the ones that speak most to you or use them as inspiration to create practices of your own.

Whatever you do, know that these practices are designed to get you *fully participating* in your experience with money. Saturn will not allow you to be the victim of your experiences any longer, nor will it allow you to avoid your money. While it's not always possible to establish a few practices, snap your fingers, and get your financial house in order immediately, know that you will build acumen and resiliency, a respect for your money, and a healthy higher perspective in seasons of financial flux. Plus the habit of setting, pursuing, and achieving goals around your financial life strengthens your self-discipline and focus, qualities that are highly valued in any professional setting. Watch your career take on a whole new life as you remain disciplined. All this will keep you out of the habit of identifying with the number in your bank account, while also building healthy new habits that will help you feel more financially secure in the future.

FIND YOUR WHY

When you have a compelling reason behind an action you're taking or a goal you're pursuing, you're much more motivated to take action. This absolutely applies to money, just as it does to everything else.

Create a list of reasons why you want to have a certain amount of money or why you desire to take control of your finances. Is it so that you can afford a certain living space? Is it because you want to contribute money to charity? Do you want to create a certain type of lifestyle? Or do you just want to feel a sense of freedom when you're spending your money?

Your own personal *why* can be a feeling or a thing.

Here are some examples (your answers will be individual to you, of course!):

- I want to have the freedom to travel and explore the world. I am working toward traveling to X place for X amount of time.
- I want to live in X city/town/area and live in a home that feels comfortable/cozy/airy/beautiful (however you want to feel in your home).
- I want to save so that I can start a family and contribute X and X to my future child's upbringing, education, etc.
- I want to save enough so that I can leave my nine-to-five corporate job and pursue my true passion and purpose. I am planning to save up X amount to leave by X date.
- I want to be able to enjoy simple luxuries, like going to coffee shops or treating a friend to dinner without agonizing over every purchase.

You'll notice that these examples are specific and descriptive. The more you can clearly visualize your *why,* the more your brain will both consciously and subconsciously help you take steps toward your goal.

Pass the Mic

I've never really met anybody who has a huge vision and isn't also developing their wealth identity because you need the resource of money to steward that vision through. So the bigger my vision got, the bigger my wealth identity got, the bigger my wealth identity got, the more that I could circulate in a healthy way. Money became less about me and I was no longer doing things for money, but I was doing them because God called me to do them. And that was a big turning point for me, especially in the self-development world, where you're literally being taught to do all these things to become a match for money.

—Victoria Washington, founder of The House of We
ALMOST 30, EPISODE 660

MAKE YOUR WISH LIST

Create a list of what you'd like to do with your money—a list of goals, if you will. Do you want to invest in your own business? Travel somewhere you've never been before? Save up for a bigger place one day? Create more room in your budget for self-care expenses, like retreats? Take some new courses in a field you've always been interested in? Do something fun with your family? Plan something with your friends? Get specific! Goals propel you forward when they are clear. Also be sure to create attainable goals. The point here is not to work toward a goal that you will never realize. Some might be bigger than others, and that's perfectly fine. But you want to create goals that you can achieve, which will beget the confidence and trust in yourself necessary to make and achieve even more, bigger goals.

Once you've created this list, notice what thoughts or emotions come up for you as you look over it—and be sure that includes noticing what's *not* on the list but should be. If you're shying away from things you want based on feelings of guilt, unworthiness, or the inability to receive them, you will sabotage your success. Your success will not be able to find you if you are cloaked in those heavy emotions. Instead, those emotions will create a self-fulfilling prophecy of more experiences that cause guilt, unworthiness, and shame. These omissions and negative emotions are offering you important clues about additional limiting money beliefs that you'll want to clear. Although it may seem odd that anyone would have a negative predisposition toward wealth, it's fairly common (because, as you now know, we often absorb these negative beliefs from childhood, and hold on to them in our subconscious mind). To magnetize abundance, you'll need to surface, identify, root out, and replace any negative or limiting beliefs you have about money.

DONATE YOUR TIME OR MONEY

The need to contribute to something larger than ourselves is hardwired into all of us. I know that at this point in your process, you might be thinking, "There's no way I can give. I don't even have enough for what I require!" I hear you. But giving has a magical effect. It gives meaning to life. It helps you feel grateful for everything you have. And when you are grateful for what you have, no matter how much you have, you will be rewarded with more of what you are grateful for. In *A Happy Pocket Full of Money,* David Cameron Gikandi shares that "gratitude is the first step to receiving and experiencing." It is the ultimate expression of faith in what is now, what was, and what is to come. When you are trying to pay off massive credit card debt, gratitude is probably the last thing you want to give . . . and it's also the most important time to give it. It might also be the least likely time to give your time or money, but I encourage you to do so anyway—even in small ways.

Giving to others is also a gift to yourself and your mental health. Research conducted at the University of Oregon and published in *Science*[30] found that when people give to charities, it activates regions of the brain associated with pleasure, social connection, and trust, creating a "warm glow" effect. Scientists also believe that altruistic behavior releases endorphins in the brain, producing the positive feeling known as the "helper's high." Giving is also associated with the release of oxytocin, which helps us feel a sense of happiness and connection.[31] The act of giving is also a declaration of what you do have. Giving from a place of "I have enough, let me give to those who need" is a powerful shift from "I never have enough" or "there isn't enough to go around." Therefore giving has the potential to attract more of what you're able to give—be it money or resources.

Your act of giving—even a small amount—can also have a huge ripple effect. A study in the journal *Proceedings of the National Academy of Science*[32] shows that when one person behaves generously, it inspires observers to behave generously later down the road, toward different people. The researchers found that altruism could spread by three degrees—from person to person to person to person. "As a result," they write, "each person in a network can influence dozens or even hundreds of people, some of whom he or she does not know and has not met."

Whether you're giving back to your loved ones, the community, or society, you'll only find true fulfillment when you start to look outside of your own needs. Giving will contribute to your abundance mindset. When you put the energy of giving out into the Universe, you will be more open to receiving and it will flow back to you.

Support causes that are near and dear to your heart, whether it's education, community development, or something specific, like organizations that empower young girls, for example.

Keeping in mind the Golden Rule, remember how abundance works, and that giving helps you to then receive more yourself. The secret to living is giving. Money, by itself, is so empty. Most people don't find that out until it's too late. Know that money has no power except the power of your giving. Give wholeheartedly, especially when you think you don't have it, and I promise that you will never have scarcity in your life—ever.

Unsexy Habits for Sexy Financials

With your mindset in check, it's time to get extremely unsexy. You'll thank me! Seriously, though, as we discussed earlier in this chapter, Saturn is here to establish some discipline in your financial life, and here's where that gets real.

"I don't feel like doing that" is a seemingly benign thought that wreaked havoc on my checking account before I figured out how to get everything under control. It's crazy how the mind will often talk us out of what's best for us, especially when it comes to wealth. What makes your money happy is not always the most fun thing to do. But once you establish these habits as ways of relating to your money, the chores won't feel as daunting. It will be like brushing your teeth—maybe not the most fun part of your day, but a simple enough habit to fall into that serves an important purpose in the end.

Money *loves* to be tasked. For example, when you put a designated amount of money in your high-yield savings account every month, that money loves the safety and security, as well as the earned interest. These unsexy practices will make your money feel respected and purposeful. Think of these automations and systems as the necessary accommodations that money requires in order to stay with you comfortably for a long time.

And might I add that these seemingly tedious habits will teach you to be resourceful, make the most of what you have, and prioritize your spending based on what is most important and beneficial. These practices have direct applications in your career. Getting darn good at skills like resourcefulness and prioritization will position you as a valuable asset to any team or organization, paving the way for leadership roles and career advancement.

GET A FULL MONEY PICTURE

The idea here is to get the entire lay of your financial landscape. If you feel intimidated at the thought of this, know that I felt the same! Every time I signed into an account, it was like a roller-coaster ride: my stomach dropped, and I held my breath. But just a few seconds into having a clear view of what was happening inside of these accounts, a wave of relief swept over me, even when the numbers I saw were disappointing. Through this, I realized that my avoidance was creating a lot more chaos than necessary when it came to my financial life.

Get a full money picture by looking at each of your bank accounts, statements, cards, and investments. I love doing this once a quarter. Once you understand where you're starting and what opportunities you have, you can start to edit. For me, this involved investing more money in the stock market and bonds, as well as putting some money in a high-yield savings account, rather than keeping it all sitting stagnant in a checking account. For you, it might look like understanding where your debt stands so that you can begin paying it off. Starting is the point, no matter what it looks like. You might do something as simple as turning on an auto transfer so that a little bit of your paycheck goes directly into your high-yield savings account every two weeks. That's it! You've begun to change how you handle your money. That's major.

Seeing things as they are minimizes the mind's tendency to create stories and falsehoods about your money situation, which will clear out some of that stuck and fearful money energy.

Journal: An Aerial View of Your Money

Think of getting the full picture of your money like getting an aerial view of your finances. Pull yourself up and out of the fray for a moment, detach from any intense feelings you might have, and just see the full picture for what it is. Take a deep breath up there. Your perspective is shifting as you get the full picture of your current financial standing.

Here are some questions to ask yourself—write down all your answers!

- How many credit cards do I have? (List them all, including their balances.)
- What perks and benefits do my credit cards offer?
- Am I earning points on my credit cards? If so, what do they go toward?
- Am I taking advantage of those perks and using my points?
- How many bank accounts do I have? (List them all.)
- How many investment accounts do I have? (List them all.)
- What are my monthly recurring expenses?

Believe it or not, no matter what the answers to these questions are, they will be liberating. Toss the truth onto the table, and you will *finally* be able to move forward. When this information lives in the shadows because you refuse to shine a light on it, it siphons energy from your mental and emotional body, whether you're consciously aware of it or not. Part of the mental body will always be wondering exactly what you have going on financially, and a part of your emotional body will be stressing about it. Therefore *seeing the facts,* written down, gives those parts of you permission to rest. You are the responsible adult, brave enough to bring consciousness to your money.

BREAK DOWN THE BUDGET

Create an Excel or Google Sheet and list all your monthly expenses by category. Get really specific, and include everything from the big stuff like rent and car payments to the small stuff like Ubers and coffees.

Once you've finished your budget, look at what it's showing you. In what area do you spend the most money? Is this area the most important part of your life? For example, if you spend a lot on wellness and that is a priority for your mental and physical health, great! This exercise isn't about restricting things that bring you joy. It's about recognizing whether or not your spending habits align with your priorities and goals.

When you're finished, review this budget with a trusted friend, partner, or professional, like a financial advisor, if you have one. Another person may recognize something about your spending habits that you can't see yourself.

CONSIDER CONSOLIDATING YOUR ACCOUNTS

Do you have several checking and savings accounts? There are pros and cons to consolidating them, which are worth considering. While having everything in one account can be simpler (assuming you're not a business owner), there are also some advantages to having multiple accounts. You'll want to think through what makes the most sense for you and your financial goals.

For many of us, too many checking accounts can make it difficult to access funds and track spending easily—and both of those should be priorities. On the other hand, if you are a business owner or solopreneur, it's a good idea to keep your business and personal accounts separate. You will definitely want to discuss the ins and outs of this with a financial advisor.

Savings is a different ball game, since you presumably don't need to access your money frequently or easily (and, in fact, it can be good *not* to be able to do this). Also, different accounts can help you separate your savings for different goals, such as an emergency fund, vacation savings, and so on. (Alternatively, some savings accounts allow you to create "buckets" within them so that you can separate and allocate your money for multiple purposes within a single savings account.) However you're saving, make sure you pay attention to interest rates so that you're earning the most money possible on your savings. Also note that these rates can change over time, so it's good to check in on the current rate on a regular basis.

SET UP AUTOMATIC BILL PAY

It's *essential* to stay on top of your bills—I can't emphasize this enough. Most companies have a grace period of about ten days for late payments, but beyond that, you'll be subject to penalty fees, and your credit score will be affected. If you're delinquent enough on, for example, a car payment, you may even face repossession. Both repossession and late payments stay on your credit report for up to seven years, which means that late or missed payments can affect your financial health for years to come. You don't want to face major challenges in the future just because you forgot to pay a bill!

This is why I like to set it and forget it by setting up automatic payments for my major recurring bills, like rent, electricity, internet, and so on. You can also opt for paperless statements and billing, which will make your bills and balances easier to keep track of (and it's also more sustainable!).

As far as the energetics of this, by creating more mental and psychic space and allowing your bills to be paid automatically, you are creating more energy for yourself by not having to think about this every month—or to feel stressed if you forget. This creates more flow and rhythm in your life.

CHECK YOUR CREDIT REPORT

Credit scores generally range from 300 to 850 and are based on a variety of information, from your payment history to the length of your credit history to how much debt you have. This number dictates how easily and how much money you can borrow for various purposes, as well as the interest rate you receive for loans. It might also be reviewed by people like landlords, when they want to understand how financially responsible you are to limit their own risk.

Here's a general guide for how to define your credit score:

- 580 to 669 is considered Fair
- 670 to 739 is considered Good
- 740 to 799 is considered Very Good
- 800 and above is considered Excellent

Pass the Mic

We have outsourced our self-worth. We look outside of ourself for validation. We look at the number on the scale, the amount of money in the bank, the car that we drive, the person that we're dating, the friend group that we have, the amount of likes, the amount of views—all that external shit is never going to make you feel worthy. The only person who can build your self-worth is you. There's a reason why that word begins with "self." It begins within your self.

—Mel Robbins, author of *The High 5 Habit*
ALMOST 30, EPISODE 460

Remember that, as with all ways that we are judged numerically, your credit score (and you!) are more than just a number. If your credit score triggers you, try to remember how wild it is that any type of system outside of yourself can potentially have the power to dictate your mood. Having said that, we live in a capitalistic society, where your credit score *does* matter when it comes to big purchases—like home rentals, purchases, and loans—so you do need to know where you stand.

You won't need to rely on your credit score regularly, but knowing what it is currently is a great thing. And if you realize that your credit score isn't where you want it to be at this moment, that's great information to have so that you know what you have to do to improve it for your future self. That way when you *are* ready to buy a house or car, or need a new credit card, you've done the work to achieve your goal as quickly and easily as possible.

When looking at your credit score, it's most important to make sure there are no errors or surprises, that your personal information is accurate, and there's no sign of fraudulent activity.

When it comes to your credit score, here are a few dos and don'ts to keep in mind:

- **Don't be afraid to check it.** Checking your own score is noted on your credit report (a detailed look at your debt and credit history that creditors will look at to determine your eligibility for things like rentals and car and home loans) as a *soft inquiry,* and thus doesn't reflect badly on you. (*Hard inquiries,* on the other hand, represent a creditor looking at your credit report to consider your creditworthiness; these inquiries can impact your credit score.)
- **Do be sure to check your score not only regularly but especially before applying for credit,** like for a home or auto loan. When you apply for a loan a credit check will be run. If your credit score is less than favorable and the loan is denied, you might not get a chance to apply for that loan again for a while.
- **Don't let credit report errors go uncorrected** because

they can lower your score. This is the easiest way to raise your score; it's such a quick fix!
- **Do contact your lenders if you fall behind on payments,** and discuss the potential for alternative payment options to avoid negatively impacting your credit score.

Healing Your Debt

Whether it's student loans, credit cards, or car loans, it's not uncommon to be in debt, so let's start by taking the shame out of it. Your debt does not define who you are, and it is not a reflection of your character. At the same time, you want to work on healing your long-term debt so you can extract that stress from your life and focus on your future.

Like other major stressors in life, debt can seriously impact your mental health. It can be a heavy burden, feel like it dictates your options and choices (especially in terms of your career), and make you feel alone and unsupported. Debt can trigger or worsen other anxieties, affect your sleep, and even have a negative impact on your work and relationships. A study from the Royal College of Psychiatrists found that half of all adults who are in debt also struggle with mental health. This ranges from a consistent feeling of anxiety and low mood to a diagnosed mental health condition.[33]

Know that you don't need to feel like you're alone when it comes to defeating your debt. Talking through your stress with loved ones is a start, and listening to experts on how to find solutions is next.

~~~~~~

Practice: Dissolve Your Debt

Many people feel guilty about their debt, so they choose to ignore it, which will only exacerbate the issue. At various points in our lives, Krista and I have both approached debt with some of the following steps. Try doing one of these this week, and I promise it will lighten your mental load and start you on the path to being debt free.

- **Start with a plan of action, baby!** I love a plan. Which area of debt shall you begin with? You might want to tackle your debts one by one, starting with the highest interest loan first. Or consider the snowball method: Start with your smallest debt. Pay it off in full as soon as you can, while maintaining just the minimum payments on the rest. Then move on to the next smallest debt. Lather, rinse, repeat. By the time you only have your last, biggest debt left, you'll be able to pay it off more easily without the other debts to hold you back.
- **Check into lowering your interest rate.** Give your lender a call and get to negotiating. Remember, there is a human being on the other end of the line. If you're a loyal customer who may otherwise take their borrowing elsewhere, you'd be surprised at the possibilities available to you. It's always worth a shot!
- **Focus less on debt and more on the abundance you can create.** By shifting your mindset from the lack of money to the money you are creating in your life (whether that is through a side hustle, selling your clothes, or getting a raise), you can align yourself more fully to the energy where you want to be rather than remain so focused on the stress of being in debt. It also gives you a sense of purpose and power in taking action toward something rather than running from something. Moving toward feels way better than running from, in my opinion.
- **Make a promise to yourself to avoid further debt.** Make a plan and stick to it. Cut up your credit cards, create a budget, and do whatever it takes to stop adding to your current debt.

And, one last thing: remember that many financial companies aren't designed to help you out of debt, because your debt keeps them in business.

This means that, most of all, you must become your own advocate and leader in this realm.

Pass the Mic

When people think about debt, it's important that they think about it in the sense that this is business. It's business for your creditors, and their goal is to keep you in the life cycle of that debt for as long as it's legally allowable. So when they tell you, "Oh, we can offer you these really low minimum payments," or "You have the option to skip payments," *don't do it*. The longer you pay minimum payments, it allows them to earn the maximum amount of money from you, as their product, on interest. Minimum payments are not your friend.

—Bola Sokunbi, author of *Choosing to Prosper*
ALMOST 30, EPISODE 301

Set Up Automatic
Retirement Deposits for Future You

It's important to start investing in retirement accounts ASAP—in your twenties, if you can—since the earlier you get going, the easier it is to accumulate wealth. *Take a deep breath!* I know that you might be reading this chapter with a little knot in your stomach and are potentially feeling overwhelmed with what you haven't yet done. Even if you already feel overwhelmed by too much debt and expense and too little income, you can still start saving for your retirement. Stashing away just a little bit on a regular basis (think the money you spend on drinks during a night out) makes a big difference, because your money will grow over time thanks to this little thing called compound interest.

Pass the Mic

For all the people who complain about what's going on in the economy, the single best thing you can do is set up automatic savings and automatic investments with proper asset allocation.

—Ramit Sethi, author of *I Will Teach You to be Rich*
ALMOST 30, EPISODE 448

Here are some small steps you can start taking *today*:

* If you work for a company that offers a 401K, ask your HR department about it. Approximately 47 percent of people between the ages of twenty-five and thirty-four have access to a workplace retirement plan like a 401K, according to a report from Stanford University.[34] So if you don't have a 401K at the moment and are curious if your employer offers one, ASK! Odds are that they do. A 401K is great because it offers significant tax savings, and it's simple. The money will come straight out of your paycheck before taxes are withdrawn, which reduces your taxable income. That means you will pay less in taxes each year. And because your contributions are automatically deducted from your pay, you won't be tempted to spend the money now instead of putting it toward your future.
* Ask your company if they match your 401K contributions. For example, if you put 5 percent of your salary into your 401K, your employer may also contribute up to 5 percent, depending on the type of program they offer. The median matching level is 4 percent. Maybe that doesn't sound like a lot, but as *I Will Teach You to Be Rich* author Ramit Sethi puts it, "That's your company literally saying: 'Hey, here's some free money, do you want to take it?' If you don't take that, you're making a huge mistake."

- If you work for yourself or your company doesn't offer
a 401K, consider setting up automatic payments into a
retirement account, a feature that most banks offer. It's an
easy way to set it and forget it. Start with a small amount
and increase it as you feel more comfortable over time. If
you start small, you'll probably hardly notice the little bit of
money coming out of your paycheck, and it will add up in
a big way. Commit to calling your bank today and asking
about this. Even $50 a month adds up!

Now sit back and watch these unsexy habits make your overall life quite sexy! Confidently checking your bank accounts on a weekly basis? SEXY! Watching your money grow for you while you sleep? YOU'RE MAKING ME HOT! The key to any of these habits is consistency and diligence. Before you know it, you'll be sharing your money systems with your friends when they ask how the heck you have your money shit together.

You Are Abundance Embodied

During my Saturn Return, I read a book that changed my relationship with both money and myself—*A Happy Pocket Full of Money* by David Cameron Gikandi. At the heart of Gikandi's philosophy is the understanding that abundance is not finite, but infinite. He posits that the Universe is abundant by nature, and so are its possibilities. This paradigm shift helped me to move away from scarcity thinking—where I constantly saw resources as limited and competition as necessary—and toward a mindset where I believe in the endless possibilities for growth, wealth, and prosperity for all. The energy of the intention will automatically create an equal effect. For example, if you want to create more abundance in your life but often think about what you don't have, compare yourself to others, or feel an overall sense of lack, you will attract more lack. You can write "I am abundant" on a piece of paper a zillion times, but if you don't feel abundant, you won't attract abundance.

I began to look outside of my bank account for the proof that *I am abundant*. And ya girl is rich! The depth of my close friendships, the love that exists between me and my husband, the pee-your-pants moments I have with my sisters, the spring flowers I saw popping through the soil on my morning walk today, my son's giggle, my good health, the conversation I had with a complete stranger that lit me up—all this makes my life rich beyond reason. No longer is money the only thing that gives me that dopamine hit. I've opened the aperture, and every day I *look* for the blessings that confirm my richness. A magic math happens when you do this. Your riches multiply.

Yes, there are steps and decisions you can take to make your financial life less stressful and more organized. And, also, always remember that wealth starts from within. It is not just about accumulating money but about reflecting your inner values, beliefs, and state of being with abundance. When you nurture a positive, abundant mindset, you will attract wealth in its many forms into your life—and your life will become more aligned in the process.

Chapter 9

THE SEARCH FOR PURPOSE

Krista

Pre–Saturn Return, I woke up in my Chicago apartment one morning and slowly peeled my eyes open. I sat under the covers quietly for a few seconds, waiting for my anxiety to kick in again. Once it started, the cycle went like this: *What am I doing with my life? Why am I here? What is my purpose?* At the time, I didn't know this was anxiety talking. It just felt like I would forever feel lost, purposeless, and alone.

And then there they were—the existential questions that made me feel like I was a prisoner of my own mind. My heart raced, and my breath quickened like it always did, but this time was more intense than usual. I kicked back my duvet and headed out to the living room, where my childhood best friend was sleeping on the couch that weekend. I completely broke down as I plopped on the sofa next to her. "I've never seen you like this," my friend said. She was right—I had never felt like this before. I had experienced and struggled with mental health, but this degree of anxiety was new. I was stuck in a loop, consumed with the same thoughts and questions, repeating over and over again.

Although it didn't feel good at the time, looking back I can see how incredible it was that I was so determined to make meaning of my life, to find my purpose. So determined that the thought of it consumed me. What's not great, obviously, is that I went through so much emotional distress as a result of this seemingly innocent desire. Before we get any further into this chapter, if you can relate to any of what I felt back then,

I want to extend to you the same reframe that I wish I'd had to help lift me out of that dark, anxiety-riddled state.

Many years later, when author and mindfulness teacher Manoj Dias spoke with us, during our conversation he quoted the great Fritz Perls, a psychologist, who said, "Anxiety is excitement without breath." As soon as I heard him say that, something clicked, and it made me think back to that previous version of me who had put so much pressure on herself to discover and declare her purpose. What if I had approached this idea of purpose with excitement rather than anxiety? As a process of discovery rather than as pressure? What if I had just *breathed*? Manoj and Fritz are right: both the feelings of anxiety and excitement produce an elevated heart rate and a feeling of butterflies in your stomach. Both can potentially make you sweat. The difference is that while excitement is connected to the emotion of joy, anxiety comes from a different emotion—fear. It is important to distinguish between the two, because when we operate from fear, we are operating from a place of survival, rather than a place where we can take advantage of opportunities and possibilities like we can when we're excited. Anxiety depletes us and has us running around aimlessly, while excitement motivates us and makes each step part of the journey and something to look forward to.

What if you're feeling those sensations because you're pumped about what you might discover, or about what the future holds? By pausing and allowing yourself this reframe, you're not ignoring or diminishing what you feel, but embracing it, even as you change your story and thought pattern. We are generally so quick to label intense feelings as bad, but often they creep up during the times and in the places where we are stepping up and stepping into a new phase of life or a new way of being. This is powerful stuff. Understanding and being okay with big feelings like this can help you acknowledge and work with them in a way that's almost fun. If you find yourself thinking, "I'm feeling a bit anxious about this," acknowledge the feeling but shift your explanation for it. Instead of spiraling and sinking further into anxiety, think about how grateful you are for this opportunity that might just open up a new door for you. Remind yourself that you're having these feelings because you care and are taking bold steps into your future. You can say, "Thank you, brain, for flagging that feeling, but I know differently now, and this is actually how I want to perceive what is going on."

Remind yourself that, right this very moment, you are in a place of possibility. After all, that's what purpose really is—it's about possibility, *your* possibility, and exploration. In the survival state, it's hard to think clearly about the big picture in the way that you want to during this time. It's hard to access the experiences and feelings that *will* guide you to your purpose—like being in a state where you can get into flow, where you can easily feel when things make you happy or bring you joy, or understand where your sense of motivation and pressure are coming from. Your anxiety can also cause you to put too much pressure on finding the right thing, right now. It's like bullying yourself into action, which may quite possibly force you into inaction because the sensation of anxiety can be debilitating.

Pass the Mic

My soul was saying that my purpose is to be in joy, to dance, and to allow other people to see me in joy. Which totally fucked with my idea of producing, of giving value, of creating all these things that will "help other people." It took me a while to process that because it was so different from how I had programmed to produce, produce, produce, produce, create, create, create, help, help, help, serve, serve, serve. This message from my soul said, "You're kind of done with that. You need to be in joy." In all the spiritual texts that I've seen, they talk about how the greatest service is living a life that's in joy and actually enjoying your life.

—Marie Forleo, author of *Everything Is Figureoutable*
ALMOST 30, EPISODE 593

I hope you can keep all this in mind as you move through this chapter, and also remember that all the things that might have felt like a failure or a miss up to this point aren't necessarily that at all. In fact, they might actually be bids for progress in hindsight. Remember that your purpose is so much bigger than just whatever job you are working at any given point. And remember that purpose is not found externally. As you embark on this journey, remember to check in with yourself to notice when a feeling makes you want to get out of bed and move, rather than focusing on external markers of success.

Saturn Return and Purpose

My friends, I want you to know how natural and healthy it is to want to incite change in the realm of your career, especially during this transformational time. Like relationships, your career path is a vehicle for growth and healing . . . if you choose for it to be so. Also, know that you're not alone as you try to figure it out. Our community members often share that they're ready for a change but don't know what their next step should be. Or they might know the next step but are afraid of making the leap, or worried about what their peers or family might think. Another thing that I both understand and see frequently is that people conflate their job with their purpose. Yes, you might think about your purpose in terms of your career, but your purpose is big enough to include all your roles and responsibilities: sister, friend, neighbor, daughter, cat mom. Your purpose is about your entire *life,* and it usually touches upon what truly matters to you, upon matters of the heart.

"Purpose" is such a loaded word. It can incite excitement, fear, anxiousness, overwhelm . . . we feel as though we should be constantly seeking and searching for it. That if we don't have it, no one will want to hang out with us, and we should cease to exist. But, on the other hand, if we don't try to find a reason for being here, we can exist aimlessly, our lives consisting of nothing more than a series of Netflix binges and hollow routines. The way to approach our purpose is to see it as a dance, a coming and going, a waning and waxing. We are born with purpose, on purpose, and yet we also seek it, find it, and lose it, perhaps many times over throughout the course of our lives.

Pass the Mic

Purpose is really a function of engaging with your curiosity and following your instincts and your intuition. I typically bristle at conversations around purpose and passion and things like that, because I think those words are very triggering for a lot of people. I think most people are walking around thinking, "I don't know what my purpose is" or "I don't have a passion in my life." They scroll through Instagram or TikTok and see all the people living these wonderful lives, and it just makes people feel bad about themselves. I know what that feels like; I've been in that place, and it's not a binary thing.

I don't think that you have one singular purpose or there's one passion out there waiting for you to discover it. I think we can have many different purposes throughout many different phases of our lives. I've been around for a little while, I'm quite a bit older than you guys. And what I've discovered along the way, as somebody who has been in career paths that were not a fit for me, somebody who has had financial challenges, and challenges with addiction, and been in some pretty dark places, and now as somebody who feels very fulfilled in what they're doing: the purpose that I feel in my life and the passion that I'm privileged to be able to engage in every day has really been a function of getting to know myself and doing the inside work so that my instincts are true.

It's not about lightning-bolt moments or overnight successes. It's really about the tiny choices that you make every single day that move the needle in your life imperceptibly. Everything that I've accomplished is the result of things that I've been working on for decades, not months or years. I'm always encouraging people to be gentle on themselves, and to be patient, and to not set themselves up against some calendar.

If there was a lesson that I would give my younger self, it would be to be patient. We tend to think of life as being short, and I guess it is, but it's also long.

—Rich Roll, author of *Finding Ultra*
ALMOST 30, EPISODE 521

You can think of your life purpose as your personal mission statement; it's how you plan to make your mark in this world. It should bring you joy and make you feel fulfilled, while allowing you to tap into your unique essence and feel like you're living in alignment. Your purpose does *not* have to change the world, but if you embrace and live your purpose (whatever that means for you), I can promise that you *will* make the world a better place, though perhaps not in as dramatic a way as you might feel you need to from where you stand right now. You can have fun and allow the process of understanding your purpose to be an unfolding, rather than a forcing.

Tapping into the next phase of your life's purpose during Saturn Return opens up a powerful period of transformation. Along the way, you may feel less sure of who you are and how you define yourself. Sometimes this process might feel inspiring, and other times it might feel confusing. I suggest *allowing* yourself to be unsure of who you are and what your purpose is, and staying open to possibilities. This time will help you to reflect on your personal and professional values, and to consider whether your current career path aligns with them—and, also, to consider whether that matters because, again, your career doesn't have to be your purpose, though it can be.

As you move forward, I hope this chapter will feel like a warm hug from a friend, a sweet remembering, and an alleviation of all that pressure you might be mistaking for direction.

Your Purpose Is Not (Necessarily) Your Job

Most people see their jobs and careers as inextricably tied to their purpose (or feel like they're a failure if their job *isn't* directly related to their purpose). It's hard not to when work accounts for forty-plus hours of the week for the majority of our lives. This conflation of job and purpose is so common, in fact, that many people don't even question the relationship between the two. This is why layoffs and retirement are often associated with an existential crisis, if not outright despair (if you have a dad who has retired you know this is real, LOL). People often don't know what to do with themselves when a job isn't dictating who they are, how they feel, and their inherent worth.

Losing your paycheck is stressful enough, but it's even worse when you associate that loss with losing *your purpose*. Here's the difference: unlike a job, your purpose belongs to *you* and you alone, fundamentally and forever. You are not your job title, which is finite, can change in a second, and is given to you by someone else. While your purpose may change over time, it will always begin within you, and nothing outside of you can ever take it away. I see purpose as the anchor necessary to survive the stressors of your career journey—but it's *not* your job, even if the two are related to some degree (and they might not be—that's totally okay too).

While this job-equals-purpose idea is something that most of us were conditioned to believe, I've found that many people are questioning and having an awakening when it comes to this relationship. Maybe you're in a position where you're already in a meaningful line of work and feel like it's your purpose. While there is nothing wrong with this latter scenario, it's helpful to consider expanding your view to include your current job as *part* of your purpose—but not all of it. Otherwise, you risk the potential of putting your self-love and sense of worth outside of yourself. When you come to the realization that the job you've been doing may not be who you are because you recognize that your purpose can be expressed in many ways, you won't despair if things end up changing. Your purpose and its expression are endless, just like you.

Tackling the Big P-Word

Maybe you already feel clear on your purpose, or perhaps you have no idea where to start. First of all, take a deep breath—this isn't a situation where putting a lot of pressure on yourself is likely to get you where you're trying to go. Remember, we're approaching this with excitement, rather than anxiety. Second of all, know that chances are, at least on some level, you *do* know your purpose. It just might not look how you think it should—it might not feel ambitious enough, important enough, or be tied to your job.

If you'd like to get some clarity, try asking yourself a few questions that might help you define your purpose in a way you haven't been able to up until now. These questions are designed to help you connect the dots between your interests, your values, your experience, and your strengths.

VALUES

Remember when we discussed values back in chapter 3? Seeing as how your purpose is part of your identity, part of your core self, it is informed by those values. What are yours? If you're already living life according to those values, you're likely already on the path to discovering deeper purpose.

Values are how you can measure and determine what a successful and meaningful life looks like *for you*. But the catch here, my friends, is that defining your values requires time, care, and attention, and that process of consciously understanding your values is just the beginning. Values are not just abstract concepts—they should manifest in your everyday life through your actions, decisions, and behaviors. When your values are in alignment with the decisions you make, you will experience a feeling of satisfaction and true authenticity. To fulfill your purpose you must make sure you're clear on your nonnegotiables (aka your values) and allow them to guide your actions on a daily basis, even when you don't know exactly what you're heading toward.

WHAT COMES NATURALLY

Although you may feel stumped at first, I think one of the most underutilized self-reflection questions out there is: *What am I naturally good at?* It seems so simple, right? But really think about how you answer this question. Rather than only focusing on what you love, consider what comes naturally to you. Interestingly, we often overlook these God-given talents precisely because they come naturally. It just feels too easy, right? So easy that you might not even realize it's a talent or skill that's unique to you. It wasn't until we started the podcast that I realized my natural curiosity, inquisitive nature, and interest in people's stories was actually a talent. There was no forcing my interview style; it came naturally to me. It was *easy*. It was a previously unrecognized gift that made doing what I do feel effortless. I can promise, you have your own set of unique skills and talents.

If you're not sure what your innate talents are, think about the activities that give you a strong sense of confidence when you're participating in them, things that flow and happen with little friction or effort. Another good way to get to the root of your talents is to ask people you love questions about what you're good at—often your friends and loved ones can clearly see what you can't. You can also do some excavation work by jogging your memory to recall all the things you have a knack for, no matter how small that thing might be.

By identifying your talents, you'll be able to narrow your focus, and you'll have a renewed energy and confidence to live your purpose because you're just being yourself and playing into your own strengths. It makes it so much easier to discover and live our purpose when we realize that it's about being more of who we are, all the time.

INTERESTS

Ask yourself what you truly enjoy doing (or *think* you might enjoy doing) and experiment from that place. Discovering what you're passionate about in life and what matters to you is a trial by fire process that takes your engagement, curiosity, and openness.

This is why it's so important to take the time to reconnect with interests you might have neglected over the years. I bet you know what they are; I'm talking about the kind of things that you might tell yourself you "don't have time for" or that are easy to push off when you're stressed or overwhelmed.

Maybe it's writing, reading, or interior design—whatever it is that makes you feel simultaneously light and free, and like there's nothing else you'd rather be doing. These interests are likely signposts, and making time for the things you're passionate about or excited by can help ignite your creative side, and potentially even support you in stepping into your most aligned career (although, remember, that's not necessarily the goal).

Pass the Mic

It's wonderful to want to impact people or empower people, but you almost have to start at the small thing that you love doing and stop putting pressure on yourself to be this grand, amazing, pitch-perfect thing. Jeff Bezos just started selling books on the internet, do you know what I mean?

The thing that makes it a big dream is your excellence and the energy that you bring to it consistently; in the way that you hold yourself to high standards, and that you give. You have to start showing the Universe you're putting your money where your mouth is and not squashing that dream. Because it doesn't sound like the big dream yet. There's so many of us looking on Instagram and we only see five careers on there, and then if your small passion and your small interest doesn't fit into one of those, you're like, "Well, it can't be that."

Let go of your grip, and when you see your own excellence coming out of you every day, you will start to trust it more and more. It's not going to be easy the first day. One of the things that's really stuck with me from my childhood is my dad always said, "You know, I can give you so many things, but I can't give you the self-esteem and the confidence that comes from making a contribution." Feel like you made a contribution every day. I think what really helps us feel more trusting, and more aligned, and more all these things, is flexing your gifts. We focus so much on what we are receiving. We're not even thinking about the fact that we're here to share.

—Jenna Zoe, author of *Human Design* and founder of
My Human Design
ALMOST 30, EPISODE 594

This doesn't mean that you should become a librarian if you love to read, or a veterinarian if you love your golden retriever, but rather that it's important to balance your life with things you love. If your full-time job doesn't incorporate your interests, you'll want to be intentional about making time for activities that are uplifting and rewarding. You'll feel stronger and more fulfilled because of it—and who knows what unexpected new paths might open up to you along the way?

MOTIVATION

Are you clear on what motivates you? This could mean different things to different people, because there are two types of motivation: *extrinsic* and *intrinsic*. Extrinsic motivation is the kind of motivation that comes from outside of yourself, like a monetary reward or an accolade of some kind. Intrinsic motivation is something you do for your own personal satisfaction, regardless of what anyone thinks or what the outcome is. Intrinsic motivation is the type of motivation that comes from within—it's that thing inside of you that drives you and your actions. It's what feels good and gives you that warm fuzzy feeling in life. It's reading a Harry Potter book for fun and because you love the idea of existing in a magical world rather than forcing yourself to read a self-help book because you think you are somehow broken and need to fix yourself. It's the difference between being motivated to do something because you want to prove your parents wrong versus doing something because you get lost in the flow when you're doing it.

We are all motivated by a mix of intrinsic and extrinsic factors at any given moment, and one is not necessarily better than the other. *But* if it's important to you that your career in some way aligns with or incorporates your purpose, you'll want to tap into that intrinsic motivation as much as possible, because it's likely to give you a greater sense of meaning. While an extrinsic motivation like your salary is finite, your intrinsic motivation for something like working with kids won't run out.

FLOW

When I think of a flow state, I think of Rick Rubin in the TV miniseries *Shangri-La*. This magical being is simply in the moment, completely focused on whatever he is creating, almost entranced by trying to piece together sometimes-nonsensical elements of music. He's Buddha-like when he's in this state, sitting cross-legged in his white T-shirt, with wild hair and a gentle smile. It's almost like he doesn't exist separate from the task at hand. It's true unity. Have you experienced this feeling? When do you find yourself in flow?

When we are in flow, we are usually doing something we love and that comes easily to us—you can think of it as the intersection between your interests and talents. If you love to write and words come easily to you, you can probably find yourself in a state of flow on the page. On the flip side, if you hate math and numbers make your brain hurt, it's unlikely you'll reach a state of flow doing accounting work. Think about the times in which you found yourself in a state of deep concentration—and truly enjoying it. It might be when you were working on a big work project that required a lot of interaction with others. It could be when you were painting, running, or playing piano.

Another part of flow is that you're probably not super concerned with the end result; instead, your focus is on the process or activity in and of itself. Notice these times because they're telling you something. They're pointing to something you enjoy doing, whether you consciously realize it or not. When you find yourself in a moment like this, notice whether it's the work or activity itself and sit with what that's telling you. When you clue into what you truly enjoy doing and those times that you've been in flow, your purpose might just become easier to identify.

Flow doesn't always feel frictionless. Some of the best flow I've ever felt has had a flavor of challenge to it—that's what helps me to stay engaged. So the next time you engage in a challenge that feels healthy, as though it is helping you to expand in some way, stick with it. That can be flow too.

Pass the Mic

Everything I've ended up doing has been a beautiful, magical, random interaction with someone that sparked something in me. I met an Ayurvedic practitioner and chef and was obsessed with this human. I was like, "I need to study her and be around her." I became her assistant in cooking classes. I was like, "I just want to learn from you and absorb you in any way possible, so let me just follow you around and shadow you." I helped her in her cooking classes and then I went on to do a yoga teacher training, which had to do with me seeing that spark of joy, and happiness, and purpose in what they were doing.

It's not that I want to be them, it's not that I want to have what they have, it's that I want to have that joy in myself, that contentment in what I have, to be able to give to other people. It's such a beautiful feeling to know that, for me, jealousy or dissatisfaction come when I don't understand who I am and I don't understand what I have to give to other people. Actually, we all just want to give to other people, and the problem is that when we don't know what we have to give, that's where the frustration came from for me. I feel like that's probably true for many people.

—Radhi Devlukia-Shetty, author of *JoyFull*
ALMOST 30, EPISODE 371

The Pursuit of Purpose

The idea that we are each born for some higher purpose (one that looks super dope on social media and makes us a lot of money) and that it's our duty to find it can be nice. But it's also a lot of pressure, during Saturn Return and every other season of life. When you feel overwhelmed, rather than focusing on big existential questions like *Why am I here?* and *What should I do with my life?*, instead try paring it down to something more manageable (and human) like *What is my next best step?* I hope you will remember that even when you have setbacks and everything feels like it's upside down, taking even the smallest of steps to find and cultivate purpose in your life offers a sense of stability and direction.

Remember that all this is not just what you do or where you are supposed to be going. Your purpose is the story of your soul. It's the story your life wants to tell when you aren't caught up in all the details. An understanding of your purpose starts with self-knowledge. It's so important to know what you are all about—about your strengths and motivators—because your unique design will ultimately point you to your purpose. This discovery process is not a means to an end, but an ongoing journey.

While there's likely not just one single purpose that will be sustained throughout your entire life, seeing yourself as worthy of the pursuit is important. It can help you spend your time more mindfully and to find more meaning on a regular basis. Purpose is not so much about the destination but about finding meaningful ways to use your time, invest in yourself, and navigate this awakening period during which you begin to understand who you really are on a much deeper level than ever before.

Chapter 10

A CAREER RECKONING

Lindsey

Up to this point, we've started most chapters by sharing some insights from our own lives. But since this chapter is all about pivoting, it's time for us to switch it up too and take a broader view. Join me for a minute in thinking about your career as a book that you're writing, and each job, each role, is a chapter in your future *New York Times* bestseller. For years, you've been writing in a genre that feels comfortable and familiar to you, following a certain plot or format—maybe because it's what you thought your story was supposed to be. But as you write, you realize there are other stories within you that are eager to be told, and other less-familiar genres you want to explore.

Making a career pivot is like starting a new chapter with a fresh, exciting plot twist (or maybe even diving into a new genre altogether). We love a plot twist! It's an opportunity to shift the narrative, to introduce new characters and experiences. This doesn't mean that the previous chapters were wrong or unimportant; they were essential parts of your story and ultimately created the opportunity to be here in this moment. But now you're giving yourself permission to write something different, something more aligned with who you are today and who you want to become in the future. Of course, you can insert these plot twists in any area of your life. And, let's be honest, they can all feel like different flavors of *Oh shit, what now?* This tends to be especially true when it comes to career, because it's hard to uncouple your job—and everything that you've been working toward up to this point—from ideas about security and survival.

To take some of the fear out of it, instead of looking at your career as a path or ladder, think of it as a portfolio. The term "career portfolio" was originally coined by philosopher and organizational behavior expert Charles Handy in the 1990s, and it's overdue for becoming a TikTok trend, because it speaks to the direction so many of us are already moving in. *Harvard Business Review* explains it like this: "A career portfolio is different in that it is not a physical entity or system. It's a new way to think about, talk about, and—most importantly—craft your professional future in order to navigate our ever-changing world of work with purpose, clarity, and flexibility. Whereas a career path tends to be a singular pursuit (climb the ladder in one direction and focus on what is straight ahead), a career portfolio is a never-ending source of discovery and fulfillment. It represents your vast and diverse professional journey, including the various twists and turns, whether made by choice or by circumstance."[35]

Plenty of people have great success in the process of pivoting. How about Vera Wang, who had an all-consuming career as a professional figure skater before pivoting to become a design icon? Her pivot was inspired when she decided to design her own wedding dress, which sparked the idea to eventually open her own bridal boutique at age forty. From there, she went on to build a fashion empire, one step at a time. Then there are the Olsen twins, who were only one year old when they were cast on *Full House,* splitting the role of Michelle Tanner. After the show, they went on to parlay their sitcom fame into an entertainment empire called Dualstar Entertainment, where they made direct-to-video movies like *Passport to Paris* and became multimillionaires before the age of thirteen. But it wasn't just up from there; they had multiple wins and some losses, which sent their company into dormancy. Following that, the sisters reemerged to launch their super chic and super successful fashion line, Elizabeth and James (and, subsequently, the line of my wardrobe dreams, The Row). As a result, the former sitcom babies are now widely respected—and ridiculously wealthy—designers who never let anyone else determine their fate. Or our friend Jay Shetty, who was a monk prior to his renowned career as podcaster, author, and thought leader. I can't imagine what his fellow monks would have said (although there's probably not a lot of conversation happening at the monastery) if he had shared with them that he saw a future in which he'd impact people across the globe, befriend luminaries like Oprah and J.Lo, and create an empire.

The point is, you're not alone if you're feeling the need to switch up the plot and pivot your career. In fact, career pivots are far more common today than ever before. Most of the parents of friends I knew in my hometown spent their entire careers at the same company, often even in the same role. But my friends? Some don't so much as allow their desk chairs to get warm. College majors? Yeah, those don't seem to matter much either. Gone are the days of picking what to study on the basis of a clear job choice or career trajectory. We are collectively expanding beyond linear plans. As most f*boys would say (and in this case, I agree) the best plan, it seems, is no plan at all. So when it comes to career, here's to keeping your options open, being noncommittal, and not taking things too seriously.

Pass the Mic

There are so many ways in which you can be successful, make money, do whatever. Sometimes I feel like the menu is so big, this is a Cheesecake Factory! But to know the self is to know what feels really good and to know what is aligned with the life you want to live.

I thought I wanted the corner office, and the high heels, and the power suits, but I really like sweatpants, and my feet don't fit into high heels. This is us working off of other people's maps. Sometimes other people's directions aren't going to help you reach your destination. In a world that has an excess of information and opinions, it's really easy for us to say, "Give me your map." But what if our destinations are totally different? What I have done is not going to lead you to the same space.

—Jenna Kutcher, author of *How Are You, Really?*
ALMOST 30, EPISODE 528

Saturn Return and Pivoting Your Career

In addition to all the other ways in which Saturn leads you to get up close and personal with who you are, it also touches upon your professional identity, which is related to your own conceptual understanding of who you are. This specific aspect of your identity is influenced not just by your past work experiences but also by your vision for your future work experiences. When you feel like your career is headed in a direction that is incongruent with your professional identity (aka when the you of today is out of sync with your ideal self), you will likely feel the call to make a change. This is where career pivots come in. Psychologically speaking, they are attempts to align your occupational choices with your ideal professional identity and self.

Pass the Mic

I just want you to start dreaming again, because I believe that most of us are so blocked by fear, by insecurity, by failures in life, by disappointment, that we have stopped letting our desires flow freely, and we do it to protect ourselves from disappointment. But when you cut off your connection to what's in your heart, you feel disappointed all the time.

—Mel Robbins, author of *The High 5 Habit*
ALMOST 30, EPISODE 595

You've read enough by now to know that this is prototypical Saturn stuff. But this experience of pivoting (and even thinking about pivoting) has a neural impact as well, and that's important to understand as you move through the process. The brain is such a powerful part of your journey, and it can either really help or hinder you as you move through this period of considering how your career might look different. Here are some facts about how your brain sees pivots so that you can identify and work with these reactions if or when they arise.

Holding two truths. Maybe you feel called to take an amazing job offer at a company you're stoked about, but this job just happens to be in a different city, far away from the people you love. The stress caused by holding these two truths at once (you are excited *and* you are scared) can cause you to get stuck in a mental loop where you don't take action because you're spending so much time and energy weighing your options. To get out of this trap, remember that there won't be one perfect path, and that you can only benefit from making a decision and moving forward. Even if the choice ends up being one you want to revise at a later date, you've still taken a significant step forward by learning about your priorities and what does and doesn't work for you.

Anchoring bias. This refers to the tendency of your brain to view a situation based on the first piece of information you learn about it. This can then affect how you interpret any information you encounter later on. Leaning on that initial information conserves energy, and your brain loves to run efficiently! So if you express interest in moving into the fashion space and someone tells you it's a really hard industry to get into (because their friend tried five years ago and was unsuccessful), that story could color your feelings about your career path potential. It doesn't matter what information you hear next; it'll all be measured against the anchor belief. By checking in with your biases and beliefs regularly, you can tune in to what is and isn't yours. Saturn Return is prime time for reviewing, examining, and reevaluating a lot of anchoring biases.

Sunk-cost fallacy. Are you holding on to a job that doesn't really fit or forward your professional identity only because you're worried that making a shift would put all the time and energy you've invested in your current job to waste? If so, this is the sunk-cost fallacy at work—the tendency to keep doing something that doesn't make sense anymore, simply because of how much you've already invested in it. If you can shift your thinking to see the time you've invested as a period of learning that was necessary for growth, then you can be reminded that no time is wasted, and it all ultimately serves you in moving forward and closer to your optimal career.

Confirmation bias. Your brain likes to seek out, notice, and remember information that confirms your existing beliefs and current reality. Once again, this all comes down to conserving energy. If you're scared to leave your job because you're worried you'll fail at whatever comes next, then stories and ideas that make your shift feel doomed won't just seem more believable—you're also more likely to notice them. Meanwhile, examples of how others have thrived through their pivot will either fly under your radar, or you'll read them as random chance happenings and forget them faster than the examples of people who tried and failed. Recognizing when you do this is half the battle. Once you catch yourself in the midst of a confirmation bias moment, consciously find examples that go against your current bias and instead support the new thought you want to reaffirm.

Now that you understand the push-pull of this period when it comes to your career, let's dig in!

How to Navigate This Pivotal Time

With the pep talk out of the way, let's get down to the nitty-gritty.

Journal: Is It Time for a Pivot?

Is it time for you to make a pivot? Only you can answer that, and here are some things to think about as you make this decision. As always, answer as honestly as you can, and give yourself freedom to reach and dream here.

- What do I like most about my current or past jobs?
- What do I not like about my current or past jobs?
- What careers or jobs do I find inspiring or interesting?
- What type of culture or environment do I want to be in?
- When do I find myself feeling the most excited about my work?

As you read through your answers, notice your reactions. Are they surprising? Or do they confirm how you've been feeling recently? Also notice how your answers make you feel. You might feel a rush of excitement or a strong inner peace and calm when thinking about a particular career possibility. Give that reaction the weight it deserves, because your body is a brilliant indicator of the direction you should explore—or stay away from. Also, know that your ability to feel into the potential means it is possible to create that reality for yourself.

Pass the Mic

I've always called myself a multi-passionate entrepreneur because there have been so many things that I've been into. At this stage of my journey, I'm really excited about letting go of anything that feels stale. Anything that feels like I've been there and done that. I'm super interested in who I'm becoming, and I don't know who that is yet. I think that there's a lot of excitement and there's a lot of possibility in saying, "Okay, great! I've had this amazing career so far. I love that. I'm grateful for it. It's all cool. But what's next? What else do I want to explore?"

When this first started bubbling up in me, it was terrifying. It was absolutely terrifying. Wait! I've gotten so much success doing this, and this is who I'm known as, and this is what I've done, and this is how I've helped people. I can't let this go!

And now I'm like, fuck it. What's next? There's so much excitement there.

—Marie Forleo, author of *Everything Is Figureoutable*
ALMOST 30, EPISODE 593

There are also a few surefire signs that it's time for a change. If you find yourself resonating with any of these situations, consider this your permission slip to seek out greener pastures.

- Your job or workplace has become toxic.
- Your work life is negatively impacting your health.
- You're feeling unmotivated or uninspired.
- You're unable to grow.
- Your values no longer align with your work.
- You wouldn't want your friends to work where you do or do your job.
- There's something that feels better to your soul.

Planning Purposeful Change

As with so many things we've discussed in this book, the more material changes in life generally start with a change in mindset. The same applies when it comes to your career. One of the scariest parts of pivoting is feeling like you're somehow only allowed to take a leap if you feel 100 percent positive that you're making the right move—that this is the ultimate job or company, where you will want to stay forever and live happily ever after. Even if that *does* happen to be true, there's no way you can know it from where you stand now. Yes, you can make a move into the next step of your career by taking all the practical measures that will assist you in your job search, like identifying your strengths, evaluating your skills and experience, exploring your options, networking, and staying committed to what you really want. But there's no way to know how a job or company is going to resonate with you until you're actually in it.

Instead of thinking that your next move has to be to the perfect job, in the perfect place, and involve the perfect situation, consider your best next step. Think about what you want to learn and how you want to grow. It's actually a lot like dating. When you're dating, you don't expect every person you encounter to be The One (and, if you do, don't miss chapter 12 coming up); instead, you understand that relationships are a vehicle for growth and to help you curate and clarify what you're really looking for and who you really are. Pivots in your career are exactly like this: you're probably not going to find your forever job at twenty-five, any more than you're likely to marry your eighth-grade boyfriend (hi, Joey!!!). But do you remember how much fun your eighth-grade boyfriend was? Remember everything you learned during that time? And I bet you don't consider it a failure that you didn't end up marrying him, right? The same applies here.

As you make this move, think about the bigger picture and all the things you can learn and experience. Think about what you want to learn and experience and where you're most likely to find that. As you concentrate on this, notice if and when you start to feel excited rather than daunted. When you let that pressure valve release, you're far more likely to make a good move—one that will allow you to stretch without feeling that this job has to be *everything,* or else it's a failure. By starting from this place of focusing on what you can learn, you're opening up your aperture, allowing yourself to consider scenarios you may not have thought of before. If you view your career through the lens of lifelong learning, your mindset will naturally start to shift to that of a student, perpetually curious and excited for the opportunity to learn. Like most things in life, if you focus on the journey rather than the destination, your career will stop seeming like a mountain to climb, with a single destination at the top. Instead, it can be a winding series of switchback paths, leading through diverse terrain, with so many new sights and experiences on offer and any number of beautiful and fascinating stops along the way.

Thinking about career pivots in this way will also help you remember that you're not doing anything "bad" or "wrong" by changing up your situation. In fact, you're not even doing anything particularly risky. To me, it feels *far* riskier to stay in a situation that doesn't require you to stretch, grow, or invest simply because, well, you're already in it. Pivots are actually essential to both your career and your personal growth. And as you walk that path, your biggest job of all is to spot opportunities for more pleasure, joy, and even *fun* (yes, really).

Successful pivoting requires you to befriend fear and be not only willing but *proactive* about stepping into change. Sure, it can be uncomfortable at first, and you may find yourself in a situation where you feel underqualified or like an impostor to begin with, but successful pivoting requires that. You are changing direction, stepping into the unknown (or, at the very least, the lesser known). Yes, you are human, so there may be some fear there too—but don't let it drive you. Instead, allow yourself to be propelled forward by your desire to grow, learn, and feel inspired. All these feelings are way more powerful than doubt, and they come with a far greater pay-off. As with any big change, it's normal to feel anxious and unsure—that's okay. The power is in understanding that's part of the process, not allowing doubt to derail you, and knowing that this process requires preparation, patience, and trust.

With your mindset adjusted, let's talk about approach. Even if your next career move doesn't have to be *the* career move, it should be one that you feel good about and that leads you in the direction you want to head in this moment. This means that you'll want to go into the pivot with a tool kit of philosophical and practical assets on your side.

Understand your skills. Whether they are directly related to your career or not, it's good to know and own what you're good at, and understand where you can add value. If you are able to clearly understand what you're good at, it makes it much easier to find a job or career that is a match. If the answer isn't clear to you, ask your friends and trusted colleagues, and think about where you've excelled in the past (the skills don't have to be limited to work either—think beyond that to any areas of life where you truly excel, because chances are it will serve you in a job that's a good fit for you).

Find a mentor or someone you can learn from. Whether you invest five figures to have a professional life coach show you the way or dedicate a few hours each week to learning about your career, industry of choice, or job of your dreams online, make sure to invest in learning from someone who has gone before you and who you can learn from. Yes, I'm biased, but I love podcasts for this reason; you can learn from some of the greatest minds for free and on a daily basis.

Cultivate a support system. Having a network of people who support your efforts will give you the confidence to make hard decisions and follow your heart. This support system is key in those moments when you feel yourself wavering or doubting your skills and abilities. This group of people can help to remind you who you are, what you're capable of, and the fact that you're not alone. These are people who can help you recenter, reground, and remember that you are powerful, worthy, and capable of big things—even if you've forgotten for a moment.

Pass the Mic

If you value everyone's opinions, your self-esteem will be destroyed. If you only value one person's opinion, who's a yes-person or your best friend, then you'd also be misled. And living in a world saying no one's opinion matters doesn't actually make sense.

I've surrounded myself in each area of my life—whether it's spiritual, business, friendship, relationship—with a group of council, like a group of mentors whose opinions I value, and who will tell me the truth. This council can always make me aware of where my ego is at. Build a tribe, a community, a council of people in your life whose opinion *does* matter, and select them carefully.

—Jay Shetty, author of
Think Like a Monk and *8 Rules of Love*
ALMOST 30, EPISODE 357

Maybe I'll Stay

For all the reasons pivoting a career can be a fantastic move, of course it's not always the right time or scenario in which to make that move. If you know that some things need to change in your work life, but you love and are engaged with your job or simply don't feel like it's time to leave, this section is for you.

Journal: Should I Stay or Should I Go?

Before we proceed, let's take a step back for a moment and get honest. Here are some questions to consider:

- Do you want to progress in this particular job or career?
- Are you good at what you do, or at least have raw talent that can be sharpened?
- Do parts of your job light you up?
- Do your working conditions support you, bring you fulfillment, joy, healthy challenge, and stability?

If you answered yes to any of these questions, then there is probably room to make some changes within your current situation. And the responsibility for doing this is all yours! If your answer to that last part is *huh?* I get it. Let me explain how you have that responsibility and what it looks like in practice.

It was the summer of 2016, and I was about to walk into SoulCycle to teach my fifteenth class of the week. At this point, SoulCycle was my whole life. Of course, that had been a pivot for me, because previously my goal was to support myself with a nighttime job so I could audition for acting jobs during the day. But when SoulCycle became a part of my routine, I knew that I felt called to audition. I was attracted to the job for so many reasons, including the company mission, culture, and the ability to be creative, move my body, and impact people positively on a daily basis. And, for a while, it was great! But two years into teaching, I was overscheduled, chronically dehydrated, exhausted from all the time I spent commuting, and uninspired when it came to teaching.

Some days, I just wanted to throw in the towel, and I seriously considered doing so. I remember driving home after teaching one class in particular, asking myself if I'd be happy if I quit SoulCycle tomorrow.

The answer was *no*. For all the ways in which I truly did feel discontented in my current situation, it was also true that I loved so much about my work, what I could give, and what it gave to me. Ultimately, I believed that I didn't have power to make change. This powerlessness made me feel depleted and out of control. But that was a lie I was buying into.

Pass the Mic

You have these fundamental needs as a human being and your body has intelligent design. It is hardwired to send you a signal when something that you need is missing. One of the most misunderstood signals that your body sends you is the feeling of being stuck.

Being stuck is a signal that one of your highest needs is not being met, and that is the need for growth. Most people feel stuck in their lives and then they're like, *I need to break up, I need to quit this job, I need to move somewhere, I need to do something, I'm stuck, I'm stuck, I'm stuck.* Before you pull the ripcord on everything, stop and ask yourself: Have I stopped growing?

As dumb as it sounds, simply signing up for a new class, going to an event, doing something that energizes you, that reengages your need for growth as a human being, going to therapy can be a way because you're learning about yourself. That is how you deal with being stuck.

—Mel Robbins, author of *The High 5 Habit*
ALMOST 30, EPISODE 460

What I learned by navigating this situation is that no matter the circumstances, you always have more control over your experience than you think. *But* to seize this power, you have to shift from victim to creator mode. This can feel nonintuitive in a hierarchical company structure, but it *is* possible (and if it's not, that's important information for you to have as well). If you can create or reimagine what your job looks and feels like on a day-to-day basis, you absolutely can bring new life to your current work. This can look a lot of different ways, so let's talk about what that might mean for you.

It might be time to take a purposeful pause. This should be normalized! A pause might mean a day off, a weeklong vacation, or a sabbatical. A pause will give you intentional time to close the open tabs in your brain and reboot your whole system. When you pull your energy out of your work for a moment, you can direct it inward to gain some clarity about your current professional situation and reach a new understanding about what specifically is and is not working for you. ("I hate my job" isn't very helpful, even if it does feel like the truth when you're exhausted.) Creating space between you and "the thing" allows you to unplug from the emotional charge that it's giving you each day, and decision-making is always easier from a more neutral emotional state. I remember taking a week off from teaching SoulCycle that allowed me to rest and shift from a state of exhaustion, confusion, and frustration to centeredness, peace, and clarity. It gave me room to breathe, recenter, and have a wider view of the situation. That wider view revealed more seasoned instructors who stepped in as mentors and walked me through how to have a conversation with corporate. From this, I learned that I had been discounting just how much room I had to make changes in my schedule that would allow me to create more of a work–life balance, and most important, provide me with more time to rest on a regular basis.

Get honest about what causes you to lose steam, connection, and/or motivation. It's easier to blame others for our own unhappiness than to take initiative and make change—especially when it comes to work. We are all creatures of comfort and convenience. Getting real about what sets off a chain of events that causes your unhappiness and sense of disconnection to your job might feel like too much work, too confronting, or simply too far outside of your pay grade. But I learned quickly that so much of career development is actually *personal* development. My experience in any job I've ever had directly correlates to the self-reflection and personal-growth work I am willing to do simultaneously.

Journal: The Cause of Disconnect

Whether it's in a journaling session or talking it out with someone you trust, get to the root of what is causing you to disconnect. To do this, I recommend reflecting on the following questions:

- Do certain days feel better than others? Why?
- What is different about my approach, attitude, and habits before, during, and after the workday?
- Is my body communicating any messages to me about the environment, people around me, or what parts of my work feel aligned or unaligned? What do those sensations feel like, and what are they telling me?
- Is there a part of myself that feels under-expressed at work? What part?
- Where do my triggers lie at work? In certain people, conversations, systems, or expectations? How might these triggers be pointing to opportunities for growth?

Know your worth. Making meaningful changes at your current job will likely require some conversations with higher-ups. Before you have any of these conversations, you first need to have a conversation with yourself about your role and impact. Begin by making a list of all your positive contributions and attributes as an employee thus far. It's important that you give yourself credit and praise for what you've done up to this point so that you can have a grounded and realistic view of your worth to the company and the job. The results of the conversation you have with your employer will hinge on how well you know and own your value at the company.

It's not about leading with the need for more money or a promotion, but about embodying and communicating why your company can't afford to lose you and how they *can* afford to make you happier in your role. This can feel intimidating, but you'll likely be surprised if you come to the table confident in yourself, what you've accomplished, and what you're asking for. When I finally talked to my programming coordinator at SoulCycle, she was more than ready and willing to accommodate many of my requests because she genuinely wanted me to be happy. This defied my underlying belief that bosses prioritize making money over making their team happy. Thankfully, SoulCycle understood the connection between its high level of success and the happiness of their individual employees, especially those interfacing with customers every day. My hope is that you work in the same type of environment—and, if not, that's good to know too!

Get clear on what you love about the job and where your genius lies. Years after I left SoulCycle, we interviewed psychologist and author Gay Hendricks at his home in Ojai, California. If you're familiar with his work, you know that this was a once-in-a-lifetime moment. Our conversation was as dynamic as it was deep, and I was awestruck by his ideas about the Genius Zone. This is the idea that we all have a genius—an innate and unique power—that we often don't recognize or underutilize. Of course, we want to spend as much time in the Genius Zone as possible. For so long, including during my time at SoulCycle, I wasn't fully leaning into or embracing my genius. Instead, I spent a lot of energy focusing on what I *wasn't* and trying to become more like other people around me.

Pass the Mic

Operating in your zone of genius is when you are doing what you love to do and doing something that makes a huge contribution to other people's lives. As long as you keep aiming your activities in that direction, I predict that you will have abundance and success beyond your wildest dreams.

—Gay Hendricks, author of *The Genius Zone*
ALMOST 30, EPISODE 554

When I zeroed in on my unique genius as a SoulCycle instructor and doubled down on the type of class that I wanted to teach and the kind of experience I wanted to create, my classes began to consistently sell out—and I had more fun and energy in the process. My genius in this role was threefold, none of which had to do with the technicalities of cycling. First, I was able to cultivate relationships with riders in a way that made them feel seen and cared for in class. I checked in on their progress both on the bike and personally, which I believe built a trust between us that translated when I pushed them during class, and which resulted in them defying what they thought they could do. My second strain of genius was in music curation. This is something that most instructors are really well trained to do, but my passion for music meant that my song choices and flow created a uniquely fun and dynamic playlist that made sense and served a specific purpose. Riders looked forward to seeing what song journey I'd have them ride next. And finally, I leaned into my humor and quirky personality during class rather than trying to fit into the template of "cycling instructor." The less I tried to say the perfect, inspirational thing during class and the more I was my goofy, expressive, honest self, the more riders felt comfortable, both with me and with themselves. I was trying less and showing up as myself more. Plus, it felt so effortless! Lean into what you love and what highlights your genius at work. Become the expert that people can turn to.

Action precedes confidence. Do you want to know how Krista and I became confident podcasters? I'll tell you the secret: we recorded and released our first episode. Then we recorded and released another episode. And then another. With every new episode drop, we instilled a stronger sense of belief in ourselves and our ability, with every new guest we spoke to our interviewing skills sharpened, and we became more comfortable and confident in our abilities and mission every time we met or connected with a listener of the show and heard their feedback.

Just *thinking* about doing something is a very human type of self-torture. To wait and mull over why it's not a good idea or the perfect way to execute an idea actually erodes confidence. Let your action be the fire that stokes competence. Start imperfectly and trust the process ahead to lead you to your ultimate vision. Whether you finally schedule a call with your boss to discuss their goals so you can focus on yours, or present a new system of organization to your team that has been struggling with workflow, your action will have a powerful domino effect. Not only will it give you more competence and confidence over time, but it will also send a message to those around you. They might appreciate and be impressed by your initiative or be inspired by it. Either way, it's a win-win!

Consider investing in therapy or a career coach. I make this suggestion understanding that it's not necessarily accessible to everyone. But even if that's the case for you in this moment, I want to plant the seed, because both therapy and coaching have made the most impact on my career overall, and I've never once regretted the investment. So often, women who are early on in their career don't consider themselves worthy of this type of support and guidance. But I would argue that these early days are a particularly crucial time to invest in your team, in those who will serve as your counsel as you navigate. It's the secret sauce. Think about it this way: How many happy hours would you have to skip to be able to invest in this, say, once a month? When you really do the math, it becomes less of a luxury and more of a real possibility.

I started therapy during year two of *Almost 30,* and by year three Krista and I invested in a business coach. Therapy has been foundational for every relationship I have—my relationship with myself, with my friends, family, partner, and to my work and purpose, my body, and change. For the last six years and counting, I have been able to funnel my limiting beliefs, questions about relationship dynamics, insecurities, goals, and more into a twice-monthly session with my therapist. Having these sessions consistently prevents me from leaking the unprocessed everywhere I go. It has given me a level of self-awareness that has served me over and over in my career. Krista and I laugh sometimes because, after having both been in individual therapy for a while now, we have conversations as business partners that are so highly self-aware and self-responsible that we rarely experience conflict—and when we do, we understand how to work it out. We have the language and awareness to navigate any situation with honesty and respect for each other, ourselves, and the greater mission we are on.

Even if you work in a more team-oriented, corporate setting than

Krista and I do, you are still not immune to real human emotions and triggers bleeding into the overall team dynamic. You're all humans, after all! Therapy can be so helpful in understanding why certain people or behaviors trigger you, and how you can work through those triggers to ultimately practice healthy communication and behavior. Therapy can also provide the groundwork for creating healthy work boundaries; as you now know, unhealthy boundaries are usually caused (at least in part) by a lack of self-worth or self-confidence. Boundaries will keep you in your genius, maximize your potential and productivity, streamline your communication, and set expectations all around.

Pass the Mic

It's not about quitting your job and saying "I'm following my passion," but just finding time and energy in your daily life on a microlevel to cultivate and do some gardening around those things that you're interested in. When you do that, the Universe will provide opportunities to deepen that relationship. And that then leads to other things. And if you're self-aware enough and aware of your environment enough, there will be opportunities for you to further explore that.

—Rich Roll, author of *Finding Ultra*
ALMOST 30, EPISODE 521

Check on your non-work-related fulfillment. You are not your job, my friend. Your self-worth does not hinge on whether you get a promotion or whether your boss is impressed by your PowerPoint skills. If you find that your overall mood and confidence plummet after a mediocre presentation in front of your team, it might be time to balance your buckets. It's imperative that you show yourself on a daily or, at the very least, weekly basis that you are THE CAT'S MEOW. Yeah, that's right, honey. What can you do that lights you up, that reminds you just how talented, fulfilled, and confident you are outside of your job? Join an intramural sports team, volunteer, pour yourself into learning something new, revisit an old passion that you haven't given time and energy to in a while. Whatever lights your fire! Notice how it makes you feel to immerse yourself in something that brings you joy and piques your curiosity. The balance that you invite into your every day has the power to bring perspective to the elements of your life that are causing stress and confusion.

Stay for the Stretch

I'm that person who used to notoriously leave workout classes before the stretch. *Gotta keep it moving—on to the next thing!* For me, stretching was uncomfortable, and the pace felt too slow. I told myself that I would do it later, but of course I never did. Looking back, my avoidance of stretching said everything about where I was at that point in my life. I avoided discomfort any time I could. But as the discomfort kept presenting itself in various forms, I realized that I had to reframe and reapproach these experiences. Today I've rebranded these moments that make me uncomfortable and that I want to avoid as "stretch seasons" or "stretch moments." Now I stay for the stretch.

Practice: Stretch It Out

If you need a change, it may very well serve you to try on this perspective. Can you view your current career experience as a necessary exercise in being able to hold more, be more, do more, find more compassion and connection, to feel more, and thus understand a bit more fully what the next best step might be? If you're willing to stay for it, soon the stretch won't be as arduous, and before long it will even become your new normal. It will be an elevated baseline from which you can share your talents and passions, lead those around you, and make a living for yourself.

Through this new lens, check in with yourself often:

- How am I being stretched right now?
- How do I want to feel on the other side of this season/moment?
- How can I ground myself in this moment and loosen the grip on what was or what will be?
- What feels good about this stretch?
- What makes me feel proud about how I'm showing up for this stretch?

After you've given stretching a try, only *you* will know whether this moment in your career calls for a pivot or a revival. It might be tempting to ask others for advice or to give you the answer you're seeking. You might build a mosaic of insights, experiences, and thoughts from others. Sure, digest all this. And *then* tune in to what feels right *for you*. Right might rock the boat, and it might feel a little scary or intimidating. Ultimately, your job—the job that matters the most—is to follow that feeling at the pace that feels good to you. The point is not for your career path to make sense to everyone else, but rather to make sense to you, to your *soul*. Know that we're cheering you on as you zig and zag on your path!

I Swear, This Can Be Fun!

It's easy to fixate on all the ways changing up your career can be intimidating. We can get so caught up in the uncertainty of it all that it's easy to forget about all the ways looking at your career through a new lens—especially in your twenties and early thirties—can *help* you and pay off in valuable wisdom and experience down the line, whether your next move ends up being your forever path or yet another stepping stone toward where you're ultimately headed.

Even if it feels like you're supposed to have everything figured out, the truth of the matter is that at this point in your life, you really are just starting out—even if you've been with the same job for a few years now. I hope that you will *always* experiment throughout your life, but particularly during this season that is uniquely designed for discovery and experimentation. Even if you sometimes feel weighed down, most likely you have more freedom to experiment right now than you will at any other point in your life. Take advantage of that! During one of our live events we had a conversation with one of our community members named Jess, who dreamed of creating her own YouTube channel. When we asked what was holding her back, Jess shared that she was embarrassed to start because she didn't have a following. As we talked with Jess, we were able to reframe her situation so that she could recognize that less of an audience actually gave her more room to experiment because there wasn't any pressure or expectation placed upon her. Your twenties are similar, which means it's a prime time to roam freely and experiment secure in the fact that there is less risk involved than there may be at later points in your life.

The more exploring you do, the more paths you try out, the more you stretch, the more of a diverse skill set you can build—and it's always a case of the-more-the-merrier when it comes to skills, experience, and knowledge. You never know when a skill or piece of information is going to pay off down the line, so trust that your time is well spent, and see each of your experiences as supporting, creating, and honing your skills—in terms of both your work and your *life*. Alleviate the pressure of having to know whether what comes next is forever (or even for the long term) and, instead, know that no matter where you end up, your future career is unfolding right this very moment as you build more knowledge, more experience, and more momentum. When you allow yourself to explore, you also open yourself up to stumbling upon a hidden passion or skill that you may not even know you possess at this moment in time.

As you think about all the ways that pivoting and reviving your career are likely to pay off down the line, remember that your work life is not separate from your life—it's part of it. The challenges and wins you experience at work will likely provide you with some life lessons that apply to *all* facets of life and will contribute to your growth. There's so much to be learned by meeting new people and trying new things—and changing up your work life is yet another way of doing that.

The next time fear or doubt creeps in, remind yourself of all there is to be gained in the long run by listening to yourself, stretching it out, and taking a chance. This applies to your career, your finances, and your purpose. And you'll carry that mindset of bravery, resilience, and abundance into every relationship in your life—your relationship to your body, your spirit, your mind, and to every other person in your orbit, which is the next frontier of this book.

Relationships

Humans are relational beings, so it's no wonder that relationships are a vehicle for so much of our personal growth and reflection. As intense as it may sound, every single relationship has its purpose. (Yes, even the ones with people you hate!) As you cross this Saturn threshold, you are being asked to reconsider any feelings of regret or resentment you may have, whether they're about current relationships in your life or those from the past. During this season, your soul wants to share more with you about the purpose of each relationship you're a part of (or have been a part of) and how you can bring more consciousness to each one of them so that you're able to experience the gifts they have to offer in real time.

Before your Saturn Return, you may have asked your bestie, parents, hairdresser, or even that one loser boyfriend: *What should I be doing?* But now, as you take control of your life, that question evolves to: *Am I doing what I'm* supposed *to be doing?* As your cosmic entryway into adulthood, Saturn also ushers more "adult" relationships into your life (even if those relationships are with the same people you already know and love). On the flip side, it's also the cosmic exit out of your current situations and situationships, and into something way more beautiful and way more *you*.

This section is all about the liberation that comes from understanding that the common denominator in any relationship you're in is YOU! Whether it feels like it at this moment or not, the power is in your hands. But first, you have to understand who you had to be in order to be loved, safe, and accepted growing up (there's that conditioning again!), and how these beliefs may very well be due for an update. From there, we'll peel back the layers of conditioning and how all these elements affect how you behave in relationships today. How did you get here, and how can you use change as a catalyst for clarity in relationships? Is this period of change meant to strengthen the bond or to untether so it can be let go?

But before we move into the future, let's first travel back to the past to understand how the heck we even got here. We'll look at your very first relationships . . . the ones you had with your family.

Chapter 11

FAMILY MATTERS

Krista

There's something wild about realizing your parents are people. It's one of the ultimate steps in growing up—and sometimes it's a painful one. When we're growing up, adults seem larger than life, almost like mythical creatures. On the playground in Ohio, one of the main bragging points was, "My dad could beat up your dad!" (My dad *did* work out, so it tracked.) I also found myself bragging about the fact that my mom had a job and earned her own living. Sure, on one hand I felt neglected because of it (LOL), but on the other it felt pretty cool and hip to have such a progressive mom, because not all moms were nine-to-fivers where I grew up.

But at some point, you realize that these parents who used to seem so big and infallible when you were a kid are just people too. It's a weird shift in perception. I liked thinking of my parents as being perfect, to be honest. It felt easier, because mere humans are layered and complex. There's also something terrifying about realizing that what drives them isn't always virtue, and that they were sometimes asleep at the wheel in life, doing their best to get by, but not without making mistakes in the process. But, of course, one of the lessons of adulthood is that there's nuance in life, and that people are never just one thing. Like other human beings, your parents have their own personal history beyond you, and they can be wrong sometimes. All this can be true, while it's also true that these are the same people who facilitated your survival. They're the ones who make a great green bean casserole, always have a tissue in their purse, and showed up to all your basketball games even if you weren't that good. Still, at some point, you will have to recognize that your parents—despite their once-apparent superpowers—are human. This understanding is a rite of passage that can bring on big feelings, but it's also not all that bad in the end. As your life progresses, so do all your relationships, including your relationship with your parents and family. Still, this transition of recognizing your parents as human—and yourself as a unique individual who likely aligns with your parents in some ways but not in others—can feel like a final loss of innocence.

Only once you experience that change in perception and see your parents as people do you fully grasp the fact that you're an actual adult, and an equal with your parents. They're real, actual people, with real struggles and anxieties, real hopes and dreams, some of which were never and will never be realized. Your parents are just two adults existing on Earth, trying their best to make it through life. And for as much as they and you would like to believe it, they're not actually invincible, all-knowing superhumans like you might have thought back on the playground.

Once you view your parents as humans and yourself as an adult, it will likely cause you to reconsider some things that you once took for granted. For instance, you may come to realize they don't have all the answers like you once believed they did. It means they probably made a few missteps throughout your childhood. And with this newfound understanding of their humanity and your own maturation process, it means that you might be thinking back to how you were raised, considering the ways in which you are aligned with your family and the ways in which you aren't, and figuring out what your adult relationship with them looks like.

You might start to notice how certain patterns that you adopted from your family are repeating in your adult life and are mirrored in your relationships with other people. Some of these patterns might be good, and others may be patterns that you don't want to carry forward with you—things like people-pleasing, seeking approval, and feeling a deep need for perfection. Your family is foundational to who you are and how you interact in your relationships in general. As you begin to untangle your own upbringing and your family's influence on who you are and the relationships you're in today, expect a period of revelation and potentially big feelings, like anger and resentment. If you find yourself in this situation, feel those feelings fully, so that you can then release them and move forward in the way that feels best and most true to you. The truth is that you cannot change your family members and how their own conditioning was patterned onto you in turn. But you *can* begin to understand why people in your family are the way they are. You can open the aperture of understanding to the lineage you descended from and learn more about the generational cycles (perhaps even including trauma) that have replayed themselves in your own life . . . and how you can begin to break the cycle. How powerful is *that*?

No matter what your circumstances might have been, rather than blaming your family for the way you are now, Saturn is calling you to seek to understand your family, the generations before them, and how all this has been imprinted onto you. The goal is acceptance, so that you can heal anything that needs to be healed. It's time to trust yourself to discern what parts of your upbringing you'd like to carry forward and which parts you want to tend to, heal, and discard in order to commit to your own way of being.

Saturn Return and Individuation

As you know by now, so much of your Saturn Return is about taking responsibility and reclaiming your power as a co-creator of your life. While you are not responsible for the imprint your family system left upon you, you *are* responsible for reconciling your childhood and your adulthood so that love and compassion can crowd out animosity and misunderstandings.

Pass the Mic

If you're still blaming your parents at thirty, you're in trouble . . . it's up to you what kind of life you make. You heal that. You can't hold people from the past responsible for who you are now.

—Jennifer Freed, PhD, author of *A Map to Your Soul*
ALMOST 30, EPISODE 553

This doesn't mean that you won't feel resistance to doing this work during your Saturn Return, because you probably will. And that resistance might even present as incredibly strong (for a refresh on how to reframe resistance, mosey on back to chapter 2). *Why should I give my parents a pass for their behavior? I can't forgive my sister for how she treated me throughout our whole childhood! I've never felt like my mom wanted to understand me; why should I invest time in understanding her?* All these and any other thoughts and feelings you might have are valid, and they're all cries from your inner child, who is rightfully resentful because she has not been validated in the ways she wants to be. It is very human and very normal to want validation for the experiences you've been through and feelings you've had along the way. We all want the acknowledgment and validation of being told, "You're right, that was fucked up and you didn't deserve that." But then what? While an apology is nice, it can't do the work for you (even if you believe it will). You are not meant to hold on to the experiences of your past as an immutable identity, and only you can release them and allow them to point the way to something new and more true. You are meant to make sense of these experiences and the people involved in them so that you can make amends with yourself. By doing this, you will reclaim so much of your creative power, and ultimately change both how you experience these relationships and make way for a whole new reality based on the acceptance of what is.

Having said that, your Saturn Return is not about figuring it all out. Instead, this time will support you in realizing that you don't have to do the things your parents did or did not want you to do, and you don't have to constantly look over your shoulder for validation from them or anyone else. During this sobering time, you realize that many of the tendencies you have as an adult were learned within your family system and begin to see and understand how these unconscious behaviors might be preventing you from feeling confident, present, and fully yourself. Saturn Return calls for all that to change, because now you are being called to individuate.

In Jungian psychology (which we also know as psychoanalysis or analytical psychology today), the intent is to move toward a deeper understanding of self and to uncover the "real" self versus the self that is presented to the outside world (sound familiar?). Individuation, or the process of self-realization, is an important part of this, and it refers to how we integrate all parts of us into a true and unique whole. Basically, it's a fancy way of describing the lifelong process of knowing and *being* yourself. And while this is a lifelong process, there are some critical junctures and growth points along the way, including adolescence, the college years, and Saturn Return (are you surprised?).

Do you experience or relate to any of the following as an adult?

* Lacking a sense of who you are and what you believe.
* Feeling self-conscious or uncomfortable going after your goals and visions for your life when they are different from what your family envisioned for or expected from you.
* Feeling disconnected from what *you* really want in life.
* Frequently feeling depressed and anxious.
* A sense of being dependent or reliant on others.
* Difficulty cultivating healthy friendships, romantic relationships, and professional relationships.
* Finding it challenging to make a decision because you don't trust yourself or feel connected to your intuition.

If you relate to any or all these feelings, it points to the fact that you're in need of individuation. There is good news here! What you are moving through now is a total recalibration of these experiences, a serious invitation to a level of awareness that will support you in properly indi-viduating and thus creating a healthier, more harmonious way of relating to your family, yourself, and others to a degree you have likely never experienced before. The more willing you are to do things differently (even if you have to fake it till you make it) and to see your awareness as a gift and an opportunity to set a new tone for yourself and your life, the smoother this process will feel.

If you are someone who has been supported and encouraged in the process of individuation throughout your life thus far by members of your family, then this part of your Saturn Return might not be as jarring and intense as it is for those who experienced more friction in natural periods of individuation during their youth and adolescence. But even if that's the case, I would still encourage you to look at other aspects of your relationship with your family to understand any underlying patterns you might have that aren't serving you. This includes how your family values or devalues certain areas of life, such as career, relationships, food, body, big change, success, failure, and so on.

See It to Heal It

Each of our families is unique, so no two people are going to have the same family-related issues to work through. But we have seen some com-mon individuation hurdles in the Almost 30 community and in our own lives: enmeshment, codependency, the Mother Wound, and the Father Wound. We're going to spend this chapter looking at each of these dy-namics, and then offer tips for establishing boundaries to break out of your role in the family pattern so that you have space to heal and indi-viduate. Notice when you find yourself resonating with a particular one of these topics, or even feeling triggered—that's likely offering you some valuable information about what relationships need to be healed and transformed in your own life to move forward as the most whole and healed version of yourself.

Signs You're Enmeshed or Codependent

At the most basic level, enmeshment is typically a blurring of boundaries between people, and the behaviors that come with it often originate in our family system. In a healthier family dynamic, there are boundaries around who is a part of or exposed to family or individual issues. The parental figures are responsible for their own actions, feelings, and emotional regulation, and there is an overall respect for the change and evolution of both the family at large and each individual who is part of the family, including the children.

Pass the Mic

A lot of women in particular have a tendency to be a boundary disaster because we're trained, we're literally raised, to be and praised for self-abandoning codependence. That sets us up to not only not know how to do this but to be afraid to do it, to think that doing it makes us not-good women, it makes us not-good friends, makes us not-good daughters, makes us not-good partners.

—Terri Cole, author of *Boundary Boss*
ALMOST 30, EPISODE 421

In an enmeshed family, children generally feel a lot of pressure to live out their parents' dream or vision. The parents' dreams and desires for their child are usually well intended, but they don't account for the fact that their child is an individual who has dreams and desires of their own that may or may not be the same as their parents'. In other cases, indirect pressure is put on the child to be an emotional support system to parents or to simply snuff out their own emotional experience because the parents' emotional needs are taking up all the space. This might look like being the center of your parents' world, or maybe both your accomplishments and your mistakes are given more weight than they should have. For better or for worse, the overall well-being of a family system might hinge on how certain individuals are doing or feeling. This is a lot of pressure and responsibility, and it can make it extremely difficult to understand who you really are, how you really feel, and what you really want. In other words, it can make it difficult to individuate.

Codependency is intricately related to enmeshment. The hallmark of codependency is abandoning yourself in favor of offering attention and support to someone else. It might also look like your emotional well-being being dictated by another person's mood or energy. It can present as a daily dance of walking on eggshells or riding the highs and lows of another person, while also being confused about or disconnected from how *you* feel. The experience of codependency (or recognizing that you have experienced enmeshment in your upbringing) can be overwhelming. If you feel that as you read through this next section, know you are capable of breaking these patterns, not only for yourself but also for the generations that follow you.

It's important to understand what enmeshment and codependency can look like in practice, so let's look at some common signs that you might have some disentangling to do.

Pass the Mic

Our work as women right now is separating out what is our essence. What is our truth and sovereign reality? And it's about wiping off the traumatic residue that we've accumulated on top of it, through our families and through the culture, because we're dealing with other humans who have their own illusions and projections as well.

—Bethany Webster, author of
Discovering the Inner Mother
ALMOST 30, EPISODE 506

SIGN #1: BOUNDARIES WHO?

A lack of boundaries within the family structure can create a lot of confusion. Oftentimes, this allows for an unhealthy, lopsided power dynamic to take shape between parent and child. It might result in the child feeling like they can't make their own decisions without their parent(s)' approval or involvement, or a loss of their own voice, opinions, and personal space.

Ever have a parent snoop in your bedroom, rather than asking you directly about the thing they're snooping about? Parents justify their actions by claiming a right to know everything that happens in their house, dismissing the adult child's need for personal space and autonomy. This situation illustrates a lack of respect for personal boundaries, where the child's need for privacy and independence is not acknowledged or valued by the parents. This behavior also damages the trust that a child might have for their parent or cause them to hide things even more. Such dynamics can lead to feelings of frustration, helplessness, distrust, and poor family communication. As an adult, this might manifest as a parent over-involving themselves in their child's life, intervening in marital matters, or other personal dynamics. It can get messy and out of control! Although boundaries can be more than just physical (like privacy in your room), so much of healing from family dynamics has to do with cultivating strong boundaries; we'll walk through other examples later in this chapter.

SIGN #2: CONTROLLING MUCH?

As annoying as it may feel sometimes, a controlling parent often acts this way out of fear, perhaps because they have felt out of control at other times or in other areas of their life. This control might manifest as hyper-monitoring of everything a child does, constantly questioning and doubting a child's choices, or inserting themselves in their child's life in ways that are embarrassing or frustrating to the child. A parent who is controlling does not honor boundaries, and thus, conditions the child to expect a boundaryless life, re-creating these patterns in their own relationships outside of the family.

SIGN #3: DO YOU FEEL RESPONSIBLE FOR YOUR PARENTS?

Did you ever feel responsible for your parents' well-being as a child or young adult? Did you ever feel like their happiness hinged on whether *you* were good or successful or doing whatever it was that made *them* feel comfortable? If so, you might have taken on an inordinate amount of pressure to make sure everything you ever did or said would make them happy—or, at the very least, not ruffle their feathers.

If a parent doesn't assume responsibility for tending to their own mental health, they often displace that task on their child. That child is now the source of the parent's happiness, worthiness, and value. This might look like a father allowing his misery at work to spill over into his time with kids, oversharing with them, complaining, or otherwise not being present. As a result, the child might grow up feeling the weight of their father's unhappiness or overcompensate to try to make their father happy and proud in any way they can at the expense of their own well-being.

SIGN #4: IS THIS YOUR FUTURE OR MINE?

It's not uncommon for parents to transfer their hopes and dreams onto their child, pinning their worth and value on their child's achievements. During Saturn Return it is particularly common to come to the sudden realization that the life you are living or the career path you're on is not actually one you desire, but one that your parents desired *for* you. Women in our community frequently discuss feeling as though they cannot pursue what they really want to in their career or follow their desired purpose in life because their parents won't understand or approve. These women are so consumed by earning the approval of their parents and keeping peace in the family that they fear their parents' response more than they fear missing out on the life that calls them. Even as they begin to realize the dynamic at play, children in this situation often doubt themselves and how they're feeling because their parents' opinions and preferences have been such a driving force throughout their life that they've never really trusted how they actually felt.

It's also really common for parents to want to mold their children into a "good" representation of the family once they go out into the world. While there's no harm in raising kind, polite children, when the intention of doing so is to make the parent look good, the child can feel that, eventually harbor resentment toward the parent, and rebel in unhealthy ways.

Pass the Mic

We want our children to be great because we want to feel great, and the reason we want to feel great is because we don't feel great and we are using our children to meet that expectation. This is what was done to us. We were all raised to be instruments of our parents' fancy, and were fine-tuned and overplayed and over-parented to become that. We were abducted from our authentic self.

—Shefali Tsabary, PhD, author of *The Conscious Parent*
ALMOST 30, EPISODE 592

SIGN #5: HOW CAN I AVOID CONFLICT AT ALL COSTS?

An enmeshed family dynamic might include brushing any issues or conflicts under the rug, or avoiding resolution, and instead, letting a situation fizzle out (and then inevitably returning to the pattern that caused upset in the first place). To have healthy relationships and true intimacy, you must survive the conflict–repair cycle that creates it. It's okay to have conflict, and if you are in a family where conflict is not allowed, it's often a sign that you must negotiate who you are in order to keep the peace in the home. A child who has rarely seen conflict resolution will often go on to avoid it as an adult. Or they might become anxious and paralyzed in the face of conflict, unaware of the fact that consciously moving through it could result in growth and a deeper connection with the other person in the process.

SIGN #6: WHO AM I OUTSIDE OF MY FAMILY?

It's so incredible to grow up in a close family, but there's a fine line between being close to your family and living in a dynamic where there is an unhealthy separation between the family and any outsiders. It can result in a culture of anxiety and fear when it comes to exploring relationships outside of the family. This can look different ways: the child might feel like they are betraying the family by engaging in relationships outside of it, or they could have an unhealthy amount of distrust for anyone outside of the family. Maybe the child wasn't allowed to have sleepovers or friends over, and had to instead spend most nights and weekends at home.

Sometimes this close-to-the-point-of-unhealthy dynamic might be masked under mottos like "Family first!" or "No one messes with my family!" Other times, it could be more subtle, exemplified in situations like when a parent feels like no one is good enough for their child. This can create a distorted self-perception for the child, in addition to affecting the relationships they engage in, like the child having an inflated view of themselves, being disappointed in other relationships that can't possibly live up to the family's standards, or putting otherwise unrealistic expectations on future relationships. A child might also worry about gaining their parents' approval of friends and romantic partners, which can prevent the development of deep, authentic relationships.

The Mother Wound

The Mother Wound is the pain—and, perhaps, trauma—that a mother carries and unconsciously passes along to her children. I truly believe that almost every mother wants to give her child a healthy, secure life. But, unfortunately, we all have blind spots and patterns of behavior that we can't even see because they're so habituated. This is what the Mother Wound is all about. It has nothing to do with intention or love; it's all about cycles that tend to be perpetuated throughout generations.

When we think of our childhood and young years, we can imagine a garden that's regularly tended to and well taken care of. The plants are provided with fresh water, and the space itself is bathed in sun, filled with little flags in the soil, and maybe there are even some smiling garden gnomes sprinkled throughout. The garden is naturally and innately ready to become what it's destined to be because it's been provided with all the environmental inputs it needs to thrive. The little seedlings planted there are able to develop into their fullest expression thanks to the good caretaking they receive. The attentive and present gardener tends to them regularly, waters them, checks the soil, and generally monitors them to ensure they're given what they need.

Compare this to a landscape overseen by a gardener who has a lot of other things on their plate; maybe the gardener travels a lot or just doesn't really prioritize the garden because they're overwhelmed by other things. Or maybe the gardener was never properly taught how to care for plants, so they try their best but don't have the sort of knowledge or experience that other gardeners might. Perhaps that gardener was previously traumatized by a garden. Okay, now we're taking the analogy a little bit too far, but you get the point: the seeds are dependent upon the gardener, and they may not grow in the same way as they could have with more attentive care. Of course, you're the seed in this scenario, and your mother is the gardener, because she was your source of *everything* from the second you came into existence. Your life and survival very literally depended on her. There is nothing more vulnerable than a newborn baby who needs everything from their mother to survive.

In an ideal world, we would all have a mother who doesn't carry unresolved trauma with her and who doesn't have to figure out how to balance caretaking with the overwhelming parts of her own life. This untraumatized mother would see the world clearly, openly, from the perspective of a secure attachment, and with a high-worth view of self. Mothers like this create gardens with fertile and nutrient-dense soil that allows their seedlings to bloom into the unique, bright, and beautiful flowers they were meant to be.

Sadly, this isn't possible for many mothers. Many mothers didn't learn how to regulate their emotions or cope with the various situations thrown at them throughout life, including those they encounter during the course of motherhood. They never learned how to meet their own needs, heal, or practice self-care. They weren't taught how to establish boundaries. Out of necessity, their relationships—most important, their relationship with their child—may have reflected patterns of codependency. Because of all this, they unconsciously projected their pain onto the child, unconsciously passing down the same modeling they were taught (and that their mother was taught, and their mother's mother, and on and on). This is how cycles are created. How your mom feels about herself becomes a blueprint for how you feel about yourself. How she feels about life in general becomes how you see life. How she relates to others becomes how you relate to others. This is why our relationships heal when we heal our relationship with our mother. The things we learn from and through her are so foundational that they impact everything else in our life.

In an ideal world, we would all have mothers who are emotionally attuned to us, meaning they would show up in our life with true presence to fulfill our basic needs. We would all have a mother who is present enough to notice and who understands what our needs are and is then able to meet them. Having this experience is a fundamental part of a child's healthy development, and it's what secure attachment looks like.

Like all mammals, humans are wired for attachment and will do whatever it takes to experience it. Our sense of self and of safety depends on it. When faced with a situation where being authentic is unsafe, we appease our parents' (and especially our mother's) expectations of how we should be so that we can experience attachment. If we are in conflict with our mom, her preferences for attitude and behavior will trump our instinctive impulse to be honest, expressive, silly, imaginative, and whatever else we naturally are—to be wild, free human beings. We also make unspoken and subtle agreements with our mothers. For example: *if I have no boundaries, you'll love me* or *if I hide, do what's "right," fit in, and don't rock the boat, our relationship will stay intact and I'll be safe.* Remember that safety equals survival.

Time and again, our mother's expectations and our biological need for proximity overpower our basic birthright and natural impulse to be ourselves. This is why a lot of healing is really unlearning all the survival patterns and limiting beliefs we picked up from a young age when we were just trying to survive.

As someone who communes with a wide variety of women on a daily basis, I have a good finger on the pulse of what we're struggling with in life. Some of the things I hear regularly are that women are feeling: *burnt out, overwhelmed, exhausted, stressed,* and *in need of a nervous system reset.* I, too, have felt all this many, many times. It seems like staying busy is a badge of honor that we women have been wearing for a long time now, even at this young age, and we're collectively trying to figure out how to get that thing off our jean jacket. I bring this up because this belief that we have to "do it all," "be everything to everyone," and micromanage and control our lives one brunch or bachelorette party at a time is often connected to the Mother Wound. Think about it: How and why did you learn that you had to carry all this?

Pass the Mic

Attachment and authenticity are the two lifelines. When attachment is threatened for a child, they will always trade authenticity. It's like: If the threat of neglect is there, who do I need to become? How do I shape-shift in some way? How do I trade who I am in order to get the connection, the love, the validation that I want? Attachment is our survival, so of course we trade authenticity for attachment. We must.

—Vienna Pharaon, author of *The Origins of You*
ALMOST 30, EPISODE 597

Tuning in to what we think our mother wants us to be, and then living that out, is an adaptive survival response. With the help of our built-in survival intelligence, we mold ourselves and our interactions according to environmental demands. If we don't adapt, if we fight back by choosing authenticity over attachment, we can be seen as disruptive, needy, selfish, and unreasonable. Even worse, we can be emotionally or even physically threatened. While this may not be true in adulthood, it certainly was in childhood.

Do you relate to this? Here are some common ways the Mother Wound might appear in your life:

- Difficulty relating to your mom on an emotional level (which can lead to difficulties relating to other women or romantic partners).
- Uncertainty about the relationships in your life, especially with your mother.
- Feeling the pressure to conform to certain specific rigid expectations of womanhood placed upon you by your mom.
- Feeling like you have to mother your mother or that you need to care for, protect, and support her more than she needs to care for, protect, and support you.
- People-pleasing and emotional caretaking, which can stem from—and lead to—codependency and enmeshment with partners or in other relationships.
- Constantly looking outside of yourself for approval or acceptance.
- A feeling of uncertainty about relationships and an inability to fully be yourself or to fully trust others in them.
- A belief that the relationships in your life are at risk if you make a mistake or do something "wrong."
- Low self-esteem or self-worth.
- Feeling as if you need to be good, perfect, beautiful, thin, successful, or anything other than who you are to gain approval and be loved and accepted by your mom and others.

- Feeling competitive with other women and unable to support or see them succeed for fear of what it means for you.

As you start to understand your Mother Wound and how it impacts your life, be gentle with yourself: all of this takes a while to unravel because it involves identifying and undoing a lifetime's worth of unconscious behavior and patterning. I've been doing this work for years now, and I still have to be aware of the pressure I put on myself to "get healing right" and to be mindful of the creeping belief that unless I do it all and do it all perfectly, life will drop me, and I will fail and be forgotten about.

The Father Wound

You've probably heard the phrase "daddy issues" thrown around almost as a joke, but the damage that our fathers can do is very real. Similar to the Mother Wound, the Father Wound can be incredibly painful, and its impact can echo throughout all areas of life. Like the Mother Wound, the Father Wound is typically the result of emotional neglect, abuse, absence, or an unattuned parent or caregiver (being attuned means that a parent is paying attention to, responding, and even predicting a child's needs in the moment).

Pass the Mic

Everything is energy, so I say the mother-father wound, because they're both one and the same and they're unique. How we relate to women is very much rooted in how we related to our mothers, and how we relate to men is very much rooted in how we related to our fathers.

—Sheleana Aiyana, founder of Rising Woman and author of *Becoming the One*
ALMOST 30, EPISODE 511

However, the impact of each of these wounds is different, because we have very different cultural models for what we expect to get from our mother versus our father (think of the expectations and stereotypes we have for women versus men). The Father Wound can be healed and handled similarly to the Mother Wound (which we'll get into in the next section), but should be approached with the societal ideals that we place upon men in mind. The Father Wound is the result of generations of conditioning that shame men for having emotions, being vulnerable, and force men to meet an "ideal" standard of what it means to be a man. As with your mother, your father's unresolved trauma becomes your own, until you are consciously aware of it. When you were little, your subconscious mind and body could not fathom that your dad's trauma wasn't something to take personally, so you personalized it; the problem couldn't be him, so it must be you. Thankfully, Saturn Return is here offering an opportunity to understand and heal what the younger version of you could not.

Our fathers have the greatest impact on our self-worth, core beliefs, and coping mechanisms, so that is generally where the wounding shows up. For women, it can be present in the relationship dynamics we create with the men in our lives. A symptom of the Father Wound, for anyone, is feeling as though you are not worthy enough and need to seek approval from others, especially other men. More specifically, women with a Father Wound may find themselves in relationships with men who are emotionally unavailable (we all know the type), especially if their fathers were absent or weren't around enough to establish a relationship with them.

Other ways the Father Wound can show up in your life include:

- Unconsciously choosing romantic partners that mimic the dynamic you had with your father (which can be unfulfilling at best, and toxic at worst).
- A need to perform, do, or achieve in order to be loved.
- Codependency and a need for approval from others.
- A core belief of unworthiness or not being good enough.

- An inability to trust men and their intentions.
- A hatred of men and desire for them to be punished, shamed, or hurt.
- A lack of self-trust or ability to make your own decisions with confidence.
- The belief that if you are not doing what your dad wants you to do, or being who your dad wants you to be, then you are not worthy of love.

Identifying and consciously releasing the coping mechanisms you've cultivated over time that have been damaging or harmful to you is big work, and it's work that you'll want support for. As you awaken to and discover these less-than-ideal ways of being during your Saturn Return and rewrite the future of who you're becoming, keep returning to compassion and kindness for yourself. The gift of the process of healing and reparenting is learning to be your own wise, loving parent—you are safe and loved because *you've* got you. Think about all the ways you can be there for yourself in ways that your father couldn't. This might mean giving yourself the approval you so desperately seek, releasing the need to perform, or letting go of that emotionally immature guy you've been texting.

But as with all family matters, the biggest key of all to healing is establishing boundaries that allow you to be the fullest expression of yourself, despite how your family dynamics may have worked up to this point.

Boundary Baddies

The way any pain or trauma you might be experiencing as you embark upon this important time of individuation is healed will vary for each of us. In some cases, it might be helpful to have a therapist to guide you through the process. But the one prescription that tends to work best across the board is establishing boundaries. I know that it might not sound particularly sexy or even novel, but there's a reason we hear about boundaries so much, and that's because they're essential to staying on your path, maintaining your autonomy, and building fulfilling, healthy, and supportive relationships. They are often especially necessary in existing relationships where you need to initiate new patterns and ways of interacting.

Pass the Mic

I can't imagine another point to life than just, over and over, becoming truer and more beautiful versions of ourselves — which ironically usually means we're just going back to the version of ourselves we were born with. Like we're trying to get that self back that at some point the world convinced us wasn't good enough, so we started trying on other identities. It's almost like we're becoming and also returning, at the same time, and that scares the shit out of people.

By definition, we have to do things our parents don't understand. If we are not doing things our parents don't understand, we are not living into the future they birthed us into. We are of two different worlds. Evolving doesn't have to be done with anger and hatred, it has to be done with boundaries. When I said *no* to my mom and made that clear boundary is the moment I became an adult. I was forty-two. And it's the moment when a mother and a daughter became two women. You are building your island to your own specifications. Your parents had their turn, and now it's yours.

—Glennon Doyle, author of *Untamed*
ALMOST 30, EPISODE 325

Not only that, but boundaries are one of Saturn's favorite things, because it's the planet that brings concepts to reality, spirit to body, and thoughts to words. That means this is the prime time in your life to put them into practice—alignment, baby! Boundaries are also particularly important as you individuate, because they prevent you from building resentment toward your family members based on things unsaid. They promote healthy, pleasant interactions, while also helping you develop into a more authentic and autonomous individual. Healthy boundaries with family members involve a mutual acknowledgment that you are an adult with your own thoughts, opinions, beliefs, experiences, and needs. As you navigate your awakening and review of all things during Saturn Return, it's crucial that you are clear with those you love about your evolving identity.

Now that you know why you need to establish boundaries, let's talk about the difficult part: how to set those boundaries. Of course we hear about boundaries all the time these days from the boundary bosses, bitches, and babes on Instagram . . . but what are they exactly? First, let's talk about what they're *not,* because most of us were never taught what boundaries are, and we definitely weren't taught how to put them into practice. Instead, we confuse defensive strategies we've built up to keep ourselves safe for boundaries, and use them in an attempt to exert power, control, or influence over someone else's behavior and experience. By doing this, we believe we might not feel so fearful and insecure when facing conflict, differing needs, separation, or intimacy. But that's not really a boundary—it's a defensive wall. Walls are solid and inflexible; a way we seek control over someone else. This is something to be particularly aware of if you experienced trauma or chaos when you were a child. Walls go up when our defensive strategies are triggered, and in addition to keeping us "safe," they can also be used to punish the other person involved through a self-protective, and often blaming, reaction. There is no way for another person to connect with your defenses because they're built upon blame and projection, are constructed of demands and threats, and they block influence. There might be an appropriate time for that, but at the 2.0 level of healing you can seek a deeper layer of connection that's more loving, while still helping you to heal and move forward.

Boundaries are parameters put in place to establish and communicate what behaviors are and aren't acceptable within a relationship. Boundaries generally bring a certain idea into form for the betterment of all parties involved. And yes, they can feel really uncomfortable when you first start to set them. I know that, for me, it felt like I was doing something wrong. That I was mean, a bitch, cold, stuck-up—the list goes on. What I didn't realize is that certain patterns had been so normalized in my family that what is healthy didn't necessarily feel "normal" to me. But I know now that part of my role in this lifetime is to rewrite some of the scripts my family has been given and to find a way to live more authentically, which involves boundaries. Since you're reading this book, I suspect that might be true for you too. Know that most of us need to establish boundaries with our family at some point. It's part of growing up, figuring out who we are as individuals, and often, breaking old patterns or healing.

Boundaries can look all kinds of different ways depending on your relationship, why you need to set the boundary, and what you are hoping to accomplish through it. Your boundaries might be spoken or simply energetic. In some cases you might need to clearly express what your boundary is to your loved ones so they understand what that means in practice. That's up to you and your situation, though; you can explain why you're setting the boundary or not. Sometimes boundaries might be permanent, or they could be temporary while you take some space to figure things out. Oh, and by the way, you get to change how a boundary looks and if it even continues to exist—you're not married to boundaries forever just because you need them at one point.

What I've learned about boundaries is that they're more fluid and energetic than static and logistical. Once you start setting boundaries, you'll find that you lose your desire to control others. There's this belief that boundaries allow us to dictate what others do, but it's more about how boundaries affect what *you* do. It's not about demanding that your mom never ask you about your dating life ever again, but about you sharing in the way you want to. Building this muscle will allow you to be more present with yourself and with others as they walk through their unique growth and healing processes. With healthy boundaries, you can tolerate other people's differences and feelings. You won't feel threatened by navigating the complexities and disappointments of intimacy. It's weird to think about it from this perspective if you're new to the boundary game, but only with boundaries in place can true, safe, secure, deep love exist.

Here are some strategies to keep in mind when it comes to setting your own healthy boundaries.

DEFINE EACH OF YOUR ROLES

One of the things that makes it most difficult for children—yes, even adult children—to set boundaries with their parents is that they don't want to hurt their parents or damage this essential relationship. And one of the reasons that children most need to set boundaries with their parents is because parents have the tendency to perpetually see their adult children as kids and treat them accordingly. If it feels right to you, I recommend that you begin to set your boundary by having a discussion that defines and clarifies the role the loved one plays in your life. If you can't have this conversation, it's still important that *you're* clear about what each of your roles should be in the relationship.

Let's say you're having this conversation with your mom. It might sound something like: "You're a big part of my life as my mom, and I want to make sure we're both on the same page about what it means for you to be in my life at this point in my journey." Not only does a statement like this establish the foundation for your conversation, but it can also help ensure that your mom isn't talking to an expired or outdated version of you. You're bringing each of you into the present moment and establishing yourself as an equal partner in the relationship. Hopefully, the reminder that you're an important part of each other's lives (even if you don't like each other all the time!) also allows you to come to the table with more compassion, with the understanding that the relationship is still secure, even if it's changing.

Pass the Mic

We are responsible for creating the boundaries that allow us to be adults and for attempting to create the boundary conversations with our parents that have them respect us as adults. And it takes time.

—Terri Cole, author of *Boundary Boss*
ALMOST 30, EPISODE 421

CONSIDER THE BOUNDARY
FROM BOTH PERSPECTIVES

Consider the boundary that you need to set not just from your perspective, but also from the other person's. How can you have compassion and empathy for them and at least consider their point of view, while also being true to your own experience and needs? How might this boundary go on to create an opportunity for a deeper relationship in the future rather than creating more division? If you don't know the answers to these questions, you can have a discussion with the other person about it. This will also help lay the groundwork for a new, healthier, and more authentic way of communication.

TALK ABOUT THE SITUATION
RATHER THAN THE PEOPLE

I really love approaching a situation or relationship as if it's the third person in the room. It's just you, me, and the problem at hand, Dad! Approaching a boundary from this perspective allows you and your family member to come at it with curiosity and openness to exploring how you can both reach a solution together as opposed to getting everyone's defenses up or descending into a blame game, neither of which are productive, nor will they create change or understanding.

EMPATHY AND CLARITY ARE KEY

Express your needs and feelings with empathy and clarity. Empathy allows you to approach your loved one more gently and compassionately, which is likely to generate a better outcome than aggression ever will. And it helps you too. When you're coming from a place of empathy, you're able to more easily understand that your parents' behavior and emotional state are not something to take personally, change, or fix. You can listen and seek to understand their point of view, but you're not trying to change anything about the situation—just relate to it.

This also opens up the door for you to share what you're experiencing with clarity. As Brené Brown famously said, "Clear is kind." Sometimes people confuse clarity with a lack of kindness or empathy, but it's actually one of the biggest acts of kindness and empathy there is. Sharing information in this way offers the best possible opportunity for everyone to win: you can have your needs met, and your parents will understand how to meet those needs.

BE HONEST ABOUT YOUR
FEARS AND DISCOMFORT

Just because you're practicing establishing boundaries doesn't mean you have to pretend to be an expert about it or authoritative in the process. Humanity and honesty are connective. Take responsibility for how you're feeling, and speak truthfully without judgment about what you're saying. You can use phrases like: "I'm feeling nervous to speak to you about this because the story I'm telling myself is that you are going to be upset with me when I share my needs. I know that you love and care for me, but I still have fear in my body that may not even have anything to do with you, or could be left over from our past."

I love to use phrases like "the story I am telling myself is" and "help me to understand" or "tell me what I need to know." Not only are these phrases great for taking responsibility, but they also help both parties pull up and out of any energy dynamics they may unconsciously be swimming in. You're also coming from a curious place that opens everyone up to more conversation, rather than blaming or shaming, which can create distance and distrust. I use these phrases with almost anyone in my life I am having conflict with, and find myself in a way better flow and even deeper relationships as a result.

BE PROACTIVE, NOT REACTIVE

Even after you've made progress establishing and operating within boundaries, chances are you're still going to hit some bumps in the road. When these challenges arise, make sure you're dealing with them on a case-by-case basis rather than letting them build up. Even if you're afraid to have a conversation about what's not working for you and what you would like to see change in the future, have the conversation anyway. It might feel scary in the moment, but it will save you a lot of pain in the future and is better for your relationship in the long run.

If you're open, honest, and speak up before things can get tense, you can avoid a lot of stress by approaching the situation proactively and clearing things up as you go. It's a lot like your home: it's much easier to keep it tidy when you put things away as you go, wipe off the counters after cooking, and put the dishes away right after a meal rather than doing a complete overhaul of the entire space after letting things pile up for weeks. Maintenance communication is key, and it will (or should) make your relationship with your family stronger and deeper as you build the habit of honest communication.

ESTABLISH CONSEQUENCES

Even if you're a boundary goddess, you can't ultimately control whether your loved one abides by your boundaries. How you handle this really varies on a case-by-case basis, but what is true across the board is that you need to hold that boundary, regardless. If you find yourself in a situation where a boundary has been crossed, you can consider having a follow-up conversation with that person to acknowledge the breach and come to a solution, detaching from the outcome, or limiting contact with this person. Most important is that you continue to set strong and consistent boundaries. If it helps, find an accountability buddy who can help you stick with your boundaries, even when it's difficult.

One caveat here is that abusive people generally do not abide by boundaries (though, obviously, not all people who violate boundaries are abusive). If you find yourself in this or any other kind of unsafe situation, strongly consider no contact, and speak with an expert source to help you through it.

Journal: Boundary Check-In

Boundaries take *practice*, especially with your family. Don't expect to be perfect at it, and be sure to celebrate yourself for putting in the work, which will pay off in all areas of your life. Here are some questions to ask yourself to check in on your progress and see where you might want to consider making some adjustments as you go.

- Have I been setting up walls or boundaries? (Hint: walls will make you feel isolated, whereas boundaries will deepen your relationship.)
- When am I setting boundaries as a reaction?
- Have I clearly communicated my expectations or desires?
- Have I checked in with my nervous system? Am I scared, angry, or vengeful when establishing boundaries? If I'm scared, how am I working with that?
- Will I follow through with consequences when someone violates the boundaries I've set?

Parent Yourself

Now that you have control over your own life, you get to act as the loving, kind, present, compassionate parent that you perhaps once so deeply desired. You've got you—and that's particularly important to remember as you do this work around individuation.

Re-parenting is the process of providing yourself with what you needed but didn't get as a child. The beauty of this practice is that all you need is you; whether your parents are in your life or not, alive or deceased, doesn't matter, because it's not about them. It's about you parenting yourself in the way that you deserved. As this kind, compassionate parent to yourself, one of the most important things is to give yourself permission to feel however you are feeling right now. One of the light-bulb moments I had through my Mother Wound healing process was realizing that sometimes my desire to "heal" was just my desire to be perfect, and to contort myself just enough so that I could be accepted, loved, or seen. That's right: even healing had to lead to perfection—and all the better if it looked perfect in the process. So, I'm here to tell you this: healing is for you. It won't always feel good, and it won't be fun at times, but underlying it should always be the intention for you to love yourself more, not less, as you guide yourself through it.

Chapter 12

RELATIONSHIP STATUS

Lindsey

D o you think he's The One?" my nana asked as we stood chatting in the corner of my parents' kitchen one Christmas.

I was twenty-one, and as you do at that age, I felt like I had learned all that I could learn and knew all that I was supposed to know about life and relationships. "Without a doubt!" I replied with no hesitation whatsoever.

I remember the feeling of those words coming out of my mouth, as if they had escaped without consulting me first. The part of me that said this so confidently was the part that believed whoever I was with at this age was the person I should marry by the time I turned twenty-six. It's the part of me that cruised by red flags "because I loved him" and avoided any opportunity for growth together (because, honestly, I didn't even know what that would look like). My college boyfriend wasn't a bad guy by any means. He was a good person who I believe really cared about me. But, like me, at that age he wasn't equipped with the communication tools, self-awareness, or the ability to emotionally connect when things got hairy in our relationship. Frankly, it's very rare that *any* twenty-one-year-old can do these things—it's more likely they can hit the last cup in beer pong.

By the time my nana and I had this conversation, my boyfriend had been out of college for two years. I planned to move to New York City upon graduation to pursue my acting career while bartending on the side (you already know how that worked out) while he attended business school over an hour away. We felt like we *should* make this work. We *should* navigate this new situation since we loved each other. We didn't realize it then, but our desire for certainty was hindering us. We were "shoulding" ourselves to death, looping through emotions, beliefs, and behaviors that were familiar, which only caused us to exist in a perpetual state of disappointment.

For years after that conversation with my nana, I continued to ignore the part of me that sensed the misalignment in myself, until eventually that part dissociated and took it upon herself to be seen and heard through less desirable means. That's when I cheated on my boyfriend. It was a delusional period of my life, during which I convinced myself that I was justified in seeking what I didn't have in my relationship elsewhere. I was living a complete lie, a double life that slowly wrecked me and would eventually wreck my boyfriend and our relationship too. I had strayed so far—away from him, yes, but also from myself. When my boyfriend found out, I was mortified, snapped out of the delusion, begged for forgiveness, and asked for a chance to make things right. I groveled and cried, grasping for his love and validation as I drifted further and further away from what was true for me. It was as if I was out of body, observing myself like my life was a movie. I felt terrible that I had deeply hurt and betrayed someone I cared about, yes. *And* I knew I had reached a pivotal moment when I could actually come to terms with what was and wasn't working in this relationship and make the hard—but right—decision for myself and let go of it.

And just like that, I was catapulted into what felt like the abyss of singledom at age twenty-four.

If God would have told me then, "Linds, you're going to be single for the next seven years," I think I would have told God, "Hey, man, I'll pass on that." There is so much growth in the in-between, and yet so often our first instinct is to wish it away. It was only after about four years of fighting this season of my life, of trying desperately to find The One, of wondering who I was without my "other half," of shaming myself for how I had handled the breakup, dating to the point of sport, and swimming in the stigma I wrapped myself in (once a cheater, always a cheater, right?) that I finally fully surrendered to being single. Not surprisingly, I was smack-dab in the middle of my Saturn Return when this shift happened, and I entered into my relationship reckoning—a period of time during which I was called (or, rather, *dragged*) into a space where I was able to get really honest about how I was showing up to relationships, what I was settling for, and the types of relationships I truly deserved and desired to cultivate. It's here in this reckoning that we are tested, driven totally crazy, and sometimes brought to our proverbial knees, only to get up slowly, one foot at a time, holding ourselves more centered and clearer than before.

It was an often confusing and sometimes sacred time of my life. In retrospect, I can see how vital this whole experience of singledom and relationship reckoning actually was. Today I view it as such an important, rich period, that I've gone on to start my own program, the Sacredness of Being Single. In our sessions, a group of women gathers together to connect with one another, dive more deeply into relevant topics, ask questions, and journal. The women who join in this circle, most of whom are in their late twenties or early thirties, have expressed a shared sense of an intense pressure to find The One. There's a focus on this seemingly validating milestone in life that catapults us into the next wave of expected milestones: marriage, home, and baby. While the modern woman has certainly challenged this linear life trajectory by prioritizing her career and having a fulfilling, dynamic life of travel, education, exploration, and community, it's still almost impossible to evade the messaging and pressures from media, friends, and family . . . and it can take a toll.

For as much as I once felt alone in my own relationship reckoning, I've seen over the years, and particularly through this group, how we ALL go through this period of in-between. Or at least we should if we want to someday enjoy a more conscious relationship—both with a partner and with ourselves. So if you resonate with this feeling of being in-between, of wanting to know how it's all going to turn out or to create a sense of certainty in your future, and if you feel like you should be moving on to the next phase of your life but you're just not, know that this in-between is exactly where you need to be.

Saturn and Relationship Reckoning

In our mid- to late twenties a question, almost an obsession, takes over most of us: *Who am I meant to be with, and where are they? WHERE ARE THEY?!* I remember living out this question to the point of total exhaustion and frustration. I had zero patience for anyone who had the nerve to say, "Oh, you'll find him soon." Or, my other favorite: "It'll happen when you least expect it." Eighty percent of my daily thoughts somehow came back to finding The One. I was seeking and searching, desperately combing the apps for The One, feeling the incessant urge to look around every public place I found myself in to see if he was around the corner. I'd be picking up tomatoes at the grocery store, while secretly staring at the dude near the onions, hoping he gave me husband vibes. When I was on a date, I looked across the table at the guy on the other side, imagining him meeting my parents and wondering if he'd be a good dad.

Two thumbs down, do not recommend this.

When you spend a date future-tripping rather than being present for who this person is and how they make you feel, you will inevitably buy into a false representation of who they are, one that you create based on what you deem ideal, rather than the truth of what is in front of you. When you walk around looking for validation in human form, hoping to fill the void of what you believe you don't have, you are neglecting to validate yourself and appreciate what you do have. Instead, what you feel you don't have will become your point of attraction, and that means you'll just get more of the not-having.

Your Saturn Return will remind you that you are meant to focus on who you *really are,* not who you feel you need to be in order to be loved. From that centered place of knowing and connection with your own being, you will attract everyone and everything that is meant for you. It (or they) will not miss you. Okay, *okay*—I know! It sounds easy or fluffy when I condense all this into a few sentences, but understand that getting to this place is a process, and it takes commitment—but will eventually become a new way of being.

So how do you know if your Saturn Return is working on your relationships, especially romantic ones?

- If you are currently in a relationship and feel as if you are suddenly seeing it with new eyes, unsure whether this person is The One.
- If you have been single for quite some time and someone comes into your life who: (1) calls you to a more conscious level of operating in relationships, or (2) is the personification of a long-standing pattern you have in relationships that needs to be changed.
- If you hit what feels like a void of hopelessness around your relationship status, and begin questioning everything and feeling like you won't ever find anyone.
- If you are suddenly and unexpectedly thrown into a single season in the wake of a breakup, unprepared and scared, because you thought that this now-ex was The One.
- If you suddenly feel an inordinate amount of pressure to find The One, and perhaps feel like time is running out or you are missing opportunities.
- If a wave of pressure from family, friends, and/or society knocks you off your feet, despite the fact that you have felt pretty good in this single season.

Although Saturn Return generally marks a period of hyperfast, multi-faceted change, the nature of who you are is *always* in a process of being redefined. Think about who you were five years ago or ten years ago! You've learned and changed so much since then. This means that it is inevitable and natural for your intimate relationships to feel the shift too. This can happen at any point, but it tends to be particularly prominent during Saturn Return, for obvious reasons: you're questioning everything and going through rapid-fire transformation on many fronts. Which is exactly what's *supposed* to happen in this season of life. In the throes of my breakup with my college boyfriend, he said to me, "You've changed." At the time, I felt so much shame and guilt for having changed from the person he knew and fell in love with. Looking back, I wish I'd had the awareness to respond "OF COURSE I'VE CHANGED!" It would've been far worse for both of us if I hadn't.

As you change and grow into who you really are, what you desire and require in romantic relationships will become clearer. Thank goodness for that, because I don't know about you, but I had been getting it wrong for so long. How this plays out will look different for all of us: some people may end their relationships, others may strengthen them; some may find a new partner who they feel more aligned with than they have in previous relationships; others may embrace being single in a new way, start to look at dating differently, or redefine what they hope to find in a future partner. All this is part of the relationship reckoning that Saturn offers you during this period.

Pass the Mic

In the longest-running longitudinal study at Harvard, they found that your relationships are the number-one determining factor in how long you're going to live. They are significantly more telling than your diet, your exercise, your sleep habits, and your stress management. All those things that definitely matter. Our relationships are more impactful. It is such a powerful thing for us to focus on. But in our society, we're usually not taught anything about how to cultivate healthy relationships.

—Shawn Stevenson, host of *The Model Health Show*
ALMOST 30, EPISODE 630

"You've Changed . . ."

The real health of a relationship is not determined by how easy the relationship is, but rather how well you're able to stay connected and communicative during growth and change. The truth is that you *must* unsubscribe from the idea that a relationship is the happily-ever-after you see in the movies. You might think that everything good remains frozen in time once that "dream" relationship has been established. But once you can begin to accept the truth that change is inevitable, the roots of the relationship will begin to grow and deepen. So what does change mean for a relationship? Well, sometimes we fight or deny change in relationships—much like I attempted to do with my college boyfriend with disastrous results. Other times, one person changes while the other remains the same, which can be tricky. Ideally, both people in the relationship are open to and embrace change—although even that doesn't mean the changes they're experiencing as individuals are propelling them in the same direction.

A woman named Zoe was in one of my Sacredness of Being Single circles and brought up this exact topic during our Q&A. "I'm in a relationship, so hopefully I'm allowed to be here," she began. We both laughed, and I assured Zoe that, yes, she was absolutely meant to be here regardless of her relationship status. Despite its title, this program is not solely designed for people who are single. In fact, I very much encourage people who are feeling the rumblings of change within their current relationship or who tend to lose themselves within a relationship to join. Zoe went on to share that she had been with her current partner for five years, since they were both twenty-three. It was clear that she loved her boyfriend a lot, but she felt unsure whether the relationship had legs. Recently, Zoe had started therapy and begun incorporating more meditation and other practices that brought her closer to herself. She talked about how she loved the clarity and openness she was experiencing as a result, and that she'd never felt more alive. All good, right? The problem was that Zoe was excited for her boyfriend to try some of these modalities as well so that he could experience what Zoe was. But he *wasn't* so excited about the idea, and Zoe was worried that their relationship wouldn't work if she continued to go deeper on this journey, understanding herself more in the process, without her boyfriend doing the same.

A big part of the issue was that the clarity Zoe had found offered her a better perspective on herself and her relationship. She was suddenly consciously aware of the fact that a sort of autopilot had kicked in, as is often the case in long-term relationships. She could see that she and her boyfriend were locked into a repetitive dance of familiar patterns together, some of which felt good, and others that did not. As it stood now, their relationship depended on these patterns to uphold it—but Zoe had outgrown them. Still, the idea of doing something different and breaking those patterns felt scary, threatening even. Zoe figured that if her boyfriend started doing the same work she was, maybe those patterns would dissolve on their own, easy-peasy, and they could move on to the next stage of their relationship without missing a beat. Ah, wouldn't it be nice if it were this simple?

Despite our feelings of fear around change, it is our soul's desire to experience growth and deepening, not only as individuals, but also in our relationships with one another. But for this to happen, *both* individuals in the relationship must be committed to their own inner exploration, willing to surrender old relationship templates, and to allow new ones to emerge. But let's be honest: this can feel scary. Especially when it involves love. It can feel like *so much* is at stake. So what happens in a situation like Zoe's when one person is willing to change and evolve and the other is not?

Pass the Mic

The more that something means to us, the higher the stakes are, which is why in relationships we hold back so much of ourselves—because we're afraid to lose it.

—Sheleana Aiyana, founder of Rising Woman and
author of *Becoming the One*
ALMOST 30, EPISODE 511

It's hard, but it's also important to remember that it is our responsibility to embody our own work, not to convince others that our way is the best or only way. It is important to stay true to who we are, what we need, and the direction we're called to move in, even when it's not clear how the relationship will weather the shift. After all, the goal here is for *both* people to be the most true and authentic expression of themselves, right? Instead of focusing on how the other person must change, we have to trust that our partner's soul, just like ours, will guide them perfectly, at their own pace, and in their own direction. It is not our job to control that trajectory or timeline. Of course, this is easier said than done. We're always changing, and those changes absolutely *can* stress a relationship—and even end it—when one person wants to break out of the existing patterns and the other does not; or when both want to make changes, but they don't agree on what those changes should be.

Pass the Mic

The most powerful form of intimacy is when you make space for yourself. If you are fully self-expressed with somebody that you are committed to, that you love, and they don't hold that space, then you'll know they're not someone for you.

When you haven't found intimacy and acceptance for yourself and then you do find someone who really loves you, you become attached to that person because you see them as the source of comfort. The relationship isn't a safe haven because in the absence of them, you're going to go straight back to feeling not loved since you haven't found it for yourself.

True intimacy is where I embrace all aspects of myself, all my flaws, all my humanity, all my imperfections, none of which are actually real.

—Peter Crone, The Mind Architect
ALMOST 30, EPISODE 542

Zoe came back with an update the following month. She had walked away from our last session understanding that she had to release her desire to control her partner by convincing him that he should do what she had been doing (and the quiet part: come to want the same changes in their relationships that she did). Instead, Zoe focused on *practicing* all the things that she had been preaching to him about. She committed to practicing honest, vulnerable sharing in the moment, so as to prevent resentment from building. Zoe's energy naturally shifted from wanting to change her boyfriend to living in a more aligned way herself, and with this she was able to more easily trust that if he was meant to remain in her life he would remain, and that if he wasn't, a natural ending would eventually come. Before long, Zoe's boyfriend asked if he could sit with her in meditation one morning, and had been joining her a few times a week since then. He told her that he noticed a difference in how he felt when he did meditate versus when he didn't. This began a really beautiful conversation. Zoe said that he also asked if her therapist would recommend a therapist for him; he was experiencing the positive effects therapy was having on Zoe and was curious to give it a try for himself. Zoe was elated and admitted that it felt really good that he had come to these realizations on his own rather than feeling pressured into them or, even worse, being given an ultimatum. It made Zoe think that the changes he made would actually stick and be as impactful for him as they had been for her.

Zoe's experience is what many of us hope for in a similar scenario. But let's be honest: not all relationships are meant to evolve beyond a certain point. And that's okay, even if it can be painful in the moment. Sometimes your growth and commitment to knowing yourself deeply can be incredibly threatening to a partner. They might feel as though your clarity will expose the parts of them that they need to tend to. They might fear that you're going to leave them, which can lead to a whole host of undesirable dynamics and situations in the relationship. They might feel overwhelmed, like they cannot possibly catch up to you, and therefore avoid any effort in self-improvement or understanding at all. Their ego might feel betrayed by you changing. And more. It can get *messy*.

I've seen in both myself and in other women who I've spoken with over the years, both listeners and guests, that the hardest part of being in a relationship that reaches a crossroads is not abandoning yourself to make the other person feel more secure in the relationship. We've discussed this point before, but it feels particularly relevant and important to highlight here. If you find yourself wanting to self-abandon, it doesn't mean you're broken; it's how you're *built* as a human being. Now of course this doesn't mean you *should* self-abandon, but it does mean it's a natural urge and that being aware of this tendency is helpful; you can recognize the inclination, remind yourself that you are safe and worthy, and make a different choice.

Your responsibility to yourself and your partner is to communicate honestly and consistently, and to release yourself from the feeling that you are responsible for protecting them from feeling whatever comes up for them. It's also important to connect with your soul on a daily basis, whether that's through meditation, journaling sessions, on your morning walk, or whatever else calls to you. Ask your soul to connect with your partner's soul as you move through this transitional season to help ensure that the weight of the relationship working or not working doesn't hinge on human you, and that the outcome is instead based in the highest interest of both of your souls' evolution. It is true that a relationship may very well end because you have reconnected with yourself. Like I was, you may be thrown into a single season that you don't necessarily want or didn't see coming (we'll get into that in a bit). Or, like Zoe, you may move into a more conscious relationship, which should be the goal for all of us, whether that relationship is the one that you're currently in or one that follows later down the road.

What Is a Conscious Relationship?

Here's the thing about conscious relationships: they aren't ever about finding the "right" person who ticks all the boxes. These relationships aren't about a "perfect match" in the traditional, surface sense. Instead, they're about a perfect match on a soul level. This means a symbiotic relationship that generates growth, evolution, and awakening. Know that a conscious relationship can sometimes feel a little uncomfortable, because you are being stretched in a way you haven't been before. The conscious relationship is not something most of us have seen from our parents, in the media, or even in history books. In fact, we have probably witnessed more unconscious tendencies in relationships than conscious ones. Ever observe a romantic relationship dynamic where one partner plays more of a parental role and the other more of a child? I saw this play out between a friend, let's call her Amelia, and her husband, who we'll call Evan. On the surface, they seem to complement each other well, with Amelia assuming a caretaker role and Evan often playing the part of the needy (or less responsible) partner. This dynamic has led to a cycle of dependency, where Evan relies on Amelia to manage not only the day-to-day tasks but also his emotional well-being, while Amelia finds value and self-worth in being needed and taking care of Evan. Neither has fully acknowledged this pattern or its roots in their individual histories. This pattern is *unconscious*.

Even if this concept of conscious relationship feels foreign to you right now, know that when you find this sort of healthy relationship, you'll know it; the difference is impossible not to feel. The hallmark of a conscious relationship isn't necessarily about staying together forever or not—it's about allowing each other to be the truest version of yourselves, to walk your own path, and make your own choices. Whether you and your partner ultimately move in the same direction or not, it's vital that each person makes their own choice in the path forward and stays true to themselves in the process. Conscious relationships are all about creating space for evolution, both for the individuals involved and for the relationship itself.

In conscious relationships:

Giving and receiving are part of the same system. There is a harmony and oneness of giving and receiving that you can feel in conscious relationships. When you give, you are also receiving love, joy, and excitement. And when you receive, you are giving your partner a sense of peace, love, satisfaction, and fulfillment. The two create a circle, with no beginning and no end, no scorekeeping or ultimate goal. Both giving and receiving are part of the life force of a relationship.

Love is unconditional. Conscious relationships are built on unconditional love, which breeds compassion, understanding, and more love. This is pretty clear, eh? But sometimes it's hard to practice. "If he doesn't propose to me by next month, does he even love me?" or "If she can't hang out with my friends more, this relationship is never going to work." Most conditional statements (and the feelings underlying them) indicate a lack of clear communication about one's own desires, dreams, and experience. Instead of communicating, conditions are placed on loving someone. Unconditional love is also experienced by the desire to love someone as they are, not who you want them to be (for all the girlies who love to fix, this one's for you). When you feel yourself placing conditions on a relationship, check in with yourself to understand: *What have you yet to make clear for yourself? What have you yet to communicate with your partner?* If you express your needs and your partner still can't meet them, then you know that the relationship is not for you.

Pass the Mic

Research has shown that couples who have the highest level of thriving are the ones who can engage in spontaneous play. When we saw that research, we wondered: Why spontaneous play? That's different from going to play tennis, where you make an appointment and play a structured game. This is not that kind of play, this is spontaneous play where you don't have a game, you're just playing with each other.

We've figured out why that's possible. Thriving relationships have one feature, and that's safety. If you don't feel safe with your partner, you're not going to be spontaneous and initiate play. You're going to monitor them to see what you can do without getting into trouble. If you're safe, you can walk in the room and say, *Hey, baby, what's cooking?!* and start to spontaneously dance with your partner. If you can't do that, then it raises the question: How are you scaring each other so that you have to figure each other out before you know what you want to say? Neuroscientists have documented that the brain can't be anxious and have fun at the same time.

—Helen LaKelly Hunt, PhD, and Harville Hendrix, PhD,
authors of *Getting the Love You Want*
ALMOST 30, EPISODE 646

Each party takes responsibility. In order to create more of what you want, you must take responsibility and be aware of all that you have created thus far—the good, the bad, all of it. It is so easy to blame the other person for the difficult parts of and moments in a relationship, but you will feel more confident, powerful, and energetically sound when you own what you have created rather than giving your power away through blaming.

Each party feels safe bringing spontaneous fun to the other. Life can throw a lot of serious things your way as a couple. Together, you'll navigate some of the highest highs and lowest lows. But how will you be in the mundane moments? Bringing fun, spontaneous moments to each other is like giving a sweet, unexpected gift to your partner. This sense of fun is communicated through the energy you bring to the relationship. Without words, you are saying that, "In this moment, what matters is our connection and the love and levity it brings to our relationship."

The Single Season

A relationship—much less a conscious one—is not in the cards for all of us during Saturn Return. Being single can feel like an in-between, but it is a sacred time. Hear me out! There is so much pressure to always be *something*, you know? *Be successful, be in love, be on purpose, be healthy, be happy,* be all these things. But what about the in-between? There isn't much praise, recognition, or support in this place. We're taught to hurry out of the in-between, to keep moving in the direction of the thing, the accolade, the title, the reward, the relationship.

But in this season of singleness, when you are in between whatever has come before and whatever will come next, you are being invited into a period of stillness that will allow you to love and let go of so many stories, patterns, and aspects of yourself. A time when you are allowed to celebrate yourself and exactly where you are and everything and everyone that influenced the journey to here. When you allow for this stillness, you'll find that it's a (mostly) gentle, heart-opening experience. But the key word here is *allow*. When you resist the stillness (as so many do), it can become difficult. (For a refresher on resistance and reframing it as expansion, take a look at chapter 2.) I hope that you allow all of you to arrive for this experience. To allow all that comes up to be felt and moved through your being. If you feel the urge to censor or hold parts of yourself back, just notice the temptation and get curious. Release that crusty, stubborn energy that is attempting to stand between who you were and the *you* you want to embody. Resistance makes everything hard, complicated, dramatic, illogical, and unsafe. But resistance loses its power when you take action toward what you really want. First, though, you have to understand the invisible forces that might make taking action more difficult. My hope for you is that you'll seize this in-between time as an opportunity to be with *you* and to explore some aspects of your relationship with yourself.

Journal: Identify the Invisible Forces

Let's begin by getting curious about the invisible forces that might make taking action more difficult.

Early modeling. What type of romantic relationships did you see growing up? Were you privy to healthy, respectful romantic relationships? What power dynamics did you observe in these relationships? How did these relationships make you feel then, and how do they make you feel now? Can you draw a parallel between the patterns you are playing out in your own romantic relationships today and what you saw growing up?

Your relationship to drama. In an honest dialogue with yourself, reflect on whether you expect drama, instability, and chaos in relationships. Do dramatic dynamics feel like home to you? Do you find yourself waiting for the other shoe to drop when things are going well? What about inconsistency feels familiar to you?

Your worthiness. Do you feel worthy of being in a relationship that feels safe and secure? Do you know that you deserve to date someone who respects you, is a healthy communicator, and inspires you to do and be better? What part of you might be afraid of this or simply not used to a healthy relationship? What part of you is not ready to embody these sort of healthy relationship behaviors yourself?

Your trust in yourself. Do you trust yourself to distinguish between what is for you and what is not? Do you doubt your ability to spot red flags? Were you conditioned to doubt or ignore your intuition? Have you been wrong about a feeling before and felt unable to trust how you feel since?

Pressure to be in a relationship. Do you feel as though you're running out of time and cannot be discerning about relationships right now? Do you feel pressure from family and friends to find a partner? Do you feel pressure from societal messaging to be in a relationship? Do you consider being in a relationship a milestone and put pressure on yourself to find one?

Pass the Mic

Beware the initial spark; normally that is our childhood wound. That spark, that feeling of home, I've-known-you-forever kind of thing. It's because that person is your mother, your father, your grandfather.

I would beware of the spark, but don't ignore it. It's not like you have to run the other way, but I think that you do need to get super honest with yourself: What's the thing you need most in relationship? What do you desire? Have a clear idea of what it is that your heart really needs. There's usually one or two things that *really* matter. And if you're not clear on that, then dating gets really muddled.

—John Wineland,
author of *The Art of Masculine Leadership*
ALMOST 30, EPISODE 327

Like so many other facets of life we've discussed in this book, the more you get acquainted with the unconscious behavior that is weaving these experiences into tightly held patterns in your romantic relationships, the more likely you are to recognize them for what they really are in the moment. When you first recognize what you're holding on to and then get clear about how you *desire* to feel, you can begin to consciously make new choices and wire new thoughts and patterns in those moments. The longer you avoid the whispers of your soul to come close and listen, and the taps from your true desires, the more entangled you will be in the strategies of the mind and the more frustrated you will be with the state of your life and relationships.

My hope for you is that if you're feeling some of the resistance I did, you see this time for what it is: potentially the most fruitful part of your life adventure yet. *Yes, really.* Here's the catch, though—you have to make an intentional choice for it to be this.

Your relationship to the unknown is a hallmark of your Saturn Return. Who are you when the path ahead is not clear? Will you be okay with being here now, even though what's to come is unknowable? Will you trust the wisdom within you when the influences around you vie for your attention? What's really cool is that when you start to collaborate with that knowing, with the wisdom of your soul, that deeper part of yourself, you're in a rhythm that creates a magnetism that will honestly change and touch all parts of your life positively—very much including your love life.

Shedding the Shoulds

Maybe you're finding yourself comparing your life to that of the people around you. You have friends getting married, starting families even, and yet it seems like you somehow missed the memo and have no idea how you're going to catch up. Where does this intense anxiety that can accompany being single at thirty come from? You know what I'm talking about:

that nagging judgment and limiting belief that where you are in life is somehow contingent on your relationship status.

I'm convinced that one of the biggest reasons so many of us resist being single is because we're reminded that the opposite is the goal everywhere we look. From so many angles and in so many ways, society (at least in America) has imprinted the idea onto us that being in a relationship is the standard. We are taught to work toward being in a relationship with another person, not to build a better relationship with ourselves. Relationships are a social construct that validates our existence. Ah, to be loved by another! It's hard not to believe that's the ultimate goal when we are bombarded with hype around Valentine's Day, romantic comedies, dating and marriage reality TV shows, engagement ring bling all over our Instagram feeds, and so much more—it's everywhere! How many brands would be out of business if we all were to prioritize our relationship with ourselves first, to truly know that we don't need anything or anyone to complete us? But instead, we desperately want to claw ourselves out of this single season by any means possible, which can result in a whole host of circumstances that lead us further away from who we really are rather than closer (which is one of the most beautiful gifts that being single has to offer). In our quest to get out of this in-between we aren't present with ourselves, date unconsciously, get into relationships that aren't aligned or with a true soul partner, and so much more. We miss out on the opportunity to potentially notice: *Hey! I really* like *being single.* Or better yet, *I really love being with me.*

The most effective way out of this pressure cooker, to see how ridiculous it actually is, is to identify your shoulds. The mind latches on to these shoulds in order to find a pathway to more comfort, even though that might sound counterintuitive, because these shoulds can be really frustrating to ruminate on. But the other option is to lean into what is now and get curious and close to your feelings, desires, and fears. This will bring on growth, discomfort, and change, which the mind is not going to willingly consent to. Latching on to an idea like "I *should* be married with kids by now," for example, puts you on a path of searching for what you've seen others create for themselves to achieve a seemingly comfortable life. But what if your path is different? What if it zigs and zags a bit so that you can unlock or heal parts of yourself that will allow more of the true you to be out there in the world, to be attracting people and experiences that bring you more life and expansion, rather than just comfort? The natural unfolding of your life, getting and being everything you want and more, is dependent upon your willingness to explore your inner world. This is a daunting task, especially if you haven't taken a peek underneath the hood in a while—or ever.

As you probably know by now, Saturn Return won't let you avoid your internal world any longer. Your relationships of every variety ALL require you to have a deep awareness of your inner landscape in order to connect, communicate, and love in a real way. Going inward is not a delay or detour. *In fact, I believe it is a superhighway to the relationship you desire and the success you are striving toward.*

Getting to know your shoulds more intimately will free you from the trap of living for the acceptance of others and society in general. Unfortunately, this is not just as easy as saying, "I release this" and *poof!* All that shoulding is magically gone. Most of our shoulds are so tangled up in our being that letting go of them is an inherently slow and steady process, one that must be undertaken with patience and compassion. It's so worth it though, because your shoulds are most likely not yours, which means they don't serve you. You're only holding on to them because you tried them on, like you would an old blazer in your mom's closet, and haven't taken them off yet. Then, before you know it, your life, how you show up, and how you feel about yourself and your relationship status all revolve around that damn blazer!

Be on the lookout for shoulds like:

- I'm [insert age], I *should* be in a relationship by now.
- I *should* be dating because all my friends are.
- I *should* be married with kids; my sister was at my age.

- I *should* be on more dating apps to increase my chances of meeting someone.
- I *should* tone down my personality so that I don't intimidate or turn off my date.
- I *should* be fully healed in order to be in a relationship.

Sit with a should that you've believed for a while now. Relax your mind and bring your conscious awareness to your heart space, as if you are taking an elevator ride down to your chest. Say the should out loud to yourself. Notice who or what experience begins to come forward. Have you seen this play out over and over in your own life? Do you see this should everywhere you go, every time you scroll? Once you pinpoint where the should originates from, can you imagine that you are taking it off—even just temporarily? Shake out your body and release any sound that wants to come up as you remove the weight of that pressure from your psyche. Once you feel complete, return to stillness and notice how you feel.

Now let's now try on a truth for size. Instead of "I *should* be married with kids by now," how about looking at the issue from a more expansive angle, like: "My path to where I am now has been so purposeful; I trust that I will meet all that I desire in perfect timing." Or, "I'm really looking forward to when I am married and have kids; at the same time, I have deep gratitude and trust for where I find myself now. I am on my path."

At first you might roll your eyes at this exercise or feel like you don't believe what you're saying. This is totally normal. If you've believed something else for so long, it might take a bit of practice to recognize truth and soften into the fact that, yes, you are most definitely on your path. Notice when your mind wants to stay stuck on a loop of adversity and misfortune. The mind loves a merry-go-round, because it gives it something to do. From this point forward, every time you notice the merry-go-round starting to spin, make a conscious effort to connect with truths from your heart. You'll know them because they feel like peace, comfort, and remembrance, rather than pressure and anxiety.

There's more. In order to take on what's really true and finally embody it, you need to address the fear beneath the should. Think of the fear as the root of the should, the feeling that keeps it anchored in the ground. You want to extract this root so that you can see and understand the complex root system that has held this belief so firmly for so long. This is critical because fear makes it difficult to operate from your center, which makes it really hard—if not impossible—to attract anything from an authentic, grounded place.

In another Sacredness of Being Single session, a woman named Nikki shared that she had recently broken up with her boyfriend of six years. She said it was the hardest decision she's ever had to make because she thought they were going to get married. But after going to therapy, both individually and together, and doing a lot of inner work, Nikki realized that while their relationship had been purposeful for a time, it was no longer supporting her growth. Nikki described an immediate feeling of regret once she broke off the relationship.

Not only had Nikki expected to marry her boyfriend, everyone else had expected them to get married as well—especially her parents. The shock of others made Nikki feel insecure about her decision, and she ended up calling her ex shortly after the breakup to tell him she had made a mistake. Confused and frustrated, Nikki's ex asked her not to contact him for a while, because he was still hurting and didn't want to engage in a back-and-forth when she had been so undeniably sure of her decision just a couple weeks before. Nikki recalls feeling so grateful her ex didn't engage beyond that point, because it forced her to feel what was actually coming up. Looking back, she says, "I truly believed that we should get married because we'd been together for so long, because I was in my thirties, because my parents loved him, because there wasn't anything glaringly 'wrong' with him." Can you hear all those shoulds? As we talked through it, Nikki got down to the root of why she had tried to hang on, even after she understood the relationship wasn't for her in the long run: she was afraid that she wouldn't find anyone who would love all of her and that she would end up being single for her whole life. I think we've all felt like this before, and it's not a good feeling. But it's also not truth. It's fear.

Once Nikki separated truth from fear, she was able to see the situation more clearly once again. She could acknowledge that her ex didn't challenge her in healthy ways and seemed to be on relationship autopilot. She went on to say that her commitment to her inner work has been the biggest blessing and has also shown her parts of herself she's afraid to share with a partner, in case she scares them away. As we talked through all this, it dawned on Nikki that this fear had actually been the missing link in her relationship: the safety and ability to be *all* of who she is, to be witnessed in her process and growth and loved and accepted every step of the way. When Nikki acknowledged and sat with it, the fear actually *revealed* what she had yet to experience in a relationship. Once she realized it was possible to call in a partner who made her feel safe and secure, I saw her body relax and her mind take a break from the merry-go-round of untruths she had been living with.

I heard someone use this acronym for fear, and it really stuck with me:

F alse
E vidence
A ppearing
R eal

I remind myself of this a lot when I'm feeling fear creep into my life and impact my decisions. Your mind will fabricate stories and evidence to prove to you that taking the risk, being vulnerable, putting yourself out there is not the best choice. Sometimes it's just easier to believe in the worst-case scenario than to muster up the courage to *try* something new, because it keeps us comfy where we are. But I believe that our conscious relationships—whether in the present or calling to us from the future— ask us to trust our *tries;* they are the keys that unlock more and more of who we are, which ultimately serves to build a solid foundation for a relationship of any kind.

Dating Yourself

Just as important as ridding yourself of what other people think you *should* do when it comes to relationships is getting up close and personal with what you actually want. I've found dates with myself to be a huge (and fun!) tool for understanding my own wants and needs better.

Dating yourself means scheduling dedicated time to do something you might normally do with another person solo, like going to dinner or a show. The chosen activity should invoke joy just thinking about it, excite you to some extent, and it might make you nervous too. Often it's that thing you've been meaning or wanting to do, but haven't had time for or have been waiting for someone else to do with you. Yes, it will probably feel a bit outside of your comfort zone at first. But don't worry, honey—this is a sweet spot. You are being called to be what you need in those moments, to find joy and pleasure in what is in front of you, to allow the truth that arises from your heart to envelop your being in these moments of enjoying on your own.

If you're not sure what this solo venture should entail, here are some of my favorite ideas. Try them out or use them to spark some ideas of your own!

- Take a leisurely trip to the farmers' market to buy flowers for yourself and ingredients for a nourishing dinner.
- Enjoy a picnic in the park or on the beach with a book, a journal, and some tunes.
- Reserve a spot at the bar of a restaurant (or even a table!) for dinner for one. Put your phone away and take it all in: the sounds, the sights, the smells, and the tastes.
- Take a fun, creative class to learn pottery, painting, cooking, or something else you've been wanting to try.
- Get "lost" in your own town. Explore shops, neighborhoods, restaurants, and landmarks that you haven't soaked in before.

- Attend a performance or event that interests you, like a show at a theater or art gallery.
- Take a day trip to a local destination to explore and play tourist.

Practice: Date Yourself

Once you have your destination in mind, it's time to focus on getting yourself in the right mindset and heart space to make this event just as special as—or even *more* special than—any other date. Here are some tips to set yourself up for presence and joy as you date yourself:

1. **Start simple.** Let's not overcomplicate this solo date—especially the first one. Minimize the mental hurdles, and make planning and committing to the date really doable.

2. **Set an intention.** Starting with an intention will change your experience because intention has the magical ability to imbue your experience and connections with whatever it is you desire to feel. Wayne Dyer said it beautifully in his book *The Power of Intention*: "When you're connected to the power of intention, everywhere you go, and everyone you meet, is affected by you and the energy you radiate. As you become the power of intention, you'll see your dreams being fulfilled almost magically, and you'll see yourself creating huge ripples in the energy fields of others by your presence and nothing more."

3. **Prioritize joy.** Choose an experience that brings you joy. The energy of joy will create a buffer between you and any anxious, looping thoughts. Allow yourself to soften into the simple joys of what you plan for yourself.

4. **Mark the date on your calendar in advance.** Make sure this time is scheduled formally, just like you would do for any other commitment.

5. **Plan, but also allow for spontaneity.** Strike a balance of structure and space for your solo date. Allow the structure to support you through moments of doubt and discomfort, and the space to conjure latent joy, creativity, and curiosity.

6. **Limit time on your phone.** It might be tempting to numb the initial discomfort of a solo date with scrolling, but I promise you that the feeling will pass more quickly if you allow yourself to be with what's there in the moment. Bring your eyes to your surroundings, and open your heart and awareness to the little signs around you that will remind you of how special this time with yourself really is.

7. **Engage with people.** The point of a solo date is not to isolate yourself. I encourage you to be open to conversation and connection wherever you are—and, of course, always use discretion! Expect synchronicities and surprises.

8. **Keep a record of your experience.** While I recommend limiting your phone time, I do think that having a record of this experience is a beautiful thing to look back on. So take a selfie, record a voice memo, or bring your journal. Capture your emotions, thoughts, and the sensory elements of the experience at any point.

When the time for your date arrives, remember that it's okay if you feel a bit awkward or uncomfortable at first. You are doing something new, and just like any other date (well, *some* other dates), this is the start of something special. Soon your discomfort and doubt will dissolve, and I'm willing to bet that this will become a ritual you naturally gravitate toward to recalibrate and spark soul connection. Allow yourself to feel all that comes up throughout the process, because it's a necessary and powerful part of this experience.

Know that this practice will be integral when you next decide to be in a relationship as well, because there is no better way to return to your own energy than by taking yourself out on a date. When you're in a relationship, taking the time and space to recalibrate your own energy (rather than existing in a sometimes-confusing combination of your and your partner's energy) will liberate you from codependent tendencies, help you communicate with your partner from a more grounded place, and provide clarity about anything that might be causing confusion or frustration in the relationship. Think of it as a car wash for your relationship: a date with yourself will bring a sense of newness and sparkle to your relationship.

Pass the Mic

We're learning how to come home to ourselves and regain our innocence to see ourselves as whole and innocent. And to be able to see others in that same way, while also holding our own boundaries; being able to be in a relationship with another person while also staying in yourself. By building this core relationship to ourselves, we're actually making it possible to have a conscious relationship with another.

When we are in ourselves, we are choosing relationships from a place of self-love, not from our wounding, not from our defenses, not from our fears. We're freeing up so much energy in our bodies to be creative, to be innovative, to be giving, to be generous, to share, and that is what makes this world better.

—Sheleana Aiyana, founder of Rising Woman and
author of *Becoming the One*
ALMOST 30, EPISODE 574

You Are the Sun

Toward the tail end of my single season, I started to attract people who were more and more aligned with what I knew I deserved. My relationship reckoning allowed me the time and space to walk back to myself and get crystal clear about what I desired in a partner. I now believed that I was worthy of respect, clear communication, vulnerability, support, intimacy, unconditional love, and FUN. Those beliefs became my point of attraction and *boom*! I began to have a different experience.

What was so cool about this new wave of connections was that each one showed me that something I hadn't experienced before was possible. I remember sitting across from this guy, Jay, who was so present and interested in knowing more about me. His questions were thoughtful, and his ability to listen made me feel so safe and seen. I remember thinking, "I love this about him." Though Jay wasn't a romantic fit, I was grateful to experience this quality in a person and to feel the impact it had on me. I knew this was something I valued and wanted in a person. So when my now-husband Sean came back into my life, I was already attuned to and very clear on how I wanted to feel in a relationship and the specific qualities I was looking for, which meant I was able to immediately recognize these things in him. Rather than searching out things that would turn me off like I had done so many times in the past, I was now super-centered and present, and could easily feel how his presence and way of connecting made me feel. For the first time in a long time, I didn't second-guess such a strong feeling because I also trusted myself, thanks to cultivating an unbreakable connection with myself during my single season. I went from bullishly resisting this single season of my life to dating myself, respecting myself, and knowing myself so deeply that from the moment Sean and I reconnected, I knew with full confidence that we would be together forever.

If you find yourself in the middle of a relationship reckoning during your Saturn Return, take a deep breath and remember that this time is *meant* to rock some of your relationships as you are called to step into your own authenticity. Know that while some relationships in your life may be knocked out of their orbit, it's so that your center can serve as a gravitational pull for new ones.

When moving through any type of transitional period, it can feel like parts of you are dying, and this is especially true when those transitions involve relationships. It's true that you may very well be letting go of parts of yourself to evolve—and you may even be letting go of other people or ways of relating as part of that evolution. But always remember that who you *really* are is never, ever lost. Don't give anyone or anything that much power. Surrender to the ebb and flow of your relationships and allow this movement to show you what is true and what is not, who is aligned with your life and who is not.

Chapter 13

FRIENDSHIP 2.0

Krista

My understanding of friendship came from shows like *Sex and the City*, which I used to watch after school, belly down on the carpet and eyes glued to the screen. Not sure how it felt like I was relating to the thirty-plus-year-old women on the show, but somehow this teenage girl from Ohio felt *seen*. Even as a high school kid, I pondered how Carrie, a self-proclaimed struggling writer, made enough money to afford both her shoe addiction and that massive, historic brownstone Upper East Side apartment. But when I myself experienced the friendship wake-up call of my Saturn Return in my twenties, I realized that her shoe collection wasn't the most unrealistic part of the show: the friendships were.

Together, the four main characters of the show, Carrie, Charlotte, Miranda, and Samantha, formed this unbreakable-bond friend group that lasted through trials, tribulations, and *time*. They were best friends for years without much rupture. The *Sex and the City* women were seemingly immune to the scheduling horrors my friends and I experienced when trying to get together (if it's not on the calendar it's not happening!). Their work schedules never seemed to get in the way, their long-term loves seemed to work seamlessly into the fold, and their group brunches were never disrupted, even when Miranda had a kid and moved out of Manhattan! No matter what, these four women seemingly always had the energy, time, and love for one another. None of their transitions seemed to breach the armor of their incredibly solid friendship. It all seemed so easy, everything felt fluid and clear.

Then there was *Girls*—the raunchier, more approachable, and way more realistic version of female relationships that appeared later in our lives. The show and its characters were messy and complicated. Listening to their conversations, it's like the scenes never felt fully complete. But the murkiness of the relationships in the show was what made it so good. I think the most powerful thing *Girls* did wasn't just show what a real woman's body was like, it was showing that friendships, even the good ones, are not immune to rupture. The cringe I felt watching *Girls* was a reflection of the discomfort I've felt in my own friendships. It showed that friendships are often contextual (hello, college sorority), and that this is especially true in our twenties. As we grow into adulthood during Saturn Return, we often move past the friendships of convenience that dominate our younger years. In the show's final season, we see a group of women who have changed completely. They are now all incompatible, and their relationships are fractured beyond repair. It's not a happy ending exactly, but it's reality. This happens, and it's time we normalized the seasonality of our friendships.

And yet, when a friendship breaks up, we don't really understand how to process or recognize it in the same way we do romantic relationships.

Despite the fact that the vast majority of us will have far more friends than spouses or romantic partners throughout the course of our lives, there's still no real public discourse on friendship. You don't hear a lot of people talking about how devastating it can be when you begin to feel distant from a friend who's on a different life trajectory, getting married to her high school sweetheart, and settling into her starter home while you're living in the big city and Taco Tuesday-ing it up with your new crew.

Friendships change, and sometimes they even end. This will be the case throughout your life, and it will quite likely be the case during Saturn Return as your path begins to diverge from those of your friends. That's natural and it's okay—but it still hurts. And just because this is normal, it doesn't mean that the world at large will understand how to support you through that pain. Unlike romantic relationships, when a friendship breaks up, there's a lot of gray area. There's not necessarily a plan to follow. There are fewer songs to listen to, fewer books to read, and certainly not the public outpouring of sympathy. It's hard to know how to respond to yourself (*Is a trip to Bali too much?*), and other people in your life almost certainly won't have a script for how to support—or acknowledge—the pain you're in. It might be more difficult to articulate (or even understand) why the friendship is coming to an end. The situation usually doesn't feel very cut and dried, and there might also be a sense of shame, no matter how unwarranted.

Pass the Mic

Adult friendship is so hard because we learn how to be friends when we're little, and the main reason why you become friends with someone is because of proximity. Your friendships have ebbed and flowed based on the patterns in your life.

We underestimate how much proximity and being physically near somebody creates friendships. Yes, there's the energy thing. Yes, there's the values. Yes, you click with some people and you don't click with others. But understand that it is also about patterns, it's about proximity, and that the second you change a job, your friendships will change, period. It does not mean that you don't care about those people anymore.

The thing that has helped me the most is reminding myself that just because I don't see these folks that I used to see all the time doesn't mean I'm not friends with them. When I see them on social media, it stings a little because I'd like to be with them, but I can't allow myself to go that step further and bash myself and allow myself to feel somehow separate or not included, because it's not true. I think that's the part that we play personally in adult friendship that makes it hard, is that we look around and say, "Something's wrong with me."

—Mel Robbins, author of *The High 5 Habit*
ALMOST 30, EPISODE 595

If you feel any of this, I hope this chapter can be your guide for dealing with friendship breakups, understanding why they're so painful, and perhaps working to guard some of your friendships from breaking up along the way. We'll guide you through new ways to perceive and reevaluate your friendships—and how to have the hard but necessary conversations to help your friendships thrive, or release those that are no longer aligned for you as you evolve.

Saturn Return and Friendship

Because Saturn can confront any uncomfortable truths lying beneath the surface and reveal anything that is inauthentic or out of alignment, friendships will feel the effects. Relationships, families, and friendships are a HUGE area of transition throughout our life, and *especially* during this period. Love is love, baby, and misalignment is what it is, so all connections and bonds are up for review. Most important, Saturn Return is a time of significant endings and beginnings, and relationships are a major part of that.

How your friendships fare during Saturn Return really depends on three things: the strength of the relationship, how well you and your friend know each other and, most important, how well you each know yourselves. If you go through Saturn Return while remaining pretty close to who you have been up to this point *and* if that's also the case for your friend, your relationship will be more likely to survive. But in other cases, you may start to feel slightly uncomfortable, like your relationship is suddenly somehow "off," or there might even be a big blowout you never saw coming. Maybe there's an imbalance in the effort being put into the friendship and things feel one-sided, or perhaps you're being pulled in another direction in life and now have the confidence to actually move on. If any of this feels true to you, know that no matter how hard it can be to see a friendship change or even end, friendships should be about alignment, authenticity, and reciprocity.

On a positive note, since Saturn Return is a great moment for self-discovery, it offers you an opportunity to get to the core of what you truly want in your friendships. You are being presented with an opportunity to redefine what friendship means to you and (perhaps, finally!) have those reciprocal, loving friends who cheer you on, are there when you need them, and love all your quirks. While this might require you to navigate some choppy waters and shed a few tears (and maybe have a few less bridesmaids than you previously intended), you will be more whole and more satisfied in your friendships in the end. I remember feeling shame and guilt that I had friendships that were transitioning during this time period, and I wish I could tell that version of myself now that it was all a part of the plan, and that better, more aligned relationships were on the way as I became more aligned with myself!

As you navigate Saturn Return, remember a few things. First, know that there is no such thing as one friend for all things. It's important to honor the strengths of your friends and to have compassion for their shortcomings. Rather than getting angry in those moments when a friend can't give you what you need, consider the fact that perhaps YOU can give yourself that thing, or that another beautiful friendship—either currently in your life or coming down the pipeline in the future—can. Whenever we put too much pressure on one person, it's hard to connect and grow together. Remember, wounds can be portals to a deeper understanding of *yourself,* and when healed, a highway to inner peace and positive manifestation. Most important, remember that all change isn't bad, and maybe this period is leading you away from lackluster, inauthentic relationships toward the thriving girl gang of your dreams.

The Friendship Audit

As Saturn Return allows you to get clear about where your friendships currently stand, a friendship audit can supercharge your process. I know the word "audit" might seem a little sterile, but it's just a way of bringing a method to the madness as you take the time to review all the relationships in your life. It's an opportunity to consciously evaluate your current relationships and how they feel, how they are supporting you, and whether or not you want to continue to invest in them moving forward. It's a way to see the landscape of your friendships more clearly and to recognize any that may not be in your highest alignment or reflect your deepest potential. Once you understand this, you can adjust your relationships consciously, rather than waiting until things either blow up or fizzle out.

I know it might sound a little weird at first, but I like to organize my friendships from a quasi-hierarchical perspective. When you stop and think about it, you're probably already doing this—there's a reason why the terms "best friend" and then "good friend" exist, rather than a specific person. We all naturally, but usually subconsciously, create ways of organizing our relationships. What I'm offering just makes this organizational process conscious, which can be a powerful practice. Harvard can back me up, since their renowned happiness study (based on a model by Aristotle) shows that there are three main friendship types—utility friendships, friendships based on pleasure, and "perfect" friendships—but we'll do an updated version here.[36] Getting clear about what type of friendships you're in and which ones fill you up will help you understand how to use your time and energy the most wisely. *Especially* now, as you need all the support you can get moving through Saturn Return. Now more than ever, it's good to know who is on your roster of ride-or-dies.

To be clear, this is not an exercise in judgment, but in expectation-setting. I think you'll find that this structure is more freeing than it initially sounds, because it will alleviate some of the expectations you have for friendships that just can't hold you in the way you need. Unconscious expectations can create resentment, confusion, and misunderstanding. When expectations aren't met, they can ruin even the strongest of friendships. But on the other hand, you will also gain more clarity about which friendships you want to pour more of yourself into.

I encourage you to approach this audit as a way of thinking about the depths of intimacy each of your friends has access to, and to what lengths you will go for them. What expectations do you have for them, and they for you? Who can you go to for what? Who will pick you up from the airport or answer their phone when you call in the middle of the night? Who is your party friend? What friend do you walk with once a week or month? When you think this through, chances are you'll realize there are some friendships you can allow to ebb and flow naturally. During some seasons, these friendships are on, and during others, they're off. Other friendships might give you pause and lead you to question whether they're living up to what you want and expect them to be.

Journal: Friendship Audit

Are you ready? As honestly as you can, I want you to go through each of your meaningful friendships, both old and new, and ask yourself these questions. Don't answer how you think you *should* or how you might have responded a few years ago. Consider each of these questions in terms of how your friendship exists today.

- What does my ideal friendship with [insert friend] look like?
- How do I feel in my current relationship with this person?
- In what ways do we support each other?
- When there is conflict, how do we resolve it?
- How would I describe this friendship in a few words?
- How does this friend help me to grow and evolve?

Once you've worked through your answers, I want you to organize each friend into one of the following friend categories.

FRIENDS WHO ARE THERE FOR . . .

A Good Time: These friends make your life fun, and their presence can be intoxicating, but they're not the ones you want to call when you're going through a breakup or get laid off from your job. They just can't swim in the deep end of the pool with you. You can enjoy seeing them when you're out and commenting on their European vacation photos on Instagram, but don't expect too much from them. It's great that you can have fun together, but that doesn't necessarily mean the friendship can go the distance!

The Long Time: These are the hometown friends from growing up who just get you in a way most people won't. At this point in life, you probably don't speak to them often, but when you do it feels like no time has passed. They may not be the first person you call, and you may not call them when you're in need, but you love the connection for the fun and nostalgia it offers. These friends will help you recall and remember random details about your childhood home, will remember your landline phone number, and won't let you forget your most cringeworthy younger moments—but they won't be as in tune with the most recent version of you. College friends might also fall into this category for some of you. These are friends who understand a certain version of you that might not reflect where you are today. You know and love these friends, but at this point you only see them once or twice a year at bachelorette parties and weddings, where you reminisce and laugh about late nights and old times.

The Nine-to-Five: These are the people who you love and bond with between the hours of nine and five Monday through Friday. They'll see you go through things most other people in your life won't, and because you spend so much time together, they just might be the ones you would expect to go deeper more quickly with. But these friendships sometimes end at the office.

The Rocky Road Time: You're navigating some rocky times with these friends but still aren't fully ready to let go. Maybe you've been through a lot or tend to have really high highs or low lows in your friendship. These friendships are meaningful, but the relationships aren't stable—at least at this point. That makes it difficult to establish any sort of solid expectations beyond to expect the unexpected. Anyone who falls into this category is likely someone you should consider breaking up with. You may have an "off" feeling about them and are left unsure if you had fun or just feel drained at the end of a hangout sesh . . . but there are enough moments of connection that you continue to stick around.

ALL the Times: These are your besties. I can imagine you're smiling as you read this, because we all love the besties, and life would be a much lonelier, less colorful place without them. Even as a full-blown adult it feels so tender to say the word "bestie." These are the friends who you have reciprocated love for, who you expect to return your calls (and do the same for, in turn), have hard conversations with, and who are as honest and understanding with you as possible at all times. You are willing to invest in them, develop intimacy, and perhaps even align your future with theirs. They receive your utmost care and attention (because they deserve it!), and know their role and place in your life.

Once you have spent time in reflection, found clarity, and finished your audit, notice if your friends actually fit into the category you think of them as belonging to or if the friendship has shifted over time. For example, it can be easy to perpetually think of Hometown Friends as Besties, even if that's not actually the case at this point in life. This is great information to have, because it allows you to adjust your expectations accordingly. Where are there opportunities to have deeper conversations, to surrender to what is, or even let a friendship go?

I recommend revisiting this audit yearly. It's okay and natural for friendships to ebb and flow between categories. Seasons change, and so do your friends. During this season in particular, expect things to shift, but trust that these shifts are ultimately for the better.

FRIENDS TO THE END?

As you do your audit you might realize that some of your friendships have expired. Obviously, the Tough Times friends are a prime category to look at when it comes to friendship breakups, but whether during or outside of Saturn Return it goes without saying that friendships can end for any number of reasons—whether you want them to or not. Sometimes there are some cut-and-dried reasons . . . and sometimes there aren't. But when I sit back and think about some of the reasons my own friendships have broken up, as well as the stories women in the Almost

30 community have shared with me, I can identify a few of the more common categories that lead to a friendship's demise. So, in addition to categorizing your friendships, it's also important to consider the current state of your relationship. Can you relate to (or are you in) any of these friendship scenarios?

The Drifter: This is the friend who you've drifted away from naturally, whether because of a move, a job, or a change in relationship or parenthood status for one or both of you. This friendship is with someone you love, but the bonds are simply no longer strong enough to keep you in contact regularly. Life just *happened*.

The Lateral: The Lateral friend and you both realize that you're growing in different directions, and now have different interests and desires. You still respect and love each other, but one or both of you are in a place where you no longer invest in friends who don't align with your core interests. Maybe she's continuing to drink and you're on your sober curious journey, or you're exploring inner child work and she's still playing childish games. Whatever the reason is, you're moving along in life, just in different directions.

The Hot and Heavy: We usually talk about hot and heavy situations in the context of romantic relationships, but they can happen in friendships too! This is when you and a friend connect quickly—platonic sparks are flying and you're obsessed with each other. Initially, at least, because friendships like this sometimes end as quickly as they start. It might have felt like you met your new bestie, but a lot of times these friendships are built on trauma bonds and burn out as quickly as they ignite. Unfortunately, hot and heavy friendships often end in drama and might include gossiping, betrayal, fighting, or other behaviors you're either not proud of or that it hurts to be on the receiving end of.

The One-Sided Friendship: These friendships are built around a pattern of one friend constantly pouring energy, attention, and emotion into the relationship while the other sits back and has their cup filled. The effort you can put into even your most important friendships ebbs and flows over time, and that's okay! There might be periods where you or your friend carry more of the effort based on life circumstances—but this should be a phase, not a pattern, and overall the friendship should balance out to much closer to fifty-fifty over time.

The Fixer-Upper: These friendships have some issues that need to be addressed. You've likely tried to explore how to fix these issues only to find you just don't have the tools to repair the rupture and mend the friendship so that you can come back together again.

There are plenty of other reasons why friendships can break up too, because life is really complicated. If you're on the brink of or recovering from a friendship breakup that fits into one of these scenarios or any other, remember that this is your viewpoint of the relationship. It's human nature to believe that we've been the best friend in the world while the other partner was mean/neglectful/distant/insert adjective. But remember that your friend may have a different perspective from yours—to the point that they might believe the friendship ended for totally different reasons from what you do.

When you're at a point where a friendship is ending, remind yourself that you don't have to be *right*, and you also don't have to agree on the reasons why the friendship is coming to an end. The important thing is to extract the lessons you can from this friendship, honor yourself, and remain as compassionate as possible toward this person who was once important to you.

Trust the seasons of your life. Remember that you—and your friends—are meant to change.

The Breakup

Maybe you're on the precipice of a breakup, maybe it's happened already, or maybe you're still thinking about Nina from eighth grade. Maybe you've tried to create change with this friend, or maybe you haven't, but either way you're at the point where you know the friendship can no longer continue. Maybe they weren't there for you when you really needed them (like when you had a blowout with your parents over Christmas break), or maybe they've just been draining your energy lately. Whatever the case is, my dear one, I must tell you that there are no villains and no heroes in this game of conscious awakening during your Saturn Return.

Pass the Mic

Every time you get triggered, you have a deep learning opportunity. I have people who will say, "I thought I was healed, but I got triggered the other day." Healing is not getting rid of triggers. Triggers are warning signs. Triggers are these beautiful radars that say, "Hey, when the world has looked like this, or I've felt like this, it has led to betrayal, pain, abuse, trauma, whatever it might be."

The trigger is telling you to pay attention. The healing of a trigger is actually when you observe it, you acknowledge it, and you respond from it.

—Mark Groves, founder of Create the Love
ALMOST 30, EPISODE 496

The breakup of a female friendship can feel as painful as if our mother were abandoning, rejecting, or not loving us. In fact, there's even a name for this, which is Sister Wound. This refers to the fact that our female relationships often trigger the same fears and longings that we experienced with our own mother. We can subconsciously project some of the old pain and trauma we felt in our relationship with our mother onto our friends. This is a tricky dynamic, obviously, but it also offers us a way to process and heal old wounds. Friendship breakups that trigger the Sister Wound can hit us from both a somatic and energetic perspective. This is big stuff and also painful stuff. Whether you or the other person is initiating it, the breakup of a friendship can leave you feeling lost, confused, sad, depressed, angry, ashamed, and feeling guilty. You might find yourself replaying certain moments in your head on repeat and the shoulds could kick in: *I should have said that* or *I should have done this*.

You might discover that you're left with more questions than answers. Whether the outside world understands it or not, it's important to approach this breakup just as seriously as you would any heartbreak so that you can support yourself in healing.

Whether you are on the receiving end of the breakup or the one doing the dumping, I hope that you can find some peace and clarity around it and know that it's ultimately the right choice by better understanding when it's time to break up.

In addition to the scenarios we've already discussed in this chapter, you also know it's time to break up a friendship when:

Your values no longer align. Your goals and priorities can change, but your values will always stay the same. Those values are there to help guide you through life following a consistent thread. They are what people will see you as and remember you by. If a friendship makes you question, compromise, or violate your values or is out of alignment with them, in some cases it may be worth a conversation. But it may very well be time to move on if you find that your values don't jibe once you've clarified yours.

You feel lonely in the relationship or like you can't be yourself. One of Saturn Return's primary goals is to help you become more emotionally mature. This maturation process and the healing it involves may result in a feeling of loneliness, even in the presence of people who used to feel like good company. You might find yourself feeling disconnected from your friends. Maybe they connect through gossip, and that's no longer your jam, or you're just not feeling it like you used to. Regardless, we should seek relationships where we feel less alone, more connected, and more ourselves, so finding those friends who you can really be *you* with is the key.

You make excuses for your friend. Telling yourself (or someone else), "Oh, that's just how Amanda is," after she proceeds to get blackout drunk and yell at you for something that's irrelevant is a sign it's time to move on. Yes, you can accept people as they are and find freedom in surrendering to what is, but you also need to notice when you find yourself repeatedly making excuses for a friend's bad behavior.

You feel bored or drained in the friendship. I know that "bored" may seem a little harsh when it comes to reasons for a breakup, but relationships are here to support and serve you in positive ways. Life is too short to spend time with people who don't allow you to be who you really are or to achieve maximum vibrancy. If you find yourself drained, it could be a sign that you're out of your authenticity or around someone who is taking more energy than you're receiving in return.

You've outgrown the relationship. This is probably the most common reason I've seen for people ending a friendship during Saturn Return. Even if it doesn't feel good, it's okay and normal if you are simply no longer seeing this relationship as a place where you can be who you want to be.

Gaslighting or abuse is involved. If you've been in a situation where you've been gaslit or abused previously in your life, this kind of behavior may feel familiar to you, but during your awakening it will become more difficult to stomach and pretend that everything is okay. Use this contrast as the chance to become even more free from these patterns and ways of being. And if you're unsure about the situation or what type of behavior you're dealing with, working with a therapist can help you spot and then heal from this type of dynamic.

When you start to lean in to consciously choosing your relationships and what you want to feel like within them, everything shifts. It is such an empowering experience and—believe it or not—even an addictive feeling! The feeling of being the person you want to be, of living out the ways in which you see yourself as a powerful, heart-centered person who is clear in your vision of who you are and who you want to be, is magnetic. For as uncomfortable and scary as it feels standing on the brink right now, for as much as you do have healing ahead of you, know that understanding when a friendship needs to end is a big and important step toward what is meant for you.

The Conversation

Remember that you're not doing anything wrong by bringing a friendship to a close; *you're doing something brave.* I say this because so often letting go of what we know feels risky and even wrong—even when we know that person or thing we're letting go of isn't in our highest good. It might even feel selfish. But it's not any of those things in reality. It's brave, really brave, to choose what is best for you and to refuse to play into toxic dynamics or outdated ways of being any longer. If you're at the point where you're hanging on to something that doesn't feel right anymore, or something that's hurting you, one of the bravest and strongest things you can do is to listen to that feeling, intuition, or call—*especially* when you have reasons to try to hold on. Letting go is a good thing and a great skill to have; one that you need to cultivate for the future. Letting go is an art form, and the only authentic route to freedom.

But I understand that the process of letting go doesn't necessarily feel good. It can feel daunting and even scary. Can you feel the tension rising up in your body now that you know it's time to end a friendship? These types of conversations used to make me go slightly batty. I'd rehearse them for weeks, practice them on my other friends, journal about it, oscillate from angry to sad and back again, and try to distract myself by doing anything *but* having the hard conversation that needed to be had. I do not advise taking this road.

For as tempting as it might be to avoid the hard conversation, what tends to happen in the interim is that nothing changes, resentment starts to build, and your boundaries are crossed so far that there's no choice but to completely erupt and eject the friend from your life in a way that ultimately won't feel good for either of you. Or maybe you're the avoidant type, and just fade into the background, leaving all your messages unread for the rest of your life. It's true that, in some cases, like a one-sided friendship, a conversation might not be necessary; there might be nothing to say, and it might be okay to just let it go and see where things settle. If, though, you are clear that you'd like to preserve the relationship,

I recommend making these hard conversations a part of your relationship DNA. Like any new practice, the more you have them, the better you'll be at them. No matter how scared or resistant you feel, Saturn Return is the perfect opportunity to clear, rewrite, and reorient yourself, which is a beautiful thing.

You're probably focusing on the moment, the conversation, the *thing*, right? What if, instead, you concentrate on how good you'll feel once you choose yourself, trust your intuition, and speak your truth? Remember, for as scary and unpleasant as it might feel, this conversation is just a moment. Those feelings you'll generate in the process of being true to yourself and acting in your own best interests (and, let's be honest, your friend's as well, at least in the long run) will leave a permanent positive impact on you.

Lindsey and I call these slightly charged but necessary conversations "clearing conversations." A clearing conversation is a dialogue between you and someone you are in a relationship with. This conversation is entered into with the intention of sharing truth from the heart, listening from the heart, and clearing any distortions in your relationship. Clearing conversations can lead to the end of a relationship or a new version of it, depending upon how the conversation goes and the state of the relationship heading into it. It's a chance to clear the air and reset the energy back to its original state (a state of love!).

"Okay, Krista," you might be thinking, "but isn't this conversation to close out the relationship? How is that going to reset us to a state of love?" I hear you. But conversations like this are an integral part of being in a relationship—and that applies to both relationships you want to grow within and to grow without. If you are not growing within the relationship, this conversation will still help you to grow in your relationship with yourself. It will provide you with an opportunity to really know if this friendship is a space where you can speak your truth, be yourself, and make mistakes; to be human, and heart-centered. And if you can't be those things? That's great to know! In doing this, you are showing yourself love and also creating space for more aligned love to come into both your life and your friend's.

Pass the Mic

We have to realize it doesn't have to be about winning and losing. The reason why ego gets involved is because we want to win. And the way I see relationships is: if I win and you lose, we both lose because we both are on the same team. And if you win and I lose, then we both lose because we're on the same team.

So, we have two choices: we either win together or we lose together. We think there's a third option of I won and you lost. No, you both lost. And so my encouragement is if you are genuinely committed to working it out with someone, bring up the conversation in a nonconfrontational, nonaggressive way.

—Jay Shetty, author of
Think Like a Monk and *8 Rules of Love*
ALMOST 30, EPISODE 583

Understanding and practicing how to have conversations like this is crucial, because as you begin to further awaken, reclaim your identity, and become the person you are meant to be, tension *will* arise between you and other people. This tension is telling you something, because tension doesn't exist between two people who are in a good space. A clearing conversation will leave you feeling liberated and clear, and it will ensure that you can be who you are at all times. It's an opportunity for growth, and for you to step further into the person you want to be. If you master these conversations during your Saturn Return, I promise it will pay off in dividends for the rest of your life.

Prep for a Clearing Conversation

This is a big conversation, so it's important to go into it prepared.

1. **Come to this conversation 90 percent processed.** This is important because it will help you stay regulated, in your body,

and confident that what you are saying is true and compassionate. You will know that you are about 90 percent processed when you can come to the conversation more neutrally, rather than in a heightened state of emotion. If your defenses are down, you can approach the conversation more from your heart than your head, with less emphasis on being right and more emphasis on understanding the other. To get there, use tools like therapy, journaling, meditation, and anything that allows you to practice emotional clearing.

2. **Set an intention.** Before you even reach out to your friend to have this conversation, set your intention for what you want to achieve from this talk. What is your deepest desire for this relationship? Do you know you want to end the friendship once and for all, or is this a come-to-Jesus talk where you put it all on the table? How do you want to feel by the end of the conversation? Being clear about your intention will help you move from a state of emotional reactivity to co-creating the experience you desire. I suggest both writing your intention down and also saying it out loud.

3. **Write down what you intend to say.** This can help quell anxiety and give you more confidence and clarity about how it feels to express your thoughts and feelings out loud, and also how your words and energy translate. Be sure to practice using *I* rather than *you* statements so that you are taking ownership of how you feel and aren't assuming anything about how your friend may be feeling. The goal is not to memorize a script but to make sure your truth is expressed clearly and from a grounded place—practice helps this happen. It will also be good practice to stay in your body while saying what you have to say aloud; I like to use my car for this and let it rip while I drive.

4. **Decide how and where you're going to have the conversation.** Is this going to be a phone call or a face-to-face meeting? Bonus points for the latter, but obviously it's not always possible—and should never be done in a situation where you don't feel safe. As you think about how to have this conversation, consider

why the breakup is happening, the nature of the friendship, and the circumstances surrounding the situation. You should honor this relationship as much as possible during the conversation, however painful it may be, because it has and will continue to serve your growth moving forward. If you don't feel safe in this relationship and feel as though you have to end it abruptly, consider finding support for yourself in this breakup process.

Lindsey and I love to have our clearing conversations on walks so that we can be in nature and move side-by-side without having to make eye contact, which can feel a bit intimidating at times, especially in more tense moments. It goes without saying that adding this kind of pressure to a situation that's potentially already tense and uncomfortable isn't helpful or productive.

5. **Cultivate compassion before the conversation.** Take some time and space to bring in the softer energy of compassion for both your friend and yourself. One of our friends, *The Desire Map* author Danielle LaPorte, says, "Compassion is judgment transformed into love." When you release the judgment, she explains, the love is waiting right there. I know that judgment might feel like a way of retaining your identity and defending your feelings and actions in a situation like this, but it is important that compassion lead this conversation. When you allow compassion to lead, your ego will soften and you will be able to meet your friend from a place that considers the experience of everyone involved. Compassion will also help you both relax, which leads to a better outcome.

6. **Breathe and pray before the conversation.** Use the time before you speak to have a conversation with your soul, God, Source, the Universe, or whomever you like to connect with to find your center. Begin by taking ten deep belly breaths. Once you've finished, allow yourself to settle into your body and normal, easy, and relaxed breathing. It's from this place that you want to share your heart and how you are feeling. Assure yourself

that you don't need to be perfect; you just need to be in your heart.

7. **Check in with yourself throughout.** Continue to check in with your body, breath, and energy during your chat. I always love to place a hand over my heart, soften my shoulders, unclench my jaw, or consciously slow down my breathing when I notice that I'm starting to feel anxious. If you find that the energy between you and your friend is heating up, feeling murky, or getting intense, feel free to give yourself a break. If you need a few moments and a restroom is available, try excusing yourself to wash your hands slowly, and use that as an opportunity to come back into your body, reconnect with your truth, and find your center. Taking care of yourself during heated conversations is important, deeply valid self-care. Remember that everything doesn't have to be perfect, and nothing has to happen all at once; this can be an ongoing process and conversation. So, if someone starts to get defensive, and things start to go off track, you can recognize that fact, slow down, take a break, and revisit the conversation when you're better resourced, both emotionally and energetically.

No matter how the conversation goes, take some time to allow yourself to feel a sense of pride once you've finished it. Conversations like this are not easy to have, nor is it easy to admit when a relationship has run its course and be proactive about acknowledging it. Regardless of how imperfect the conversation might have felt, know that you have served everyone involved by providing closure in an honest way.

Healing from a Friendship Breakup

So, you've had the clearing conversation, and it showed you it's time to release this friendship and move on with your lives separately. When Amy Chan, the author of *Breakup Bootcamp: The Science of Rewiring Your Heart*, came to chat with us, I found it very affirming to learn that there is actual science about breakups and how they impact us on a neurological level. While we discussed breakups in the context of romantic relationships, I believe this information applies just as much to platonic breakups. Know that any pain you might be feeling right now about the breakup of your relationship is in your head . . . *literally,* from a brain chemistry perspective.

Pass the Mic

The part of the brain that's activated is the same part of the brain as a drug user's fiending for their next fix. You're literally in withdrawal . . . you have neural pathways that have been wired together [with your friend, based on your shared experiences and habits]. Even though you know the friendship is over on a cognitive level, your body doesn't. It is in a state of shock. It's used to getting dopamine and feel-good chemicals from this person, so even after the breakup you're going to crave it.

—Amy Chan, author of *Breakup Bootcamp*
ALMOST 30, EPISODE 400

Yes, any pain you might be feeling is real, and yes, you can heal it. Here are some healing tools to help you during this period, whether you are the person who initiated the breakup or the friend who was broken up with.

Feel your emotions. Consider this your permission slip to embrace the fact that a friend can really break your heart. And if you need a reminder, you can even write yourself a permission slip and put it up somewhere you'll see frequently. I love to use quotes like this as a reminder: *Holding on is holding you back.*

A friendship breakup might make you angry, resentful, sad, or any number of emotions. You need to process this experience instead of holding it all in; otherwise it could leave you feeling bitter about the situation in years to come. If you get no further in the chapter, know that this is the single most important thing you can do for yourself. Make space for your emotions (*all* of them) and tend to them. Invite them for tea. Let them move through you like a wave. This is how you process and heal them. And a bonus fun fact: the life cycle of an emotion is 120 seconds—anything longer than that is an attachment to the emotion. In other words, if you feel the feeling, but then dive into your former bestie's Insta, you're drawing out that initial feeling (which just has to be felt) by attempting to feed those old neural pathways rather than starving them to create new ones.

Share your emotions. It's okay to express how you are feeling to others. Some of us need support to process difficult feelings and situations. Find a trusted friend, family member, or therapist to work through these feelings. The only caveat here is to avoid talking to people who know your friend in order to avoid further or more widespread pain or conflict on either side.

Forgive both yourself and your friend. Forgiveness is freedom, because it allows for the energetic release of unprocessed emotions and pain. Forgiveness doesn't mean accepting or condoning behavior that might have hurt you; it means releasing the hold a person or their behavior has on you. To support this process, try releasing any anger, resentment, or any other negative emotions you'd like to expunge through a somatic practice such as ecstatic dance or a loving kindness meditation.

Be your own best friend. Focus on empowering yourself, and stay busy by doing things you love. Do things by yourself that you would normally do with your friends (flip back to Lindsey's ideas for dating yourself in the previous chapter for some inspo). Remember those old neural pathways? This will support creating new ones, and it will also help you get comfortable being in your own energy. Your aura changes when you do this, which will attract aligned people who will support you.

Take accountability for the role you played in the friendship. Once you've worked through processing, it's time to reflect on the part you played in your friendship dynamic. *What has this relationship shown you about yourself?* Here I use my favorite example: *Mean Girls*. Regina George, Cady's frenemy, is a harsh stand-in representing a very particular kind of relationship that we will all experience at one point or another: the manipulative mean girl. When Cady realized she was being manipulated, she reflected on *her* role in it, rather than focusing on Regina.

While it's easy to place the blame on the other person in a situation like this, it's a huge missed opportunity to make positive changes in your own life and friendships.

Recognize and identify the patterns that you were in. Since the friendship ended, most likely both you and your friend were in a pattern or way of relating that no longer serves you. Taking time to think about and process the way you were engaging with each other and identifying what behaviors and dynamics you don't want to carry forward is a powerful way to become a conscious creator of your future relationships.

Create your own closure. Even if you had a clearing conversation, you still may not feel like you have closure around the friendship. Unfortunately, this is life. You might not always get an apology or even an opportunity to talk about the demise of a relationship. But you can give *yourself* closure. One way I like to do that is through ritual. Try this exercise as a way to align your brain and body to the moment so that you can solidify the feeling of closing out a chapter, which will allow you to find freedom and move on.

Amy Chan suggests writing a letter based on the following prompts:

- What are the facts of what happened?
- How did I feel?
- What am I going to let go?
- What have I learned?
- What's changed for me?
- What am I grateful for?

Once you have finished this letter, burn it as a symbol of releasing the past and moving on from this point.

Keep your heart open. Don't let this situation stop you from opening up to new friends when your heart is ready. If you find yourself wanting to close your heart, remember you're in a new relationship and it's a new day as you begin to move forward into new friendships or deepen existing ones. This new friend is not the same person your old friend was, and you are not the same person you once were either!

Moving On

One of the beautiful things about past friendships is that they can inform your future friendships, if you're willing to reflect on and learn from them (and I know you are). Someday you will look back and be grateful that the space opened up in your life to embrace important new relationships, even if some heartbreak was involved in getting to that place.

As you reflect on and begin to move on from your previous friendship, it's important to remember that it takes two to tango. As much as I love to indulge in a little I'm-a-victim moment, Saturn Return is about leaving that mindset behind. The truth of the matter is that the friendship you've ended probably impacted you both positively and negatively. But even that is sort of irrelevant, because you can't change the past. What you *can* change is the way in which you move forward. If you want loving and supportive friendships, that means looking at yourself and discovering the ways that you can be the friend you dream of. To attract what you want, you must embody it. If you want to have nourishing, loving friendships, that means you must learn to be a better friend yourself.

Saturn Return is a great opportunity to recalibrate the ways in which you engage with friends so that you can become your most stellar, loving, supportive, and present self. This will help you attract friends who are aligned and like-hearted.

Pass the Mic

Healing only happens in the body. There's no way for you to think your way out of your suffering. That's what healing is about. People want it to be more esoteric, but it's really not. Feel every feeling in the body as it arises, and before the feelings claim a story or get tangled with the story. Be with them, breathe with them, let them come up and out.

—Sah D'Simone, author of *Spiritually Sassy*
ALMOST 30, EPISODE 608

Here are a few practices and mindset shifts that can support you to attract the friendships you desire.

Do your own work. When you focus on your own personal healing, you're showing up in your relationships much more secure and in your power. This will help you be more compassionate with yourself and more empathetic toward your friends.

Treat your friendships as a soul contract. Look at your friendships this way: you are souls who chose one another to heal. This friendship is a sacred contract for the higher good of both your souls. You have chosen to meet in this lifetime and traverse these interesting human waters! There is a magic to the fact that you found each other in this lifetime, and even if it's painful, you've been given lessons that can bring you closer to who you're meant to be.

Heal in community. It's beautiful to witness other women truly supporting one another, holding one another accountable, reflecting back to one another, growing together, and coming back to themselves in community. This is also a place where you can bring all that solo work you've been doing into practice, to observe, hold space, share compassion, and feel what it feels like to be seen in a way that feels tender and new.

I know that this work isn't as easy as it seems when it's just written on a page. But let me tell you: the ability to have healthy, honest, loving relationships with the women in your life will be one of the richest experiences you will ever have—one that will potentially continue to nurture you throughout the many seasons of your life. These friendships will allow you to be held, seen, heard, and supported in a way that sometimes doesn't feel possible in other relationships. I bet you'll also find that immersing yourself in these types of relationships will also lead you to a deeper, more stable, and more loving relationship with yourself. Saturn loves that for you.

TL;DR: We Still Don't Have It Figured Out

As we get older, there's this belief that we should have friendships figured out (ahem, *Sex and the City*). But when a friendship doesn't work out, there can be a sense of shame that we couldn't fix it. You might even feel like you did something wrong. I get it, I've been there. Know that you can heal from the pain and become stronger from friendship breakups, but it takes time and self-care. I sometimes still get a pang in my stomach when I think of old friends I've lost along the way—and I think that's normal. We want to be liked, we want to live in community, and when we have to leave others behind, it's just plain sad.

But I have some hopeful news: eventually, when you pass through your Saturn Return and enter your thirties, you'll age out of the friendship-collecting game, which tends to peak in the midtwenties, during that bright-eyed and bushy-tailed phase of life when you think that more is merrier. That time when you're still spending Saturday nights playing games at a random stranger's house, and long, luxurious Sunday afternoons nursing hangovers at brunch with friends you don't really know. Now it's a new game of depth, authenticity, and intimacy, and the goal is to settle into the business of embracing and basking in the friendships that have survived as you put down roots and navigate your Saturn return with grace.

THE END . . . AND THE BEGINNING

One Sunday in January, we were cozied up at a quaint Parisian-style cafe in Brooklyn eating quiches when Krista had a core memory moment à la *Inside Out*. Midbite of an egg-based pastry, it felt like time stopped, and everything got clear.

This moment wasn't big, just simple and profound.

"You know what I just realized?" Krista said. "Our lives are completely different than they were at the beginning of our Saturn Return. I'm not sure I would have predicted this, but I sort of love that for us. Isn't it wild?"

Lindsey nodded as she glided the stroller back and forth across the tile floor with one arm, while her baby stared at both of us like a little doll. He appeared curious about our conversation as we caught up on life during one of Krista's regular trips to the city. Our late lunch conversation had oscillated between the exploration of when to move off the dating apps into text messaging, to breastfeeding and sleep schedules.

"You're right." Lindsey smiled. "Look at God."

Lindsey was finding herself empowered and excited about her new life on the East Coast, with new friends, priorities, and perspectives. She was now married with a baby, spending her days covered in sweet potato and yogurt, hair sometimes brushed, watching in awe alongside her husband as their son developed into a little person by the day. Krista was living solo in Los Angeles, going out most nights and weekends, deepening her female friendships. She was truly living la vida loca, traveling the world and exploring what it meant to be single for maybe the first time in her adult life. While Lindsey was originally known as the "perpetually single one," and Krista the "relationship one," we had swapped roles. It felt like the landscape of our lives had done a complete 180 from where we were before our Saturn Return, and we knew that was true on the inside too. For both of us in that moment, there was potential, possibility, excitement, and liberation, mixed still with moments of loneliness and insecurity (which may seem surprising to say in a conclusion when you just want to read about the happy ending, but, hey!—this is nonfiction).

If it's not obvious, we have to tell you that we didn't do our Saturn Return perfectly. If you don't believe us, we have more cringe moments available for you to review online than any normal human should. But we really let that time of life move us, sculpt us even. Whether it was figuring out how to get ourselves out of debt, learning to accept and cherish our bodies, developing deep intimacy with our female friends, or understanding how to love our parents as they are, we went all in.

Seeing as how all endings are a mix of all the things and also new beginnings, don't let the title of this book mislead you. The two of us can attest to the fact that the guidance in these pages will continue to help you along the way as you navigate *any* period of change—well beyond your almost-thirties. We hope you will keep it close at hand to open up to a random page when you are moving through life and want some clarity. Some of these principles and practices will become a part of who you are and how you move through the world. Others, you will make your own and pass on to those around you simply by embodying them fully.

For us, prior to our Saturn Return, life felt linear, like a color-by-numbers book. We're told to do this to get that, as if existence is fully cause-and-effect. We're told to work really hard to get the promotion. Go on a hundred dates to find The One. Work out seven days a week to get a hot bod. Wake up, coffee, hustle, girl dinner, repeat . . . then, eventually you *may* be happy. But once you feel the rumblings of change, transformation, and growth as you step into your Saturn Return, things get shaken up quite a bit.

If those two women in a café, one with a stroller and the other with a dating app, could tell our younger selves a couple of things, we would say:

1. **Among the challenges, you realize that you are a multidimensional human living a multidimensional existence (pretty cool, right?).** You may be experiencing the truth of what that means right this very moment as you begin to consciously understand the layers that make up who you are, and all that you bring to every dream, every goal, every relationship, every *moment*. With this, the pursuit of the life you desire becomes less about the end goal and so much more about the invitations to get curious about *who you are* in both the big and little moments. During this time, it's more important than ever to get good at sustaining and tolerating fear of the unknown.

2. **In this very moment, practice letting go of the belief that you're lost and doomed to live a life you don't love.** Suspend the ideas around who you're supposed to be and approach this next period as an adventure, the great mystery of life in action, we'll say. We all know deep down that sometimes the best things in life are the things we didn't see coming. Those cosmic surprises and magic moments bring so much to our experience on Earth. So put this book down, take a beat, close your eyes, and be with the excitement of what is to come.

Throughout all this, there might be a nagging feeling of experiencing too much change all at once, and many moments of feeling out of control. By using the tools in this book, our hope is that you can pursue both stability and change simultaneously. That means consciously changing your life gradually and reasonably, with intention and purpose. It's all about incremental changes done with purpose, and creating habits as a foundation for self-love. It's a good practice to continually imagine the person you desire to be, and then taking small baby steps toward that person. Journey in grace, with intention and awareness, and know your soul is there to guide you all the way.

Remember this: there is no such thing as a "successful Saturn Return." This old idea of success that we've grown accustomed to is so 2D, flat, and uninteresting at this point. It's not about getting the thing, the accolade, the promotion, the partner, the money. Although we technically have all the things we wanted and the answers that we were looking for, we continue to seek in life. We're never really "there" and we never truly arrive. Our thirtysomething selves feel more at peace than ever before . . . and, yet, we wouldn't say life is perfect on the other side. You just find yourself more content and satisfied that you've become more you.

When we do the deep diving like you've done throughout the course of this book, the *feeling* of success becomes more important and more specific to *you*. Success becomes something that you know in your heart and are more attuned to than what an outcome looks like.

Our hope is that you choose yourself throughout Saturn Return and use this time to become even more you, even more awake, and even more clear. It only requires that you look at things a little differently from how you have been.

Saturn Return is a bit of everything all at once, but remember that the heart of it boils down to a few key things:

1. Redefining your relationship to change
2. A lot of unlearning and looking at the things you've been avoiding
3. Figuring out what you value in life
4. Moving forward knowing life is a journey not a destination

Yes, this could all live on a poster in your bedroom or Post-it Note on your mirror, because it's timeless and true. Sometimes the biggest truths are the most cliché. As corny as it sounds, it can be profoundly transformational to be grateful for what you have while you're working toward what you want. If we only knew during our own Saturn Returns that everything we needed to be satisfied with life was right in front of us. If only we were able to take the time to appreciate the simple pleasures, like nourishing our bodies, taking a walk in nature, or calling our long-distance best friend to laugh about a meme we saw.

Because when you can do that, this process can be a whole lot more enjoyable—and, dare we say, fun!

Pass the Mic

Saturn Return taught me so much about how to build my life as I wanted to. And I think if Saturn Return can give us anything, it's that this is your life. You are going to die. That's what Saturn tells us. You are not going to be here forever. You have a very short amount of time here; look how fast your twenties went by!

It's going to go even faster in your thirties. And if that is true, what do you want to do with this one precious life? This is yours to define and shape if you have the privilege to do so. And if you do, that privilege is a great responsibility.

That I think we have to take seriously.

—Chani Nicholas, author of *You Were Born for This*
ALMOST 30, EPISODE 299

You might feel as though you are moving through this period alone, reading this book in your private corner of the world. We sure felt alone for most of this process. But you are not. We know that it can sometimes be isolating, and growth doesn't always feel comfortable. But when we zoom out, we can see that we've collectively been moving through Saturn Returns for centuries (yes, even our parents had their own Saturn Return season). Part of what brought this book into your reality was the other people out there also connecting with these words and experiences. Your energies have attracted one another. You've gathered around the proverbial campfire to read this book in order to *remember. Together.*

GRATITUDE

We've come to a point in our lives where we want to give thanks to everyone and everything because technically it brought us to this very moment of connecting with you through this book. But we don't have the word count for that, so we'll spare you the thank-yous to the ex-boyfriends who broke our hearts and the egomaniac bosses who trampled our confidence, only for us to cultivate it ourselves!

We'd like to first thank God. Every prayer has been answered with what we needed, not always what we wanted. And for that we're so grateful. Thank you for placing the Almost 30 vision and mission in our hearts; it has changed our lives and the lives of hundreds of thousands of others for the better.

To our Almost 30 community, who proudly call themselves #Almost-30Nation, you have inspired every move we make. How are you so cool and kind and authentic and just so down *always* to know yourself more deeply and laugh with us while doing it? We are in awe of your hearts, and we honestly smile thinking about every one of you. Whether you're listening to the podcast on your commute to work or on your morning walk, getting together with fellow listeners in your city, joining us on tour, attending our retreats, DMing us the most heartfelt messages and hilarious memes, or coming up to us in the wild for big hugs and sharing what the *Almost 30* podcast has meant to you . . . just know that we could not have done any of this without you. Thank you for truly *seeing* us and believing in us and the mission.

To all the guests we have had on the podcast, many of whom you heard from in this book, we are forever grateful that people like you exist on Earth right now. More often than not your teachings and expertise, stories and experiences have come into our lives and the lives of our listeners at the most perfect moments. Your messages have been heard by millions of people, and we are so thankful you trusted us to facilitate the conversation. So many of you have become dear friends in podcasting and in life.

Thank you to our book agent, honey pie, Tess. *Almost 30* has a way of bringing us the right people at the right time. It's kind of freaky how this happens. Tess, you reached out to us at a time when we *knew* we were finally ready to write our book. You *get* us, and we have felt so confident and supported with you by our side through this process. Can't wait for more books, *together*.

Nikki, our book sensei. We love you so. The joy we felt when we found you! We knew that we wanted to write this book ourselves. Yet we craved an experienced guide and support system as we did so. Thank you for giving us the confidence to write this, for the insight that helped shape a guidebook for generations to come and for your heart. We always felt your heart in our work together, which made opening our own to this book that much easier.

Shout-out to our therapists, who might not ever read this because it's probably some therapist code of honor never to read a client's book. But Christina and Joanne, what the heck would we do without you?! It has been through our sessions with you over the years that we have discovered so much of what we've shared about in this book. We'll see you Tuesday.

Team Almost 30 of past and present, you are soul family, no doubt about it. *Almost 30* has attracted some of the best, brightest, and most heart-centered people in their field. You always go above and beyond for us, the community, and the vision at large. We love you dearly.

Gratitude from Lindsey

Sean and Maverick, my boys. My two greatest gifts, thank you, God. :) Sean, you have always encouraged me to shine, to be more of myself, to create, to rest, to express, to trust myself, and to care less about what people think and more about how it feels in my heart. You are my rock, and I love the way you love me. Mav, I wrote a majority of this book in your nursery with you in my belly. Two creative assignments at once. I love getting to know you every single day. I love you both forever, beyond measure.

To my family—you have always been my biggest fans, no matter the creative pursuit and no matter how weird. While it might not have always made sense to you in the moment (recording on a closet floor for what?!), you never doubted my abilities and potential. I know that having a public-facing part of my life has not always been easy, and it has been a learning process for me, but woo, I'm so grateful for the ways in which it has brought us all closer together now. Thank you for being exactly who you are. It is a beautiful thing to understand now, as an adult, the profound parts each of you has played in shaping who I am. Love you all dearly.

Krista, my girl. We found each other yet again, hehe. Many lives, baby, and here we are in one of our most profound ones yet—sure beats the one where I was your drunken sailor husband. Our relationship will always be a place that I know I can feel safe to be myself, to express honestly, to share my heart, to laugh like psychopaths, to dream delusionally (and have it come true) and to change (and still be loved and supported). I love that life is long and we've only really begun our relationship in the grand scheme of things. To more everything. I'm here for it and for you and I love you for-ev-er.

Gratitude from Krista

To my friends and the dear women in my life: a list fifty pages long. Thank you for seeing me when my vision was blurry. I have found such deep meaningful love in each of our relationships, and without your encouragement, love, support, and laughter this book wouldn't be possible, and neither would I. I love you very deeply.

To my family, for their respect and grace through this journey as a podcast host and someone who speaks for a living (LOL). Thank you for your trust in me, and allowing me to become the person I came here to be. Brynne, Mom, and Dad, I love you very much!

Lindsey, you are truly a home to me wherever we are. Our friendship has been one of my greatest life gifts, and the standard for me. Thank you for always reminding me of what is true in this life. For laughing with me when things get hard (and we could be crying), sharing a bed with me on tour (because I hate sleeping alone), answering all my calls (no matter when), and being one of the most conscientious, kind, pure, and loving people I'll ever meet. Creating *Almost 30* would never have been possible without our unique soul formula and the weaving that happened to allow us to create this amazing dream of a business which is now a freakin' book! We did it, baby! I love you.

NOTES

1. James S. House, Karl R. Landis, and Debra Umberson, "Social Relationships and Health," *Science* 241, no. 4865 (1988): 540–45, https://doi.org/10.1126/science.3399889.
2. Laura Marie Edinger-Schons, "People with a Sense of Oneness Experience Greater Life Satisfaction," American Psychological Association, April 11, 2019, https://www.apa.org/news/press/releases/2019/04/greater-life-satisfaction.
3. Agnieszka Bozek et al., "The Relationship Between Spirituality, Health-Related Behavior, and Psychological Well-Being," *Frontiers in Psychology* 11 (2020), DOI: 10.3389/fpsyg.2020.01997.
4. David P. Fessell and Karen Reivich, "Why You Need to Protect Your Sense of Wonder—Especially Now," *Harvard Business Review,* August 25, 2021, https://hbr.org/2021/08/why-you-need-to-protect-your-sense-of-wonder-especially-now.
5. Helen Payne, "Our Body and Mind Are One," *LINK* 1, no. 1, November 12, 2014, https://www.herts.ac.uk/link/volume-1-issue-1/our-body-and-mind-are-one.
6. Lindsey Simcik and Krista Williams, "Episode 349: Baring It All with The Birds Papaya," *Almost 30,* August 11, 2020.
7. Lindsey Simcik and Krista Williams, "Episode 575: Prioritizing Mental Health, Body Neutrality + Knowing What's in Your Supplements," *Almost 30,* January 17, 2023.
8. Lindsey Simcik and Krista Williams, "Episode 151: Go with Your Gut for the Healthiest You with Robyn Youkilis," *Almost 30,* September 25, 2018.
9. Colin A. Capaldi, Raelyne L. Dopko, John M. Zelenski, "The Relationship Between Nature Connectedness and Happiness: A Meta-analysis," *Frontiers in Psychology* 5 (2014), DOI: 10.3389/fpsyg.2014.00976.
10. A. Pritchard, M. Richardson, D. Sheffield et al., "The Relationship Between Nature Connectedness and Eudaimonic Well-Being: A Meta-analysis," *Journal of Happiness Studies* 21, 1145–1167 (2020), https://doi.org/10.1007/s10902-019-00118-6.
11. Ampere A. Tseng, "Scientific Evidence of Health Benefits by Practicing Mantra Meditation: Narrative Review," *International Journal of Yoga* 15, no. 2 (2022): 89, https://doi.org/10.4103/ijoy.ijoy_53_22.
12. Melinda Beck, "Delayed Development: 20-Somethings Blame the Brain," *Wall Street Journal,* August 22, 2012, https://www.wsj.com/articles/SB10000872396390443713704577601532208760746.
13. Lindsey Simcik and Krista Williams, "Episode 370: Immunity + Your Microbiome with Seed Founder Ara Katz," *Almost 30,* October 22, 2020.
14. Beck, "Delayed Development."

15. T. Johansson et al., "Population-based Cohort Study of Oral Contraceptive Use and Risk of Depression," *Epidemiology and Psychiatric Sciences* 32, e39 (2023), https://doi.org/10.1017/S2045796023000525.

16. National Research Council (US) Committee on Population, *Contraception and Reproduction: Health Consequences for Women and Children in the Developing World* (Washington, D.C.: National Academy Press, 1989).

17. S. A. Robinson, M. Dowell, D. Pedulla, and L. McCauley, "Do the Emotional Side-Effects of Hormonal Contraceptives Come from Pharmacologic or Psychological Mechanisms?" *Medical Hypotheses* 63, no. 2 (2004): 268–273, https://pubmed.ncbi.nlm.nih.gov/15236788/.

18. Julia A. Wolfson and Sara N. Bleich, "Is Cooking at Home Associated with Better Diet Quality or Weight-Loss Intention?" *Public Health Nutrition* 18, no. 8 (2014): 1397–1406, https://doi.org/10.1017/s1368980014001943.

19. Lindsey Simcik and Krista Williams, "Episode 621: How to Navigate a Corrupt Food Industry," *Almost 30,* August 22, 2023.

20. Cleveland Clinic Health Essentials, "How to Quit Caffeine Without a Headache." November 10, 2023, https://health.clevelandclinic.org/how-to-quit-caffeine.

21. Astrid Nehlig, Jean-Luc Daval, and Gérard Debry, "Caffeine and the Central Nervous System: Mechanisms of Action, Biochemical, Metabolic and Psychostimulant Effects," *Brain Research Reviews* 17, no. 2 (1992): 139–70, https://doi.org/10.1016/0165–0173(92)90012-b.

22. A. A. Alsunni, "Energy Drink Consumption: Beneficial and Adverse Health Effects," *International Journal of Health Sciences* 9, no. 4 (2015): 459–465, https://doi.org/10.12816/0031237.

23. Lindsey Simcik and Krista Williams, "Episode 566: Meet Your Self with Dr. Nicole LePera," *Almost 30*, December 6, 2022.

24. McDonald Center for Student Well-Being, University of Notre Dame. "Absorption Rate Factors," https://mcwell.nd.edu/your-well-being/physical-well-being/alcohol/absorption-rate-factors.

25. John Anderer, "Survey: The Average Worker Experiences Career Burnout—by the Age of 32," Study Finds, September 18, 2020, https://www.studyfinds.org/average-worker-career-burnout-age-32/.

26. Lydia Saad, Sangeeta Agrawal, and Ben Wigert, "Gender Gap in Worker Burnout Widened Amid the Pandemic," Gallup.com, July 21, 2023, https://www.gallup.com/workplace/358349/gender-gap-worker-burnout-widened-amid-pandemic.aspx.

27. Mayo Clinic Staff, "Chronic Stress Puts Your Health at Risk," Mayo Clinic, August 1, 2023, https://www.mayoclinic.org/healthy-lifestyle/stress-management/in-depth/stress/art-20046037#:~:text=The%20long%2Dterm%20activation%20of,-Depression.

28. H. Yaribeygi, Y. Panahi, H. Sahraei, T. P. Johnston, and A. Sahebkar, "The Impact of Stress on Body Function: A Review," *EXCLI Journal* 16 (2017): 1057–1072, doi: 10.17179/excli2017–480; PMID: 28900385; PMCID: PMC5579396.

29. Amanda Ruggeri, "The Downsides of Perfectionism," *BBC News,* February 28, 2022, https://www.bbc.com/future/article/20180219-toxic-perfectionism-is-on-the-rise.

30. William T. Harbaugh et al., "Neural Responses to Taxation and Voluntary Giving Reveal Motives for Charitable Donations," *Science* 316, 1622–1625 (2007), DOI: 10.1126/science.1140738.

31. American Psychological Association, "What Happens in Your Brain When You Give a Gift?" December 9, 2022, https://www.apa.org/topics/mental-health/brain-gift-giving.

32. James H. Fowler et al., "Cooperative Behavior Cascades in Social Human Networks," *Proceedings of the National Academy of Science* 107, 5334–5338 (2010), DOI: 10.1073/pnas.0913149107.

33. Mental Health Foundation (UK), "Debt and Mental Health," https://www.mentalhealth.org.uk/explore-mental-health/a-z-topics/debt-and-mental-health.

34. "Sightlines Financial Security Special Report: Seeing Our Way to Financial Security in the Age of Increased Longevity," Stanford Center on Longevity, https://longevity.stanford.edu/sightlines-financial-security-special-report-mobile.

35. April Rinne, "Why You Should Build a 'Career Portfolio' (Not a 'Career Path')," *Harvard Business Review,* October 12, 2021, https://hbr.org/2021/10/why-you-should-build-a-career-portfolio-not-a-career-path#:~:text=A%20career%20portfolio%20is%20different,purpose%2C%20clarity%2C%20and%20flexibility.

36. Arthur C. Brooks, "The Best Friends Can Do Nothing for You," *The Atlantic,* April 7, 2022, https://www.theatlantic.com/family/archive/2021/04/deep-friendships-aristotle/618529/.

ABOUT THE AUTHORS

© Heather Shane

LINDSEY SIMCIK is a creative entrepreneur and cofounder of the ac-claimed *Almost 30* podcast, a global platform that has inspired millions. Known for pioneering conversations on topics like hormones, self-development, and birth control, Lindsey also created The Sacredness of Being Single, a program empowering women to embrace singlehood with confidence. Now a mom to her son, Maverick, Lindsey has launched New Mom on the Block, offering resources, products, and community to help moms navigate motherhood with confidence and joy.

KRISTA WILLIAMS is a cofounder of *Almost 30*, a globally renowned podcast and community with more than 100 million downloads. She is also the cocreator of the podcast *Morning Microdose* and leads luxury wellness retreats while speaking internationally for top brands. Through her courses, The Life Edit and Metamorphosis, Krista has inspired thou-sands to embrace self-love and transform their lives. With a passion for growth and connection, Krista continues to guide others toward their highest potential.